Literacy, Not Labels

Literacy, Not Labels

Celebrating Students' Strengths
Through Whole Language

Kathleen Strickland
Slippery Rock, University
Slippery Rock, PA

Boynton/Cook Publishers
Portsmouth, NH

Boynton/Cook Publishers, Inc.
A subsidiary of Reed Elsevier Inc.
361 Hanover Street
Portsmouth, NH 03801-3912
Offices and agents throughout the world

Every effort has been made to contact the copyright holders for permission to reprint borrowed material where necessary. We regret any oversights that may have occurred and would be happy to rectify them in future printings of this work.

The author and publisher wish to thank those who granted permission to reprint borrowed material:

"The Labeled Child" by Karen Morrow Durica was originally published in *The Reading Teacher* (March 1994). Reprinted by permission.

Reprinted by permission of Constance Weaver: *Reading Process and Practice: From Socio-Psycholinguistics to Whole Language* (Heinemann, A division of Reed Elsevier Inc., Portsmouth, NH 1994).

Excerpts from "Whole Language and Foreign Students: The Integrated Classroom," an unpublished manuscript by Rhonda L. McKissock. Reprinted by permission.

Library of Congress Cataloging-in-Publication Data

Strickland, Kathleen.
    Literacy, not labels: celebrating students' strengths through whole language/Kathleen Strickland.
        p. cm.
    Includes bibliographical references and index.
        ISBN 0-86709-354-4 (acid-free paper)
        1. Learning disabled children—Education—Reading. 2. Learning disabled children—Education—Reading—Case studies. 3. Language experience approach in education. 4. Language experience approach in education—Case studies. 5. Literacy. 6. Literacy—Case studies. I. Title.
    LC4704.85.S77 1995
    372.4'8-dc20   94-46635
                                                                          CIP

Editor: Peter R. Stillman
Production: Melissa L. Inglis
Cover design: Catherine Hawkes

Printed in the United States of America on acid-free paper
99 98 97 96 95 EB 1 2 3 4 5 6 7 8 9

For fathers who teach their daughters to dream—
Ted Paterson, Bill Walker, and Jim Strickland.

CONTENTS

ACKNOWLEDGMENTS

More and more I realize that writing is not a solitary act. From the first, others have supported me by responding to my ideas, posing questions prompting me to probe more deeply, and encouraging me to continue. As I depended on others for response and reassurance, I learned over and over how recursive the writing process can be. This book could not have been written alone.

In my classes, I try to help our pre-service teachers understand that we are life-long learners in our profession: we learn from our students, from research, and from our colleagues. I have been fortunate to have learned from some wonderful teachers—some, like Ken Goodman and Donald Graves, have been inspirations through their writing; others, like Donald McAndrew and Ann Hunter, have invited me into their classrooms. As my teacher, Don modeled for me what good teaching is and taught me how to search for answers to real questions. Although I cannot even acknowledge Ann by her real name, in order to protect the privacy of her students, I want to thank her for teaching me that *all* students can learn if we believe in them and help them to believe in themselves. Teachers like these make ours a profession to be respected.

I would also like to thank Eugene Shultz, an educator and former middle school principal, a visionary who believed in teachers as professionals and empowered them to make decisions about curriculum and the teaching process. In 1980, I remember Gene coming to my classroom after school just to lend me a book by a researcher named Lev Vygotsky; Gene had found the newly translated work while browsing in the university library and thought of me and my interest in language. That's the kind of leader he was. He was always looking for ways to support his teachers; he considered them the experts. Over the years I've come to value the things he did, his courage, his idealism, his willingness to change, even when others saw change as dangerous.

I would also like to thank my husband James, who has worked by my side throughout the research, writing, and editing of this book and who has read every word of it many times. This book would not have been written without his support and expertise. Jim is one of my best teachers—over the years he has helped me believe in myself as a writer, encouraging and modeling for me what writers do and how they do it. He is my colleague, my cowriter, my editor, and most importantly my best friend, the love of my life.

I have had the privilege once again to work with Peter Stillman, my editor, who has added so much to our profession through his own writing and his support of others who write about teaching and learning. I have benefited from his encouragement, and I appreciate his commitment to providing resources for teachers who believe in their students' right to literacy.

A word of thanks also goes to those at Heinemann who have worked diligently to present this book in a timely manner, especially Melissa Inglis, my production editor, Richard Korey, my copy editor, and Nancy Sheridan, my proofreader.

INTRODUCTION

Some day we may look back on what we have done in creating special groups and special instruction and see it as comparable to what teachers did fifty years ago when they forced left-handed children to write with their right hand. Education has been molding rather than liberating.
Susan Stires

After almost twenty years of teaching, first as a public school teacher and later as a teacher educator, I have come to believe, as does Donald Graves (1985), that all children *can* write, and that all children can read if they believe that they can and are given the opportunity to do so. I also believe, as does Frank Smith (1988a), that learning is natural, a process starting from birth, something human beings do throughout their lives to meet their needs. Yet, I have heard others profess that there are those who are variously "disabled" and "handicapped," who *cannot* learn, who do not *want* to learn, and who *must* be taught in "special" programs with special techniques, programs informed by a belief that these "unfortunates" cannot learn as "normal" people do. I have come to realize that the labels "disabled" and "handicapped," vague as they are, tell the world more about what students *are not* capable of doing than what they *are* capable of doing. And more importantly, such labels become who these people are.

Equality in the Classroom

While research continues to suggest that children indeed learn in different ways and at different times (Clay 1967; Piaget 1971; Vygotsky 1978), too often education tends to be molding instead of liberating, as Susan Stires (1991) argues. Before going to school, most of these "disabled" and "handicapped" students were able to learn to speak and otherwise communicate their thoughts, needs, feelings, and ideas, as most children do. They learned syntax and semantics as they learned to communicate orally. These children were able to acquire reading and writing behaviors as they "read" environmental print, scribble-wrote their names in coloring books, and talked about all they planned to read and write about once they got to school. When they arrived at school, however, everything changed; a handicap was diagnosed, usually through standardized testing. These children learned that they were different, and they were taught that they could not learn. And being different makes all the difference.

Primary programs in many schools attempt to make all children the same instead of celebrating and building upon their strengths and differences.

Such programs in kindergarten and first grade are driven by a desire to teach children based on what adults know, instead of what children know. Glenda Bissex (1980), in her book *GNYS AT WRK*, argues that "the logic by which we teach is not always the logic by which children learn"; thus, we should be looking for ways to teach that are "developmentally appropriate practices," as outlined by the National Association for the Education of Young Children (1991) (see the Appendix for a summary of those guidelines). Interestingly, Bissex is referring to the logic by which all children learn, not just those who fit between certain stanines on standardized tests. Older "disabled" and "handicapped" children (fourth grade and beyond) who have been repeatedly told what they *can't* do by their teachers, school psychologists, and numerous specialists must be afforded the opportunity to recover the ability to learn that they possessed naturally as preschool children. All children can learn to use language as they continue to grow as speakers, writers, and readers; however, they must be given the opportunity to do so.

An Opportunity to Learn

> I never used to like to read. Amelia Bedilia is so funny—do you know her? This is my first book that I ever read myself.
> *Debby*

These words were spoken during a conversation with a twelve-year-old girl, one whom many educators would label "learning disabled" according to standardized test scores, which place her reading level as several grade levels below the norm. Debby has, in fact, been labeled "emotionally disturbed" both clinically and educationally and was, at the time of our conversation, institutionalized in a state-supported home for youth. In addition to the burden of being labeled "emotionally disturbed" and "learning disabled," this girl faced endless frustrations both in- and outside of public education. Debby had wanted to learn, as all children do (Smith 1988a), but prior to this year, she had been convinced by the methods of instruction she received that she was incapable of learning. Although she had never learned to read and write through previous participation in traditional programs, she was, nevertheless, learning to read and write in a whole language classroom, one that used literature as the means by which students learned to read. Along with her classmates, she was not only responding to what she read but was beginning to think of herself as a reader. As is demonstrated by her own words, she was succeeding for the first time—both in her eyes and in the eyes of "the system."

Her success can be attributed, in large part, to the philosophy of teaching literacy that governed her current classroom. The use of real literature to provide what some call a "literature-based" approach to reading instruction—trade books as opposed to basal readers—gave the students in her classroom meaningful opportunities to interact with print, to listen and to become part of the stories, and to realize that worlds can open to those who read.

The approach used in Debby's classroom is based on a philosophy of teaching and learning that grew out of a shifting of beliefs about how people learn and consequently how they should be taught. In this book, I tell stories, many of which took place in Debby's classroom with her teacher, Ann Hunter. The students in this classroom, the ones all others had given up on, learned to read, to write, and most importantly how to learn. They learned to believe in themselves and to recognize what they *could* do, even after years of being in classrooms where they were continually told what they were incapable of doing.

In this book, I describe the teaching of literacy to students who are often referred to as "at risk"—those with "special" labels and so-called handicaps. I begin by illustrating how the use of literature in this classroom served as a vehicle to broadening students' schemata and a vehicle to learning; I also note, when possible, how this instruction compared with other literacy instruction the students had in the past. Through the use of what Harste, Woodward, and Burke (1984b) call "language stories," I look in detail at the literacy learning of four students who grew as readers and writers in a classroom where "real" reading was central to learning.

1
Whole Language
Literacy for *All* Students

Individual growth, not achievement of absolute levels, is the goal.
Whole language teachers accept pupil differences. They plan for
expansion of effectiveness and efficiency in language, and expansion of
knowledge and understanding of the world in each child.
Ken Goodman

I met Ann Hunter at a whole language workshop that I conducted as an in-service program for teachers. When our workshop began we were a diverse group of teachers whose only commonality seemed to be an interest in the title of a workshop promising to address whole language in secondary class-rooms. Ann and one other colleague were the only special education teach-ers in the group of twenty-five. Ann told me later that she had attended my workshop because she had always been "nontraditional" in her approaches to teaching and wanted to find out what whole language was all about. She also knew that much of what she had been taught in her teacher training program had not helped the students in her classroom learn. Her special education/elementary education undergraduate and graduate training had concentrated on getting the students to stay in their seats and complete workbooks and dittos that, according to testing, should help "remediate" them. Early in her career, Ann intuitively discovered that such approaches did nothing to help students learn, so she began using nontraditional tech-niques, such as reading aloud to her students, talking about books, and encouraging them to write about what they had read. She knew that her approach, simple as it sounded, was making a difference for her students, but she was unsure why.

Ann told me later that she was skeptical when she began the workshop, but my workshop was unlike previous school in-service days she had attended. My workshop was conducted over a period of several months, allowing teachers the time to try changes in their classrooms based on the philosophy we had been discussing. At this time, Ann began to put the pieces together. The workshop gave her a research base for some of the tech-niques she was using in her classroom that supported literacy, and she gained the courage she needed to go further once she understood the "whys" of such instruction. Most importantly, Ann realized that this was just a beginning. She was facing what amounted to a shift in paradigms—belief systems—and she was beginning to reexamine much of what she had been taught about teaching and learning. When we discussed how children learn to read, based on research by Ken Goodman (1986, 1987), Yetta Goodman (1978, 1986), and Frank Smith (1988a, 1988c), Ann began to see why techniques such as reading literature aloud to her students, talking about literature, and responding as real readers seemed not only to make a difference in their attitudes toward literacy, but in their actual reading ability as well. When we discussed using a thematic approach to instruction to make learning more purposeful (Pappas, Kiefer & Levstik 1990), Ann realized that her content area "units" (which were often much longer than she had intended) were successful because they progressed according to the needs and interests of her students. Ann also reexamined how she assessed and evaluated her students, changing the way she wrote Individualized Education Plans (IEPs) from being very behavioral to more holistic in nature (Harp 1991).

One evening, as we traded stories of successes and disappointments in our classrooms, Ann shared with the group how she was discovering the power that books could have in her students' lives. She told us of one student, Blake, who was an unusual student even in a class of emotionally disturbed adolescents: he was a walking demolition man, destroying everything he touched. If he were given a new pair of pants, he ripped them. If he were given a game, he broke it. School books, notebooks, pens all looked as if they'd been recovered from a disaster site. Counseling and therapy didn't help; he treated everything with disdain. During the course of the workshop, Ann gave him a copy of an S. E. Hinton novel, *The Outsiders*. For weeks, Blake carried that book around with him, and it remained in perfect condition, though it was obviously being read. Finally Ann couldn't stand it any longer and asked the obvious, "Blake, how come nothing's happened to the book?" He looked at her and simply answered, "No one ever gave me anything that was worth anything before."

Following the workshop's six sessions, Ann left determined to learn more. She confided to me that she felt she was only beginning to understand a philosophy that could make a difference for kids like those she taught. Weeks after the workshop, Ann called and invited me to visit her classroom to see what was happening and to offer suggestions about where she could go next.

When I visited Ann's classroom one day in December, I was impressed; I saw a teacher with knowledge and expertise, one who was dedicated to working with "labeled" students, one who was using literacy in her classroom as a tool for learning about the world, about people, about feelings, and about life. Ann shared the philosophy of Donald Graves (1985), Mike Rose (1989), and Glenda Bissex (1980): Her students were capable language users who should be able to continue their language growth in her classroom. Ann saw needs as possibilities. She believed that students learn to read and write by reading and writing, much the way Frank Smith (1988c) believes. Ann defined reading as meaning-making interacting with text, and she knew that phonics drills and "workbook, basal approaches to reading, writing, and speaking present only a fragmented and technical approach, . . . restrict[ing] the ways children come to see literacy as a tool for their own empowerment" (Wood 1988, 178). She knew that language was more than "a decoding device, useful in understanding what we are told"; language was "for making our own voices heard" (178). Ann gave her students an opportunity to discover for themselves all that books had to offer to enrich their lives, without worrying about what these students supposedly couldn't do.

Ann's Class—Possibilities, Not Deficiencies

When I first entered Ann's classroom in December, I met seven students who had begun with her the previous fall; two more arrived in the early winter, and one other, Gary, arrived as a new student the following September. As happens with many classrooms, Ann's students came and went, depending on placement and personal circumstances.

All of the students in Ann's class had attended a variety of public schools before arriving at the present institution. Six of the students had been labeled handicapped and had been taught in resource rooms by special education teachers. The rest of the students had been mainstreamed, and some, such as Robb and Cole, had received instruction in reading from a remedial reading teacher.

Having been institutionalized, these students brought with them terrible problems from the outside world, problems not unlike those that students around the country have to face in public school classrooms. Most of them, when they arrived in Ann's class, had had very little success in school due to a combination of factors ranging from psychological problems to transient living. Many had been in and out of foster homes most of their lives. One thing the students had in common, however, was that all had been labeled— emotionally disturbed, handicapped, educable mentally retarded, and even gifted. Ann told me she did not even look at the academic records of the students when they first arrived, but instead tried to get to know them as individuals first. Ann understood that these students were people, not labels, and the labels often clouded who they were as individuals.

I was interested in knowing how the students' perception of Ann's classroom differed from previous experiences they had had in other schools. After several weeks of visits, once the students seemed to feel comfortable talking with me, I spoke with them about how literacy experiences in Ann's classroom compared to the way they remembered being taught reading and writing in their old schools. I was amazed at the consistency of their descriptions, even though each student had come from a different school.

Figure 1 summarizes how the students compared their past literacy experiences with their present perceptions of Ms. Hunter's classroom, a place where they read "real" books, enjoyed reading, and felt themselves to be capable readers. During my talks with the students individually and during class discussions, they described reading in previous classrooms as using "reading books" (which I interpreted as basals), and they remembered "reading in a circle" (round-robin reading), "low" reading groups, book reports, workbook pages, and various programmed approaches, such as Standard Reading Activities (SRAs). The students also remarked that they had not known how to read before, and they never used to like to read.

When the students described reading in Ms. Hunter's class, they all mentioned the fact that they got to read silently (during Sustained Silent Reading [SSR]). Many mentioned that Ann read to them every day, not just when they had "earned" it, as was the case in Gary's previous school. Many of the students described reading in Ann's classroom as "fun" or as "interesting" and stated that they could read much better since coming to Ms. Hunter's class. Several mentioned that in this class they got to read "real" books, like Blake's favorite, *The Outsiders*, not just stories in reading books (basals). They admitted to reading in their spare time, just "for fun."

The students also compared their previous writing experiences with learning to write in Ms. Hunter's class. In their descriptions of writing in their old schools, most referred to work sheets and said they did not "have writing"; they had language out of a book. They told about answering questions and practicing handwriting. It became clear to me that what most of the students were describing was penmanship and grammar exercises. When describing writing in Ann's class, they cited writing stories, keeping journals and logs, and writing poems. One girl, Tanya, said that she surprised even herself, putting "more effort into her writing" in Ms. Hunter's class, continually practicing because she was always writing. A classmate, Cole, said he was allowed to "write as much as [he] wanted" and has learned to "expand on [his] ideas." Robb was pleased that when he wrote in this class he got compliments, and he stated that this had helped his "self-esteem."

FIGURE 1   Student Perceptions of Previous Classroom Experiences Compared with Experiences in Ms. Hunter's Class

DESCRIPTION OF PREVIOUS CLASSROOM		DESCRIPTION OF Ms. HUNTER'S CLASS
not as much attention read reading books went to special ed teacher copy out of book after reading copy off the board practice cursive (mostly a list of activities)	Debby	gives us time reads to us reads with us taught me so much I've come a long way she helps me she talks to me (describes class through role of teacher)
used to have cursive writing-books read outloud in circle (round robin) never used to like to read reading class no writing, only handwriting	Tim	here I get to silent read (SSR), now I like it no reading class—read at all different times during day get to write books here she teaches us things about things we like, like baseball; I get to read about baseball and even do math about baseball no book reports—journals instead I get to write down my feelings
never made us read had to write a whole page of w's (penmanship) I flipped pages to pretend I was reading answer page of questions after reading no SSR book reports so we could get pizza (I copied them out of book)	Robb	SSR we go into more detail than in public school when we read a book we get to do a whole project on it you get to read for fun stuff we do here picks up my self-esteem when I write stories here I get compliments
it was like you'd have to get up to a table and like read (reading groups)	Gary	she reads out loud to us Ms. Hunter & Miss Rowe help me read

Description of Previous Classroom (cont.)		Description of Ms. Hunter's Class (cont.)
[we read] out of a reading book; it wasn't like no story book plenty of workbook pages, they were math, they were social studies; they were language I liked them, they were easy stories, we had to put in order if we were good we get a treat like popcorn. If we were good for a week or a month we got a movie or pizza if we wanted a book read out loud to us we'd have to earn it	Gary (cont.)	it's fun & interesting everyone is fair I'm trying here I like the books here
we would do books that said now turn to this page and then do this page and what you didn't finish you'd do for homework (content area reading) I went to a special teacher for reading we used reading books book reports mostly we did worksheets in reading class we wrote poems, never a story	Cole	you don't read out of textbooks I've read a lot of books now I read in my free time here I get to write as much as I want; I get to expand on my ideas now that I read about things I want to study more about them, like spiders in *Charlotte's Web* Ms. Hunter & Miss Rowe have taught me a lot I didn't know
we hardly did any reading & writing before in school we played games and did math packs I don't remember what we did in reading; I went to a special reading class I didn't know how to read we didn't write stories. . . .We did, like, we answered questions	Shannon	Ms. Hunter reads to us we get to read by ourselves (SSR) I learned how to read so now I read Ms. Hunter works with us I write because now I can spell words on my own you get more future here; you get to read
we used reading books and reading workbooks gave me sheets and told me to do them	David	we work in groups we read regular books, not reading books reading's more fun here

we didn't have writing we did language out of a book	David (cont.)	we read books I like Ms. Hunter brings books to my attention; the ones she thinks I'll like she (Ms. Hunter) doesn't put the high people with the high people; she puts everyone together in a group it's more positive; the teachers are more supportive, they help I don't get in trouble as much I'm learning more I'm tryin' more for some reason
we don't have pages like "was" and "were" had a separate teacher for each subject mainly they'd read out loud, everyone reads their part (round robin) we had SRAs (Standard Reading Activities) you had to fill out a whole sheet on it never wrote stories; it was always worksheets	Jeffrey	she (Ms. Hunter) teaches reading the good way I read a lot more books I do better on my reading I'm listening more, reading, and having a lot more fun I'm writing stories; even after school we keep journals and logs I don't have to read out loud if I don't want to the way we get into books is pretty interesting
we'd read at our desks; it was more structured we read harder books (textbooks) didn't read books on our own we had like math & social books—thick books (textbooks) writing was how to make cursive	Tanya	now I read books like *The Outsiders* I read a lot of books in Ms. Hunter's class reading's more fun now I read books Ms. Hunter shows me 'cuz she knows what I like now my handwriting's better now 'cuz I'm always practicing; I'm always writing! I'm surprised but I put more effort into writing it's fun

It is obvious that the students' descriptions of literacy experiences in previous classrooms echo the "scenario for failure" that Ken Goodman (1991) describes in his article, "Revaluing Readers and Reading." According to Goodman, students with reading difficulties get caught up in a cycle of failure:

> The students are not doing well in school. The less well they do, the more extensively the teacher applies the program. If the students aren't doing well on the worksheets, flashcards, drills, and remedial exercises, then the teacher repeats the same ones or provides supplementary, similar ones (129).

When skill and drill exercises do not result in improvement, the vigor of application increases, and students are given more of these exercises at the expense of other, more meaningful activities, such as free time for reading, music, or art activities. Students are even required to use their "own" time—recesses, lunch periods, after-school hours, and even vacation periods—to work on remedial exercises and programs. Goodman explains that the teacher often gives up, and the child is abandoned to remediation, very much the way Ann's students—Debby, Tim, Jeffrey, Gary, Cole, Shannon, and Robb—had been. Once referred to remediation, the students are subjected to a battery of tests, the purpose of which is to reveal patterns of weakness and deficiency. Of course, at this point the remedial exercises that are prescribed to eliminate weaknesses are even more fragmented than the exercises that failed to work in the original classroom.

Ironically, at the beginning of remediation there seems to be an upsurge of achievement and enthusiasm, offering parents and teachers a false hope. Goodman explains this phenomenon as due in part to the special attention given by the teacher. I found Goodman's explanation helpful in accounting for Gary's enthusiasm over the work sheets he was given in his old school: "there were *plenty* of workbook pages. I liked them; they were easy."

Goodman goes on to say that as the remediation program continues, the "scenario for failure" continues. When the same dull, repetitious, tedious exercises—work sheets, flash cards, and drills—do not work, the teacher gives the students more of them. To compound matters, the student actually misses out on important opportunities, especially in literacy learning, during the period spent out of the classroom for the remediation program. In the meantime, when students meet with failure and frustration again, they are told that they must not be trying; some are even told that they are lazy. Consequently blame and guilt are directed at the student; the remediation program itself is never questioned.

The remedial student's inability to succeed with the program seems to promote misbehavior and attention problems. One of Ann's students told of always being in trouble in his previous school. He said he was frequently given the choice of whether to receive a paddling or be suspended (corporal punishment is still legal in our state), and knowing the dangers that awaited him on the streets or back in his abusive home, more often than not, he chose to receive the paddling. He did, however, make the teacher chase him around the room to paddle him, he bragged. This student told me, in his own way, how he tried to survive in a system that told him he was a failure: He copied book reports off the covers of books; he pretended that he was reading when he was just flipping pages; and he acted up and caused trouble because he hated school. Another student, David, who had also been labeled a "troublemaker" in his old school, confided to me that he did not seem to be getting into as much trouble in Ms. Hunter's classroom, but he did not know why. Ironically, Goodman theorizes, the student who rebels or acts up in class may be exhibiting a more healthy attitude than the student who meekly submits or withdraws.

Goodman explains that a rebellious student shows a healthy resistance to accepting full responsibility for the failure; once the student begins to succeed there is no longer a need to resist the classroom. Gary, the student who liked the work sheets in his previous school, said that he was "trying here" in Ann's classroom, unlike his performance at his old school. One explanation might be that the "scenario for failure" had changed for these students when they were in Ms. Hunter's classroom.

Along with these changes came changes in attitude, not only toward literacy but also toward themselves as learners. It would seem that the students each saw a difference between the way literacy instruction was approached in their previous schools and the way they were taught reading and writing in Ann's classroom.

Beliefs Shape Perception

Teachers teach in a particular way because of how they believe learning takes place. Their beliefs about learning, much like any other belief, are strongly held convictions, resistant to inconsistencies or contrary observations. In fact, Thomas Kuhn (1963), a physicist, discovered how difficult it is to change belief systems or paradigms, even in the face of unexplainable anomalies, inconsistencies between beliefs held and evidence uncovered by research in a particular field or academic discipline. The textbooks that teachers employ reflect their model of learning (and some say actively shape that model). New teachers and preservice teachers adopt a set of beliefs and learn the tradition from what is taught in their education courses, from their cooperating teachers, who sponsor them during student teaching, and from their mentors, who take them under their wing and guide them through prescribed curricula taught with prescribed textbooks. The system is self-perpetuating. In fact, I found that students who leave the university without a strong personal philosophy of education quickly adopt the teaching methods and tacit philosophy of the experienced teachers with whom they work (Strickland 1991a). So great an influence does this assimilation process have that new teachers are all but told, "never mind what you learned in college; this is the real world." Thus, the system remains stable, in Kuhn's (1963) terms, until research presents overwhelming evidence to contradict accepted practice or presents enough shocks to the system to cause the traditional way of seeing things to become unreliable, unsatisfactory, and generally perceived as being out-of-date. It is only then that a paradigm shift can occur.

Frank Smith (1988a) suggests that some of the problems educators who follow a traditional program in reading and writing face are caused by a misguided reliance on psychology rather than on anthropology. Early educational psychologists such as Ernest Hilgard (1956) looked at the psychology of learning as a science that used the measurement of variables under control as the basis of its experimental designs. Simple observation and induction were not considered acceptable scientific methods by such psychologists, who believed that "scientific" research was based on the study of animals in controlled laboratory settings. Such studies, concerned as they were with the behavior of subjects "learning" to pass through mazes and hit buttons necessary to release food pellets, concluded that motivation and reinforcement were necessary for the rote memorization and recall that they believed was learning; the philosophy of early educational psychology was behaviorism.

Benjamin Bloom (1956), a behaviorist and follower of B. F. Skinner (1953, 1957), developed a "taxonomy of learning" in which he theorized that "stimulus-response" learning, or rote memorization, is the easiest type of learning and that applying and evaluating knowledge is the most difficult. This taxonomy has become the basis for much of what is done in contemporary teaching and learning. For several decades, American schools have followed behaviorist approaches to the teaching of reading. According to behaviorist theory, children learn to read by learning to decode the language; understanding follows after the code is broken and the component parts are mastered. Its theory informs the belief that children learn to read by first making sense of the smallest components of language (letters) and then progressing to larger components (sounds, words, sentences). For that reason, such a philosophy supports learning from a part-to-whole premise.

This component part-to-whole approach has been especially applied in teaching children who have had difficulty learning in school, those who have been labeled "remedial," "disabled," etc. According to standard behaviorist approaches, children are required to begin with lessons that focus on phonics (letters, combinations of letters, sounds, and rules), tightly controlled vocabulary, and short reading passages followed by numerous "skills" exercises, each having one correct answer. The reading is usually taken from a basal reading program, a kit consisting of "readers" (collections of short stories and essays), explicit and elaborate teachers' manuals, and workbooks supplemented by dittos of practice skills. In traditional classrooms, when children are asked to respond to work sheets and tests that assess "mastery" of minute skills, they are not actively involved in reading and writing authentic texts that have meaning for them; they are not psychologically engaged in the process. Basal reading programs, though used in 90 percent of American classrooms since the 1920s, have been criticized as being "sequential, all-inclusive sets of instructional materials [devised to] teach all children to read regardless of teacher competence and regardless of learner differences" (Goodman, Shannon, Freeman & Murphy 1988, 1). Such programs, it has been said, ignore the fact that learners do not all learn the same way and at the same time (Piaget 1971) and that teachers are trained professionals who, while working with children, are able to assess their students' strengths and needs and, with their students, make curricular decisions to meet individual needs.

The Paradigm Shifts

Over the past fifteen years, the paradigm has begun to shift in education away from behaviorist philosophies that employ a transmission model of teaching and learning toward a philosophy that employs a transactional model, commonly referred to as whole language (Goodman 1986; Strickland & Strickland 1993; Weaver 1990). As a result, when educators were confronted by anomalies that could not be explained by behavioral psychology, they turned to other fields for insight into learning, such as anthropology, sociology, linguistics, and developmental psychology. Recent theoretical work and research in these fields have provided a research base to whole language advocates, those who embrace the paradigm shift in education away from a behavioral transmission model toward a whole language transactional model. Unfortunately, the term *whole language* itself is often misunderstood. Whole language does not refer to a methodology; it is a philosophy. Rather than a program to be followed or applied, whole language is a set of beliefs. To understand the place of whole language in today's educational system, it may be helpful to understand its origins—where whole language came from.

Whole language has deep roots both inside and outside of education. As far back as the seventeenth century, an educator named John Amos Comenius believed that learning should be pleasurable and rooted in students' real lives. In contemporary education, the progressive education theories of John Dewey (1916) and the social educational theories of Russian psychologist Lev Vygotsky (1978) have defined teachers' roles as supportive coaches or guides. Donald Graves (1983), a pioneer of the classroom writing movement who encouraged teachers and children to write together daily for real purposes, also advanced a transactional model of teaching and literacy learning.

According to the transactional model, the student actively engages with or transacts with the external environment—including people and books—to learn (Cambourne 1989; Hall 1987; Holdaway 1979; Smith 1988c). An important aspect of the transactional model is the idea that learning—and the teaching that stimulates it—proceeds from whole to part to whole rather than from part to whole. Thus, language learning is "whole." Children simultaneously learn language and literacy in environments that permit them to read, write, listen, and speak for a variety of authentic purposes.

Children learn to read by reading, which is a "creative and constructive activity having four distinctive and fundamental characteristics—it is purposeful, selective, anticipatory, and based on comprehension" (Smith 1988c, 3). Experience with stories is critical preparation for learning to read. The more readers know of stories, the better able they are to predict and adjust their expectations about characters and events in new stories (Hickman & Cullinan 1989). Experience with literature helps children build the sense of story they need to be able to recognize conventions and patterns of language.

"It is important to help children discover the ways authors create meaning, rather than to superimpose an adult concept of literary analysis" (Huck 1977, 367). Because children are active learners, they do not need to be forced to memorize facts *about* literature; in a literature-based approach to teaching reading, students are afforded opportunities to work *with* literature. They discuss, discover, consider, represent, and reread to make meaning. Unlike basal instruction, literature-based reading instruction does not look for "one-answer" readings of story. In fact, some suggest that the reader—child or adult—creates meaning in the act of reading and that neither literary analysis nor one-answer comprehension questions are appropriate responses to reading (Probst 1992). Response to literature is an active response—a transaction between the reader and the text, according to Louise Rosenblatt's (1978) theory. The words on the page are cues from the author, but readers make meaning through personal knowledge, associations, feelings, and experiences as they transact with the texts.

The Paradigm in Writing

Like the teaching of reading, the teaching of writing in American schools has also been dominated by behaviorist theories for decades. The traditional paradigm for the teaching of writing has been characterized by Richard Young (1978):

> [Its] overt features . . . are obvious enough; the emphasis on the composed product rather than on the composing process; the analysis of discourse into description, narration, exposition, and argument; the strong concern with usage . . . and with style; the preoccupation with the informal essay and research paper; and so on. (31)

Those who adhere to the traditional paradigm believe that competent writers know what they are going to say before they write, that the most important task before writing is to organize content, and that the composing process is linear. Finally, and this is what has strongly dominated the traditional paradigm, advocates believe that to teach editing is to teach writing.

Maxine Hairston (1982), in her landmark article "The Winds of Change: Thomas Kuhn and the Revolution in the Teaching of Writing," points out that the traditional paradigm began to become unstable in the 1950s owing in large part to the psycholinguistic theories of Noam Chomsky (1957). Chomsky concluded that the rules by which language is generated and that determine how language is learned are too complex to be regarded as "habit learning." In a point-by-point rebuttal of behaviorist approaches, Chomsky showed that B. F. Skinner's view trivializes language and learning. At the historic Anglo-American Seminar on the Teaching of English held at Dartmouth College in 1966, educators from the United States, Great Britain, and Canada, adopting a Chomskian perspective on language, "deemphasized the formal teaching of grammar and usage in the classroom and emphasized having children engage directly in the writing process in a non-prescriptive atmosphere" (Hairston 1982, 19).

Over the next two decades, the research of scholars such as Mina Shaughnessy (1977), Janet Emig (1971, 1977), James Britton (1975), and Linda Flower and John Hayes (1980) changed the way writing was studied and conceptualized. Subsequently, educators took what composition researchers had learned about the process of writing and the process of learning to write, and they showed teachers how cognitive and developmental research affects the teaching of writing to children (Graves 1983; Calkins 1986; Atwell 1987; Rief 1992).

Whole Language—A Set of Beliefs

Whole language, as stated earlier, is not a methodology; it is a set of beliefs. Rather than a program to be followed or applied, whole language is a philosophy, a major tenet of which holds that language is best learned in authentic, meaningful situations. These situations are ones in which language is not separated into parts, but remains whole. The beliefs about language learning that underlie whole language have resulted from practical applications of theoretical arguments arising from combined research in fields such as psycholinguistics, sociology, anthropology, child development, composition, literacy theory, and semiotics. Various remarks by Ann's students may help to make some of these beliefs more concrete:

1. Robb loved the book, *The Outsiders*; he understood the feelings of its characters. He told me, "I used to live the kind of life he did; not the same—I didn't fight Greasers and Socs, but I used to fight the Crips and the Bloods."

Students learn by constructing meaning from the world around them, a view quite different from the behaviorist view of learning by imitation, which is based not on observing how children learn but on how animals respond to "stimulus-response" in controlled laboratory settings. In the real world, in contrast to the world of laboratories, people learn what is worthwhile, useful, and easiest to learn, as Frank Smith (1988b) reminds us in *Joining the Literacy Club*. People learn by building on what they already know (schema), and literature helps to connect their world to other worlds.

2. Cole said, "Mostly we did worksheets in reading class," and Shannon said, "We didn't write stories, . . . we answered questions."

Language learning is not sequential, but reading and writing skills develop simultaneously along with oral language skills. In a behaviorist classroom, reading is taught as a progression of standardized skills, each of which is designed to elicit an appropriate response in a reader that might be objectively tested before moving on to the next skill. For example, in a traditional kindergarten classroom, children would be taught all the letters of the alphabet and their sounds before they were given the opportunity to react to whole texts. Regrettably, the teaching of writing often follows this same premise of learning from part to whole. The subskills of spelling, grammar, and sentence structure have been taught through drill and practice prior to allowing students to attempt real writing.

3. Tim explained, "I think . . . if the teacher does a subject, like a History thing, and they go into it with books and reading it as a group . . . then I think people will get into that topic and read. I know when we did the Civil War and I got real interested about that, I read three or four books on my own about the Civil War."

Curriculum in a whole language classroom is not a prescribed course of study; instead, learning occurs when students engage in purposeful activities that connect to their lives and experiences. Teachers demonstrate reading and writing by being readers and writers themselves, people who use reading and writing for real purposes. Conversely, in the behaviorist classroom, students are expected to operate within their teacher's assumptive bounds and their learning is controlled by a curriculum that is decided outside the classroom. "Teacher-centered approaches . . . do not encourage true learning, only adjustment to someone else's expectations" (Reid & Golub 1991, 84).

4. Cole decided, "I think for people who want to start writing or reading, I think they just have to try it, and it's not going to come overnight or in a few days. . . . It takes practice."

Language is best learned in an environment encouraging risk taking; error is inherent in the process. Students learn in a language environment that provides opportunities to transact with print, to think of themselves as readers and writers, and to learn about language as they are immersed in it and using it. In a behaviorist classroom, students are expected to learn the rules of language before they are allowed to use it, and children are taught that there is one right way to use language—the teacher's way.

5. Tanya found a purpose for reading: "I like *The Outsiders* because it shows how the world really is."

Reading and writing are context specific, reflections of the situation in which learning is taking place. Young children approach written language expecting it to make sense. Harste, Woodward, and Burke (1984b) clearly demonstrated that children, as readers, transact with environmental print, and their responses are functional, categorical, or specified, depending upon the children's previous experience. This same natural functional approach to language learning continues as a student uses reading and writing in the whole language classroom for real purposes and for real audiences. In a behaviorist classroom, children are expected to read and write about topics of the teacher's choosing and for purposes dictated by the teacher or the prescribed curriculum. Often children's knowledge about environmental print is generally ignored rather than built upon.

6.   Cole thinks, "Just reading a book, period, is helping you learn how to read. . . . It's like when I read, it gives me ideas how to write," and Jeffrey concluded, "I'm listening more, reading, and having a lot more fun."

Instruction in a whole language classroom includes all aspects of language learning—students learn to read while they are writing and they learn about writing by reading. Students may also learn about reading and writing while listening, but not when listening exclusively to their teacher lecture, an activity designed to help adults more than children exercise their language abilities.

Whole Language for ALL Students?

In the last two decades, the adoption of a transactional philosophy has been evident in teaching at all levels: from primary grades through postsecondary instruction. While it is impossible to deny that the traditional paradigm is still very much a part of American education, a shift toward a new paradigm is supported by the majority of recent research findings. And yet, for as many educators who have accepted the new paradigm of language learning and teaching, there are teachers and researchers who still disagree among themselves about methodology and about how a transactional approach to teaching and learning should be implemented in the classroom. The methodology disagreement is especially heated when considering students who have had difficulty learning to read and write in school (Goodman 1991; Graves 1985; Smith 1988a; Taylor 1991; Mather 1992). Many educators still insist that some children, especially those labeled "learning disabled," need systematic phonics instruction or what is called "code-emphasis" (Chall 1967). Some educators maintain that students identified as word-blind or dyslexic require special techniques to learn to read. For example, in "Whole Language Reading Instruction for Students with Learning Disabilities: Caught in the Cross Fire," Nancy Mather (1992) cites research (Hulme 1981) contending that "subjects with learning disabilities remembered words better when they were allowed to trace them" (91). Never mind that throughout much of her article, Mather considers dyslexic students as those having a visual perception problem, rather than those who have, by the very definition of the word, an unexplained reading difficulty. What strikes me as I read such "research" is the obvious paradigm difference between those who accept the behaviorist's medical-clinical models of reading instruction and those who believe in a socio-psycholinguistic model of reading (Goodman 1987; Weaver 1994). Behaviorists, because of their conception of reading and their belief in how it is learned will never come to accept a "whole language" philosophy because it is based on a completely contrary philosophy of language learning. Consequently a great difference exists between instruction and environment in behaviorist classrooms and those classrooms that are based on a transactional or whole language philosophy (see Figure 2).

According to a medical-clinical model of reading, students with reading problems are placed in special classes and their instruction is most often informed by behaviorist theories. These classes are frequently "pull out" in nature, requiring those labeled "remedial" to leave their regular classes for special services. These students, especially those who are labeled "at risk," "learning disabled (learning support)," or "handicapped" are grouped together homogeneously, supposedly to better meet their needs. Such labeling and grouping may be done with the best of intentions, "but the effect has been more damaging than beneficial," because as Susan Stires (1991) points out, "all of the categories define students in terms of their limitations" (xiv). Conventional wisdom holds that students who have difficulty in literacy learning are best helped through the traditional "part-to-whole" skills approaches. Yet those who have not been successful in school reading programs—students Ken Goodman (1991) refers to as "readers in trouble" (127)—are more likely than other students to be the victims of too much skills instruction and too much instruction based on behaviorist principles. In fact, so much time is spent on such remediation that little time is left for actual reading.

The net effect of such instruction is that students are led to believe that reading *is* skills rather than an "act of meaning construction" (Wells 1986). This was demonstrated to me in Ann Hunter's classroom when the students spoke about how they were learning to read. For Gary, a nonreader prior to being in Ann's class, reading formerly consisted of controlled vocabulary, programmed books, and word-attack skills. He confided that at his previous school he had to read "out of a reading book; it wasn't like no story book." In Ann's class, he developed a larger concept of reading—at the meaning-making, story level. Jeffrey added that he had SRAs (Standard Reading Activities) and remembered that "you had to fill out a whole sheet on it." David said, "They gave me sheets and told me to do them." The others in

FIGURE 2   Contrasting Models of Education for "Disabled" Learners

Transmission Philosophy Traditional Classroom		Transactional Philosophy Whole Language Classroom
1. Stimulus/response model of learning based on research in behavioral psychology.	Basis of Philosophy	1. Cognitive/ social model based on research in developmental psychology, linguistics, sociology, anthropology.
2. Dispensers of knowledge: Teachers tell and convey the impression that there is one correct answer or interpretation—the teacher's or the manual's.	Teacher role	2. Facilitators: Teachers demonstrate what it means to be a reader and a writer by reading and writing in and out of the classroom and by sharing literacy experiences with students.
3. Students strive for "right" answers and regard success and learning as completing one workbook and going on to the next "level."	Students' View of Learning	3. Students are risk takers. They see learning as an exciting opportunity for open-ended response and critical thinking.
4. Literacy is the product of a prescribed curriculum. Emphasis is placed on skills such as vocabulary, spelling, and grammar, skills which must be mastered before students can effectively read and/or write. Functional literacy is the goal.	Literacy	4. Literacy is taught in a meaningful context. There is an emphasis on meaning and "making sense" in oral and written communication. Students' schemas help them to connect to new experiences.
5. Reading is skills based and takes place in remedial classes. The emphasis for what little writing is expected is on correctness. The teacher chooses the reading selections and writing topics.	Reading and Writing	5. Students are expected to read and write every day. Students have the opportunity to choose what they read and write about and make choices from a variety of literature written by adult and student authors.
6. Phonics exercises, grammar exercises, spelling and vocabulary lists and tests.	Skills	6. Skills are taught in the context of language.

7. Students work independently; often grouped homogeneously be "levels."	Grouping	7. Students work cooperatively in groups that are formed for many reasons, including shared interests.
8. Environment (desks in rows) is designed to promote behavior management. Programmed learning is the basis of the curriculum: Teachers give assignments, correct papers, and construct spelling charts. Students work on exercises or do homework from a text.	Environment	8. Environment is designed to promote literacy development. A variety of language materials are readily available for student use and student work in progress is displayed. Classroom becomes a clustering of literature and writing groups where peer groups of individuals work and teachers conference.
9. Teachers evaluate primarily by grading products or by giving tests. Students are labeled according to standardized test scores. Evaluation tools focus on student deficiencies.	Evaluation	9. Teachers are "kid watchers," evaluating and assessing student progress based on observation, focusing on what students can do. Teachers work with students to establish attainable goals.
10. Primarily behavior management techniques—rewards/punishments; students are kept separated; the emphasis is on control and maintaining quiet.	Management	10. As students are engaged in learning students become responsible for their own behavior. Students learn to respect and rely on their community.

the class admitted that they never understood what those "pages" of skill sheets had to do with reading; they just did them so they could move on to the next book or in some cases to "get a pizza."

Did Ann Hunter teach skills in her classroom? Not in the traditional sense of isolated exercises; but during shared reading time, Ann talked about language, sharing techniques for learning or using words that were unfamiliar to her students. She encouraged them to use a variety of strategies, and they did so in context of real reading, not in exercises. Did they have to know each word when they read? No (what real reader does?), but they did learn when it was important to figure out a word essential to meaning and what strategies they could use as readers to figure out unfamiliar words. For example, sounding out a word and hearing whether it sounds familiar was one strategy that Ann taught her readers. (For more information on the role of phonics in a whole language classroom, see the National Council of Teachers of English [NCTE] publication *Looking Closely: The Role of Phonics in a Whole Language Classroom* by Mills, O'Keefe, and Stephens 1992.) Looking at unfamiliar words and seeing how they are similar to known vocabulary was another strategy. These strategies were discussed in the context of real literature *after* attending to meaning, not through exercises or meaningless workbook pages.

Unlike the traditional basal reader and other programmed approaches to teaching reading, literature-based reading instruction uses *real* literature to teach reading, often literature of a student's own choosing (Goodman 1986; Smith 1988a). A literature-based approach uses strategies such as oral reading by the teacher and shared reading to support a student's reading development (Holdaway 1979). More importantly, readers are given opportunities to think about what has been read through the use of writing and talking and are able to make connections with the reality of their own world (Smith 1988b). Literature-based instruction, in contrast to skills-based instruction, teaches that the purpose of reading is "making meaning" rather than skills. Using a "whole-to-part-to-whole" approach, students are taught to read by reading—literature rather than basals—and are encouraged to react to literature as readers do—by discussing it, thinking about it, and applying it to their lives.

Ann gives her students opportunities to make meaning through the reading of literature. One of Tanya's favorite books was *The Outsiders* (as it was for Blake, mentioned earlier, and for so many young teens since the 1960s). From talking to Tanya, it is easy to understand why this S. E. Hinton book had more of an impact on her than the homogenized basal stories she previously had been subjected to. Was the novel on her "independent reading level"? No. Could she read it? Yes! After getting "hooked" by hearing Ann read the first few chapters of the novel aloud while class members followed along in their own copies, Tanya would not put the book away. She was absorbed in that book; it spoke to her about what she knew and felt about the world—about conflict and violence, about loyalty, and about love, in the context of the lives of city kids very much like herself. Could she make meaning when she read this book? Of course she could; even if she could not read every word, she understood the story of the teens in the book. Novel after novel reached out to Tanya who, before entering Ann's classroom, had confessed that there had been no place in her life for reading.

As one might guess, literature-based instruction founded on a transactional philosophy is not a common practice in remedial reading or special education classes. Nevertheless, many educators, prompted by current research in the field of language learning, recognize a need to do more to ensure that all students learn to read and write—including those labeled "at risk," "learning disabled," and otherwise "handicapped." Hollingsworth and Reutzel (1988), in their article "Whole Language with LD Children," confirm that "practices consistent with whole language theory . . . help LD students become literate users of language as a communication medium" (477). Many teachers, Marie D'Alessandro (1990), for example, and others whose stories are told by Susan Stires (1991), recount tales of success with whole language practices for labeled students. We need to apply what we know about how children learn to read and write (Smith 1988c; Harste, Woodward & Burke 1984b) to how such learning might be facilitated for all students in the classroom (Atwell 1987; Calkins 1986, 1991; Goodman 1986, 1991). Whole language is not a methodology used with *some* learners; it is a philosophy of teaching and learning that holds as a major tenet that *all* children can learn when such learning is purposeful and when they are supported by a teacher who *believes* they can learn.

2
The Teacher's Roles
Supporter, Model, Facilitator

Teachers consistently report that their major and most reliable source
of information inside the classroom is their personal interaction with
their students, even if these interactions are not usually classified as
part of the curriculum.
Sara E. Freedman

Ken Goodman quips that he didn't find whole language; it found him.
Nevertheless, teachers frequently ask, how does one become a whole language teacher? Ann Hunter, the teacher I worked with, did not consciously
decide to become a "whole language" teacher; she did not consciously
choose to abandon approaches to teaching literacy that she had been taught
as part of her teacher education and those modeled for her by her teachers.
To move from a skills orientation in teaching reading and writing to a holistic one involves a fundamental shift in a teacher's personal pedagogical philosophy. Ann Hunter became a whole language teacher when she embraced
a different philosophy of learning. That's what Ken Goodman meant, whole
language found Ann Hunter.

Developing a Philosophy

A change in philosophy frequently begins with a general sense of dissatisfaction, an uneasiness that comes from asking too many unanswered questions.
Ann Hunter was dissatisfied with what was not working with her students.
She was frustrated with traditional approaches to literacy instruction that
she knew from experience were inadequate—approaches based on a transmission or behaviorist model of education. An entry Ann wrote in the
reflective teaching log she kept reveals her growing disillusionment:

> After my teacher training, I was convinced that teaching was a
> rather simple, cut-and-dried process. You tested, identifying very
> clear weaknesses and shining strengths, and you used those strong
> skills and learning channels to "fix and repair" weaknesses.

> Simple—like writing prescriptions or building a model—follow
> the directions and go step-by-step. HAH!

In the log, Ann continues to explain her dissatisfaction with the skills-based approaches she used in her early years of teaching:

> No one ever said that real, flesh and blood people with dyed-in-the-wool attitudes and feelings would be in my class. [My] first group [of students] had been tested, prescribed, and remediated to death! Each succeeding group was so defensive and so beaten down by all our "scientific" methods that I realized that something had to change and change fast or these kids would be lost forever. That first year, and for seven years after, I learned from the kids to abandon that test/teach/test method and . . . to incorporate literature into our daily routine.

Ann said she sought out workshops like mine, ones that were offered at the university, simply because she was "looking for some answers." By the time she took my workshop, Ann knew enough to recognize that she needed to know more.

Yet dissatisfaction alone is not sufficient to guarantee a change in philosophy. When teachers change, the transition is often gradual, and those going through such a change require support of various kinds (Vacca & Rasinski 1992). Ann, like other teachers, often had doubts about her teaching and about her shift away from what was familiar and comfortable. Very early in our relationship, after a particularly difficult afternoon, Ann confessed in her journal:

> It's tough to keep planning all new books and activities. I feel nervous that I'm not providing my kids with a cohesive education. I'm having trouble building on prior knowledge. Maybe [it's] because I'm new to whole language.

And most of all, Ann worried that what she was attempting to do might not be appropriate for all the students in her classroom. In September, she wrote in her log:

> Gary is quite lost. The whole language thing seems to be way over his head.

Ann continued to worry that some students might still require a skills-based approach to be able to read, students such as Gary who were nonreaders, even though she knew that Gary's problem was comprehension, not decoding. Ann needed someone to validate what she was doing, someone to tell her she was on the right track, someone to confirm her best instincts. For many teachers, especially for those like Ann who teach in places where help in whole language pedagogy is virtually nonexistent, it is incredibly difficult to shake that persistent feeling of loneliness and insecurity. Ann needed support and encouragement. That may have been one of the first functions I had in Ann's classroom; while Ann experimented, questioned, and took risks, I acted as a cheerleader, coach, and supporter. After all, when I think about it, Ann was beginning to look at teaching and learning in ways totally different from what she had been taught in college. She was completely retraining herself. Ann was behaving as any learner would in a new and uncharted region, and I was there to help in any way I could.

In addition to the support that I offered personally and pedagogically, Ann turned to another nontraditional source for help in working through her questions and insecurities—her students. Ann allowed her students to spend time discussing their learning. Ann let them work through strategies and reflect upon how they learned. She felt that they needed to metacognitively work through the process of learning itself.

Ann's students provided additional support concerning her decision to drop the "skills" instruction that used drills and workbooks. During a class discussion, Ann told the students that she still worried about not giving them more phonics instruction, and she asked how they felt about not receiving drills and workbooks in class and if they felt that they needed such instruction. In response to her query as to whether they had missed these phonics worksheets, Tanya asked, "You mean that 'eee, ah, ah, ah, oh, oh, oh' stuff?"

"Those stupid 'eee' words?" asked Robb, and the rest of the class giggled, making guttural noises and faces as they imitated the vowel sounds.

"Well," asked Ann, "do you think that learning phonics rules and practicing the sounds helps you to become a better reader?"

Tim responded, "No; I don't think that stuff helps you learn."

Tanya turned to her classmates and took a quick poll, "Anyone who thinks that 'eee' stuff works, raise your hand."

When no one did, she turned to her teacher, satisfied, and concluded, "See Ms. Hunter, we don't think that stuff works." The other students all agreed, even Gary who earlier in the semester had shared with me that he thought those phonics work sheets were fun, even Gary who never read books before he came to Ann's class. In fact, not only did Gary now like reading books better than doing phonics work sheets, but he also did not seem to see any connection between the two activities.

Ann continued to have misgivings, but she told me that when she heard such positive statements from the students themselves, it gave her the strength and the support she needed to keep moving forward. "In my heart, I believe it because I can see it," Ann said, "but it's difficult because it's not what I was taught to do, and sometimes I get nervous."

As Ann and I talked about her philosophy and how it was changing, she realized that there was a professional component to her pedagogy. She had begun reading professional books about whole language, written by classroom teacher-researchers who helped Ann make another connection. Ann joined a teacher's professional organization, the National Council of Teachers of English, a group providing her with support through association and publication. This growing sense of herself as a professional in a community of professionals gave her confidence in the changes she was making.

Ann even began to conduct workshops herself for area teachers and participated as a workshop leader at a spring conference of NCTE. She felt that as a special education teacher her participation in the workshops might be particularly valuable for her colleagues, those special education teachers who were still being trained from a behaviorist orientation, teachers for whom the philosophy of whole language was new. "I'm certainly no expert," said Ann, "but at least I can share what I've learned with others. I'm more convinced than ever that this is the way to teach reading and writing, and I guess I can tell other people about what I'm doing and how my kids are progressing." Our friendship, her reading, and the national and local connections with other professionals all provided the support she needed as she developed her philosophy and evolved into a whole language teacher.

Supporting Individual Needs

As a consequence of embracing a whole language philosophy, Ann felt a strong desire to support not only the needs of her class as a whole but also the needs of the students as individuals, a conviction that produced more uncertainty. "Some of my greatest fears and insecurities about my abilities," Ann wrote in her log, "arise from the daunting nature of [supporting student needs] and facing [this task] on a daily basis." And yet, much of what Ann did to meet the needs of her students came so naturally to her that she was almost unaware of how she was doing it.

During classroom visits, I saw Ann attending to the needs of the students as individuals when she conferenced with them, when she encouraged them as they contributed in a discussion, and when she used opportunities or "teachable moments" to broaden their schemata, widening their worlds through stories, explanations, and recommendations. Ann was doing what I believe many whole language teachers do, often instinctively: interacting with her students instead of transmitting knowledge to them, facilitating learning in a way that she was unaware of many times. Since I was aware of the anxiety she felt about supporting her students' needs, I took the opportunity during our discussions after school to mention to Ann instances in which I had noticed her supporting their needs as learners. After one of our talks, Ann wrote in her log about why teachers have this difficulty, especially ones who have been trained to identify needs through testing and then to proceed through remediation:

> In the past, tests and teacher observation identified each kid's [specific] weaknesses, which were then addressed on an individualized basis by programming them through workbook pages and other prepared exercises relating to the particular skills [which they were] found [to be] lacking. Very little interaction, except student/teacher/aide interaction, was incorporated into the remedial process. Now, theme-based instruction through literature permits more group instruction. It allows us to address some of the gaps in the kids' social and cultural development and it forces them to increase their oral skills so that they can communicate with others. . . . When using literature as a basis for instruction, the efforts to meet those needs are less obvious and less contrived and more a natural movement from one aspect of a topic to another.

For example, Ann realized, as the class read Katherine Paterson's novel *Bridge to Terabithia*, that she did not always have to directly address students' needs, but that their needs would be met when she, as a facilitator, provided opportunities for students to learn and discover through literature. Ann reflected on this in her log:

> The literature itself can also meet individual needs. Books that address problems common to adolescents can be springboards from which rich problem-solving opportunities can arise. Kids can find heros to relate to and identify with. Many of the books and stories we read allow them to delve into cultures quite different from their own, thereby allowing comparisons and value explorations in a nonthreatening way.

Ann continued looking for ways to assess student needs as a means to drive instruction. She felt that if she could monitor student needs in a more methodical way, she would be better able to support those individual needs.

Toward this end, Ann read books, such as *Assessment and Evaluation in Whole Language Classrooms* by Bill Harp (1991) and *The Whole Language Evaluation Book* by Ken and Yetta Goodman and Wendy Hood (1989), as well as numerous articles that appeared in *Language Arts*, NCTE's elementary teachers' language arts journal. Ann also learned strategies she could use in the classroom on a daily basis by attending a 15-hour workshop on the philosophies of holistic assessment and evaluation that was provided through her Intermediate Unit (a state-level educational affiliate that encompasses multiple districts).

One of the first assessment strategies that Ann implemented was anecdotal records, a systematic collection of remarks written as she reflected on her students' needs and progress, short notes jotted down that she wished to remember, anecdotes that later proved to be helpful in piecing together the "larger picture." These dated entries were typical of Ann's anecdotes:

> 9-11 Loretta is bored and wants textbooks—Tanya has the same problem. Maybe I can work in the old science texts when we talk about [the five] senses. . . . I'll have to try to "wean" them away from these gradually.

> 9-16 Tim . . . seems to be enjoying independent reading. . . . I think I'll try the dialogue journal with him. It may make him feel special and he needs that attention right now.

> 9-17 David is a puzzle—very angry! Directing that anger to other kids—acting superior and condescending. He is reading more though. I'm not sure how he feels about what he reads, just as I'm not sure what he feels about anything.

> 10-16 Shannon *still* has great difficulty putting ideas down [on paper]. There's some improvement but I have to work with her on some prewriting strategies. Maybe if I get her to talk more before writing it will help.

These anecdotes, short, written quickly, and therefore taking little of the time so precious to a busy teacher, helped Ann begin to see threads throughout.

As we spoke after school, Ann would often share observations with me about student behaviors and attitudes that she was noticing on a day-to-day basis. Her comments during these discussions resembled the tone of her anecdotes—reporting, questioning, and projecting. Ann was learning to let the students' needs drive her instruction. She said that writing in her log and discussing what she observed helped her sort things out; it was a type of writing for discovery. Ann was always trying to find out from her students what they knew, what they could do, and where they needed help. Often, as she reported and questioned in her log, she would come up with a teaching strategy she wanted to try. For example, as Ann wrote the following entry, she was reporting her observations and thinking about where to begin:

> Gary is *really* preying on my mind. He's having so much trouble with language . . . I think I'll try having him talk into a tape recorder for some of his stories. That may not be any better though, because he rambles so much. He decodes at about a third grade level I think, but I don't think he has much more than surface comprehension; is he capable of more? He must be. He has great difficulty tracking—I'm not sure he has left-right progression. I'll try the marker approach and model how to track with my finger. His handwriting is illegible and he is unhappy with it—I'll try dictation.

Ann's use of words such as *try* and *maybe* reveals that she doesn't believe in easy answers. Her actions show that she is a risk taker; working with her students, talking to them, and discovering their strengths and weaknesses, she tries to identify strategies that might support them as learners. She never blamed students for what they did not know or tried to make them fit the system. Instead, she assumed responsibility for discovering ways that supported them and met their needs at the time; it appeared that she understood that these needs would be continually changing as the students developed.

Teacher as Literacy Model

Research suggests that teacher modeling in the classroom is a great influence on students' literacy learning. When teachers support learning by modeling, they begin by first reading together with the students. Gradually the students move from the teacher's modeling to working together to support each other and finally to independent reading and writing. This procedure follows a developmental pattern that Lev Vygotsky (1978) typified as "what a child can do in cooperation today, he can do alone tomorrow" (89).

When working with adolescents who consider themselves nonreaders, providing support often means actually reading to the students, a first step in the modeling of reading. Ann chose to do this through a technique commonly called "shared reading" (Weaver 1988; Holdaway 1979). During daily shared reading, Ann or the students choose material for the class to read as a group—a book, an article, a poem, a song. The entire class would have access to a copy of the text, either in book form or, in the case of shorter selections, as a photocopy or projected overhead transparency. After discussion in preparation for reading, Ann read the text while the students followed along. When students volunteered to read, Ann and other students supported them. Sometimes during the reading Ann paused to ask questions, thereby supporting meaning-making while inviting personal response to the text. For example, Ann asked during a reading of *Bridge to Terabithia*, "Why do you think Jess said that?" giving the students an opportunity to reflect and respond as readers do and welcoming various opinions and predictions. Other times, the students interrupted to ask questions about the story or about specific vocabulary they wished clarified. In either case, Ann would stop to discuss the story line or to explain words within the context of the story. These pauses in the reading were not planned or programmed; they occurred naturally during the reading whenever Ann or the students saw a need.

During these shared reading times, Ann modeled reading behaviors for the students, and they became involved in the text through talk and discussion. Ann read with enthusiasm and interest, and when she stopped to question, it was with a genuine interest in how other readers were responding to the text. Even students who would not have been able to read the book independently were reading because they were just as involved and immersed in the story as the other students. They all came to know the characters and the plot, and each had personal reactions to the text, as all readers do. At several points during my time with Ann's class, I saw the students keep running lists of the books they had read during the year. Without exception, all the students included the books read in class during shared reading as well as those read independently. The reason for this, I believe, is that the students had come to view reading not as saying or decoding words or as a solitary act, but as interacting with text. They felt they had "read" them because they had interacted with the story and had made the text real through their personal experiences, sometimes independently, but often in a community of readers.

When Gary first entered her class, Ann noticed that he knew how to decode some words, but he had never, to Ann's knowledge or Gary's recollection, been given the opportunity to really read and never been supported as a reader who interacted with text. When "reading" *Charlie Skeedaddle*, Gary was not able to decode the text independently, but he did follow along as others read, his eyes or finger tracking along the lines, turning the pages at appropriate places. More importantly, when Gary brought meaning to the text by interpreting and connecting Charlie's experiences to his own experiences, he transformed the text into what Louise Rosenblatt (1978) calls a "poem." When the text becomes a poem, it is a unique literacy experience made possible by the encounter of a reader: "A text does not become a poem until a reader comes along and, by reading it, makes one out of the experience" (Probst 1992, 56). Most importantly, as the students made "poems" by interacting with text, they came to *believe* that they were readers and that they were capable of reading. So many of them were convinced before coming to this class that they couldn't read, and they credited Ann and her modeling for helping them learn to read. This was evident when I asked Debby what she thought of reading instruction in Ann's class: "I would say she helps you out; there's a lot of books in here. Ms. Hunter really brought me a long way. A lot of the kids she brought a long way."

Cole agreed, "I think just reading books, period, is helping you learn how to read. They used to teach you how to sound words . . . you know, those vowels 'e' and all those; it just don't teach you."

Tim explained, "When I read now I get a picture in my head. I could never do that before."

"When I first came here," Shannon said, "I didn't know how to read at all, until I started reading with Ms. Hunter. I mean, I knew how to read, but not that much; but I started to read with Ms. Hunter, and when she was saying the words I was sorta saying them under my breath and then I just knew them."

Ann was helping the students build skills, but they were doing so in the context of real reading. When looking at the students' writing it was obvious that their vocabulary was increasing as they read, most obviously when they began to use words that were not in their spoken vocabularies, words such as *paranoid, barriers, humble, shocked, unique, predators,* and *relate,* among others. Ann did not teach this vocabulary directly through word lists. Instead, her students learned new vocabulary as they read and used the words that were necessary in discussions and in their writings. Ann had modeled an interest in words and encouraged risk taking in the daily use of language in the classroom. She often took time after the reading to talk about words found in the stories, as points of interest, not as lists. She promoted in her students an interest in language, in words, not as an assignment but as enjoyment.

Frank Smith (1988c) explains that to learn to read, students must be given opportunities to read. Unfortunately, in many classes little real reading actually takes place (Goodman 1986). Ann, an avid reader herself, felt it was extremely important to model for students the value she placed on reading and the importance it had in her life and in her classroom. Her enthusiasm was evident as she shared reading experiences with her students and recounted reactions to books she had read as an adolescent. Many students wished to read these books, often borrowing the books Ms. Hunter liked "when she was a kid," and offering their opinions of them to her. Ann was always sharing books with the students that she had read or was reading. She accomplished this in a variety of ways. During discussions, Ann would often refer to a book she had read that related to the topic; she would bring books to class that she had read; and during Sustained Silent Reading, she would read for pleasure with the students.

SSR has long been considered "a way of increasing reading proficiency and sustaining an interest in reading that will lead to lifelong reading habits" (Weaver 1988, 314). During SSR, a half hour usually set aside just before lunch, the students read for pleasure rather than to "learn" content material. They sat around the room wherever they were comfortable—on the floor, in the bean bag chair, in the rocking chair, or in chairs in the corners. Ann would take a few minutes to find out what students were reading and to make suggestions if they had no book, were unsure of what to read next, or were dissatisfied with what they were reading. Ann encouraged students to choose another book if the one they were reading was not enjoyable, aware of the importance that interest has for success at reading.

The students read books their classmates recommended and began to establish informal literature groups on their own. For example, both Tanya and Robb decided to read a mystery novel entitled *The Snowman*. Since Ann had two copies in the room, Tanya and Robb could read it together. They decided how many chapters they would read in a day and then discussed their favorite parts of the reading, usually while they walked to lunch. Their sharing seemed to be modeled upon the way their teacher talked about the books she was reading. This book sharing was not unlike what Nancie Atwell (1987) called "dining room table talk" (19), conversations where real readers talk about what they are reading for reasons they feel are important.

Being well read, Ann often seemed like a storehouse of information. During social studies lessons, for example, Ann might tell a story that recounted a famous historical incident. "How do you know that?" the students would ask. Sometimes Ann would quote a source, but more often she would simply say, "Oh, I read about it somewhere." The students began to see that Ann, a person they respected and regarded as intelligent, not only enjoyed reading but learned much of what she knew from reading.

The students began to see reading as a tool they could use. For instance, Cole shared how he felt about reading to learn. He said, "I keep things in my mind that I enjoy reading, and I don't like stuff from textbooks, and I like *Charlotte's Web*, and I learned a lot about spiders, and it's in my head now, and it's probably going to stay because I like it." In fact, after reading *Charlotte's Web*, Cole became the spider expert in-residence, reading all he could about spiders from any source he could find. Other students also used reading to find information. Once during the writing of a story, Robb got up and went to the bookcase to look for a book on rap music. Since rap music was featured in a part of his story and he needed some specific information, he was going to "look it up." He had internalized the assumption that what he needed would be found in books and that the information would prove valuable to his writing.

All Ann's students were realizing that reading was a tool that could be used for a variety of purposes, and they were learning the power of reading as they entered what Frank Smith (1988b) calls the "literacy club." In this community, with Ann as a model, the students had learned the use of reading for a variety of purposes, and one of those purposes was to learn. This realization did not come as a result of any lesson Ann had directly taught her students concerning research skills or the use of sources in writing; rather, it came as a result of their learning through experience about sources of information (texts being just one) and about how to use literacy to learn about things that were important to them.

As months went by, Ann was learning to be a model for writing as well. It was not as easy or natural as it had been for her to be a reading model because Ann said that she did not actually consider herself a writer. When we first met, I shared with Ann a copy of *Writing: Teachers and Children at Work*, in which Donald Graves (1983) points out, "Teachers don't have to be expert writers to 'write' with children. In fact, there may be an advantage in growing with them, learning together as both seek to find meaning in writing" (43).

Ann wanted to include more writing in the curriculum and increase the actual amount of time that her students spent writing, but because writing was not something she was used to doing, Ann seemed to write neither as often nor as regularly as she would have liked. For Ann, writing would not immediately happen as a natural extension of her teaching as it did with reading. She spent class time conferencing or teaching mini-lessons rather than writing herself, although she verbally accepted the idea of the importance of writing when the students wrote. This is understandable, I think, due to the fact that she was still uncomfortable with her own perception of herself as a writer. Ann began slowly; she had to consciously plan to write. It seemed easiest for Ann to freewrite with the students as they reacted in their literature logs to the chapters that the class had read. She still felt insecure about the teaching of writing and hoped a workshop approach would allow her to be methodical and organized about her teaching. She invited me to "jump in" when I saw ways to support this learning about writing.

One day, as the students were struggling with the idea of revision, I brought in drafts of a letter I had just written to my dean at the university. I explained to the students that this was an important letter and would be "published," insofar as I was going to send it to the dean. Because the dean was, in essence, "my boss" (a term the students understood), it was important that the letter say exactly what I meant it to say and that the form be perfect. For these reasons, I told them, I revised the letter several times and asked my husband to revise it once with me before I wrote the final draft. I showed the students several drafts of the letter as well as the finished product, and they were amazed at how "messy" the drafts were. With comments, cross outs, arrows, insertions, and word changes, the drafts were all marked up.

"You let your husband do that to your writing?" Tanya inquired incredulously as she looked at one of the later drafts my husband had edited.

I explained, that as a writer, I appreciated such support and that I did the same thing for him when he wrote. The students were amazed and quite interested. We put the drafts up on the wall as well as the finished product and continued to discuss the importance of revision.

Several days later Ann said that this brief discussion and demonstration seemed to be having an effect on the students' perceptions of revision. Tanya was not quite so defensive when Ann or a student "wrote" on her draft or offered verbal response, and other students seemed to be looking for "more ways to make it better." Ann admitted that she recognized the importance of sharing writing experiences and expressed the hope that she would be able to do more of that in the future. "I guess I still don't enjoy writing the way I do reading," Ann explained.

Many teachers feel the way Ann does about a part of their teaching and then feel guilty. Teachers are like everyone else—when they feel insecure, confused, uncomfortable, or not accomplished, the safest route is often avoidance. The biggest problem is that our insecurities often lead us to abandon something we know is important. Teachers need to be risk takers too. Nancie Atwell (1987) recounts in her book *In the Middle* how she reached out to others, examining what she was doing, assessing her own teaching, identifying her weaknesses and her strengths, and turning to her students for help as she learned alongside them. She took risks and moved forward—we all have to keep learning and looking for ways to improve our teaching. That's what makes us professionals.

Teacher as Facilitator

As I watched Ann and her students and listened to them express what they were learning and how that learning was taking place, I was convinced of Ann's importance as a facilitator, a vague term, difficult to explain. Many researchers emphasize the importance of being a facilitator, a role integral to student growth in literacy, but they are less clear about what exactly the term means (Atwell 1987; Calkins 1986; Goodman 1986; Newman 1985). In Ann's classroom, I learned what it meant.

As a facilitator, Ann demonstrated the purposes of literacy by participating in literacy events. Ann facilitated reading by being a reader herself and by being an active part of the reading community in her classroom. Shannon said that in Ann's class, she "started reading other books by [her]self" and that this "has helped me more because you're learning something and you want to find out what happens." David and Tanya learned sophisticated word identification strategies—ones that accomplished readers use often—as they read daily in the classroom. They began to see the purpose of word identification as a tool for reading and that identifying every word was not always necessary in constructing meaning. When they encountered unfamiliar words in reading, they had two strategies: "Ask Ms. Hunter" (David) and "Skip it" (Tanya). When I asked if it was more difficult to understand the story if she skipped a word, Tanya assured me it wasn't. "But if it is, then I try to figure it [out] by looking at the letters or thinking if I ever saw that word before. If that doesn't work, I can always ask [my] teacher." Ann facilitated learning these strategies that readers employ by giving her students opportunities to be readers.

As a facilitator, Ann empowered her students to begin to take control and ownership of their own learning as she negotiated curriculum and met student needs. The students in this class shared the books they chose to read and told me of favorite authors and genres. These students had the opportunity to make the kinds of choices real readers make. When I asked Tanya why she thought she was a better reader in this classroom, she had no doubts. "I'm goin' to tell you the honest-to-God [truth]—Ms. Hunter. She lets us read more. We read more books in here." Debby concurred: "Ms. Hunter, she helped me; she brought me a really long way. . . . I can read books myself now." Ann believed in empowering students by giving them the tools with which to make the choices literate people make, and she supported and encouraged them as they learned to make these choices.

As a facilitator, Ann provided a classroom that was a literate environment where reading and writing were used for real purposes. After reading *The Cay* and other books by Theodore Taylor, Ann and her students decided to write to Mr. Taylor about his novels and their reactions to them. The students threw themselves into this letter writing. After reading Taylor's books, these readers felt as if they knew Mr. Taylor, and they had questions and opinions to share with him (see Figures 3 and 4). After a few weeks, Mr. Taylor answered each letter personally and the students were thrilled—a real, live author had written to them! What an experience; two years later Gary still carried the response he'd received from Mr. Taylor in his wallet. Ann had taught letter writing—not just the mechanics but the power and purpose of such writing—through an experience that was real and meaningful. What a contrast to earlier lessons in other classrooms when these same students were forced to write phony letters as exercises when the curriculum called for that "lesson."

FIGURE 3   Gary's Letter to Theodore Taylor

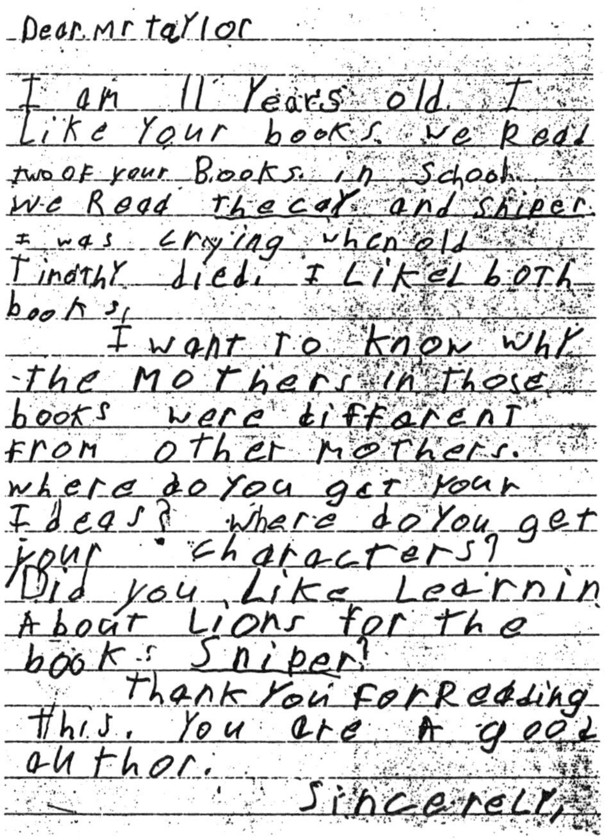

Dear Mr Taylor

I am 11 Years old. I Like Your books. we Read two of your Books. in School. we Read the cay and Sniper. I was Crying when old Timothy died. I Like both books.

I want to know why the Mothers in those books were different from other mothers. where do you get your Ideas? where do You get your Characters? Did you like Learnin About Lions for the book Sniper?

Thank You for Redding this. You are A good author.

Sincerely,

FIGURE 4 Shannon's Letter to Theodore Taylor

Jan, 20

Dear Mr. Taylor:

How are you? I hope fine. I read some of your books. They're very interesting if you ask me. What I wanted to know are the people in your book real or did they come in your mind? At the end of the Sniper there seems to be something good happending. I wanted to ask if you can write another book for the Sniper. You could put some things that happened to Ben's parents when they went on their trip.

The Cay was pretty good. I liked it and I hope to see you around some day. By

Sincerely,

Write Back
please

As a facilitator, Ann supported students as they grew as learners by recognizing students' strengths and building on them. In a system that usually looks at deficiencies, teachers must begin looking at their students from a different perspective: What can they do? What are their interests? What about their abilities outside of school? Ann did this for every one of her students, and sometimes it was difficult. Tanya didn't like to read and in the beginning showed little interest in books of any kind. Later, Ann discovered that Tanya liked "real" books, nonfiction, and combining this with what she knew about Tanya's athletic interests and abilities, Ann steered Tanya to books like the autobiography of track star Jackie Joyner Kersee. It is only possible to support students if teachers know who their students are as people and look at all that each brings to the learning situation.

As a facilitator, Ann encouraged risk taking by setting up a supportive community and by believing in many possible answers to questions instead of one right answer. Ann's students, like those in so many schools across America, had been taught that to be a good student you had to know "the answer." It's sometimes difficult to convince students that in a whole language class there are different ways of looking at problems, at literature, and at life. Ann helped her students learn to accept this in each other by modeling as she responded to students' views during class and literature discussions. Literature was a safe way to start building this trust. All readers have personal opinions and reactions to literature they read, and response logs and literature response groups in Ann's class helped students begin to feel comfortable with experimenting and working through their ideas.

As a facilitator, Ann recognized that learning is individual, although supported by the group, and that learning takes time. It doesn't happen sequentially or in the same way at the same time for all learners. As a facilitator, Ann was patient as well as supportive. When she wrote about Tim in her journal, she commented, "He is only reading about sports heroes, but at least he is reading! It doesn't seem to be just to please adults either." It's often difficult to be patient. The old paradigm led us to believe that we could "fix" students by following a formula. We have to accept the fact that real learning takes time, and we have to have the patience to provide that time for the learners in our classrooms.

Defining what is meant by the word *facilitator* is difficult, but what I saw in Ann's classroom was a personification of the word. As I tell the language stories of four students in Ann Hunter's classroom in the following chapters, the role of teacher as facilitator will become more clear.

3

Gary
Story Schema and Oral Language

*When we say we cannot make sense of something, we mean that we
cannot find the story in it or make up a story about it. We look at life
in terms of stories, even when there is no story to be told. That is the
way we make sense of life: by making stories. It is the way we remember
events: in terms of stories. Without stories, there would be no events.*
Frank Smith

Over the years I have had, as every teacher has, students who I can only
describe as difficult—not so much difficult to work with as difficult to support academically. Typically, they have been tested, retested, diagnosed, and
labeled year after year. These are the students who have been told in the
past to "sound out" problem words, to "slow down" their reading, and to
"think" before speaking. Of course, the conventional advice only seems to
make progress for them more difficult and learning less of a possibility. Gary
was such a student; he was difficult to teach, and his "language story" tells of
Gary's growth as a reader and a writer immersed in a literate environment.
He was supported by a teacher who concentrated on what Gary *did* know,
disregarding labels, profiles, testing, and remediation, and who supported
Gary's oral and written language development by using strategies within a
reading/writing workshop.

The Baby

When Gary came to the school as a new resident in late August, he immediately endeared himself to everyone around him. Eleven years old, he was
the youngest student in Ann's class at the time and had many of the child-
like qualities typical of elementary school students. Gary wanted to please
his teachers, whether that teacher was Ann, Emily the aide, or me, and he
loved affection and individual attention. When I walked into the room, he
would run to me, throw his arms around me, and tell me how glad he was
that I was there. He would pull his chair as close to Ann's or mine as possible and often lay his head on a shoulder as we read. In those first few weeks,
Gary seemed to require almost constant reassurance; he liked someone to sit
with him all the time and he would constantly say, "I don't get this," or "I've

never done anything like this before," or "I'm scared, I don't know how to do this." In fact, Gary seemed so used to having one-to-one assistance with everything that he seemed to truly believe that he was incapable of working independently. The rest of the class accepted Gary as "the baby," a role he seemed comfortable with, although at times it was evident that he wanted to be like the older guys. This was especially obvious in gym class, where he told what we all believed to be fabricated tales of his athletic feats. To be accepted, he pushed himself to impress the others in individual sports events, such as running, and he sought camaraderie by shouting team-bonding expressions loudly ("Way to go, man!") when points were scored in a game by David and Robb, two older boys who were his heroes.

When Gary arrived in Ann's class, it was evident that although he had learned to survive and knew how to "play school," Gary was what could be termed a nonwriter and had a very difficult time comprehending anything he read. All his standardized test scores were low, and his IQ score—in the low 80s—placed him on a level that bordered "low normal." At his previous schools Gary had been labeled many things, including LD (learning disabled) and EMR (educable mentally retarded). Gary's records, which were sent to Ann, contained lengthy descriptions of his academic and emotional problems, but they included nothing positive to build on—a trait typical of school records, Ann told me. The test scores and reports painted a discouraging picture of what Gary supposedly could not do; they were obviously going to be of little help to Ann in teaching Gary. Ann said that she was more interested in what Gary *could* do and she was determined to look for ways in which he could demonstrate his abilities. In fact, Ann says now that having taught twelve years she rarely even looks at the incoming students' permanent records anymore; she doesn't wish to be biased about a student's supposed disabilities by conclusions drawn from test results and procedures that she herself has doubts about.

Ramblings

One of Gary's immediate difficulties showed during class discussions; he had trouble participating in the morning deliberations that were so much a part of Ann's class. Each day began with a type of oral sharing time, and the class talk often focused on current events, reports the students had seen on television, or incidents in the news. Ann believes that all students need opportunities to talk and to know that their opinions are valued in her class. Her students typically spend days discussing current events; for example, when I was with the class, they discussed topics such as the confirmation of

Clarence Thomas to the Supreme Court, the political changes in Russia, the retired steel workers lobbying in Washington, and important sporting events. The students even discussed political parties and offered opinions about how they would vote if they were old enough. Ann's students, by their own choice, often watch the news after dinner just so they can participate in discussions of what's going on in the community and in the world, and many of their discussions would be considered lively by any standard. All the students had opinions that were listened to, and they learned that what they said would be accepted by the group if they could offer evidence such as "I saw on the news last night. . . ."

It became obvious to everyone early in the school year that Gary was having a difficult time with these discussions. It was not simply a matter of having a limited background, something that was true of most of the students; Gary's problem seemed much more complicated. Whenever Gary would discuss anything, be it during a current events lesson, in a literature response group, or even while casually talking before class or during lunch, he would "talk in circles," as the other students described it. He would ramble on and on, sometimes starting with a topic under discussion, but going off in directions his audience was unclear of, directions that even he seemed confused about. While talking, Gary would frequently fill in pauses with the phrase "What am I trying to say?" as he looked at the ceiling, seeming to collect his thoughts. Early in the school year when I would speak with Gary, casually questioning him about things he had experienced in school, he would have a difficult time answering or explaining things to me. Although he loved the time we spent together and seemed comfortable with the experience, he would ramble to the point where I had trouble figuring out what he was talking about.

The other students in the class were, to some extent, patient with Gary, but I could tell from some of their expressions that they were sometimes exasperated by his ramblings. In fact, it was not uncommon for one of them to raise a hand before Gary was finished simply because they had "tuned him out." It was difficult for us as teachers to discourage this, as we were often at a loss as to how to stop Gary once he embarked on one of these verbal trips to nowhere. When interrupted, sometimes even Gary himself breathed a sigh of relief, knowing that he was unable to figure out "What am I trying to say?" and just as unable to bring closure to a topic he had long lost sight of.

This same type of verbal confusion was evident in Gary's reading. Most or all of his previous experience in reading classes had been graphophonemic exercises—phonics drills. In fact, Gary was upset when he first came to Ann's class because there were no phonics workbooks. He liked them, he said; they were easy. When reading orally, he seemed adept at word-calling and he used only one reading strategy, decoding. As a result, Gary was lost when it came to discussing what he had read or even trying to retell a story or paragraph. While Gary might be able to remember a detail or two from a story he was trying to retell, he would have no sense of what the story was about. In fact, the way Gary would retell a story was very similar to his retellings of previous events in his life or day-to-day occurrences.

Story Schema

Putting together Gary's language behaviors, I hypothesized that perhaps Gary had no story schema, no sense of the general framework of the elements of a story. Story schema is what readers or listeners use to attend to certain aspects of incoming story material, helping them keep track of what has gone on before. Story schema plays an important part in retrieval as well, allowing readers or listeners to follow the familiar framework of typical stories to recall information. Story schema is what Mandler and Johnson (1977) describe as the "set of expectations about the internal structure of stories that makes both comprehension and recall more efficient" (Rand 1984, 377).

Children acquire a sense of story in preschool years by being immersed in an environment surrounded by language, both oral and written. They develop a story schema by listening at dinnertime to their parents recount "how their day went" to those around the table, by hearing children's tales such as "The Three Bears" told to them, and by being read to from the time they are very young. But Gary seemed to have no knowledge of children's stories, nursery rhymes, or fairy tales; it seemed he had no sense of story, no framework with which to recall or retell the stories that he heard or read. Vygotsky (1978) stressed the importance of the social aspect of language learning, but there are some children who spend these formative years with little language interaction. Often such children have their primary needs of food, clothing, and shelter met, but they spend much of their time alone or with younger siblings who cannot contribute to their oral language development. This can even happen in households with parent(s) who are home but separated from the child, using television as a babysitter and interacting only by giving directions or commands. Although these children have the innate ability to develop a sense of story, to use oral language to recount and sequence events in their lives and the lives of others, they have not been provided with the opportunities to do so. In cases such as Gary's, it is possible that the social aspect of language learning was absent. Somehow, perhaps because of Gary's unstable home and educational background, this part of his language framework had not developed. In his conversations, it seemed that Gary could not logically recount, in story format, a single event in his life, either in the past or the present.

Ann and I discussed my working hypothesis about Gary's ramblings, and with that thought in mind, Ann developed a strategy for Gary, an approach unlike traditional remediation programs. She decided to immerse Gary in *stories*. Ann, Emily, and I began what Ann termed "filling in the gaps"—helping Gary acquire a sense of story, much the way we would for a preschooler, based on what we knew about emerging literacy from educators and researchers (Cazden 1972; Halliday 1975; Harste, Woodward & Burke 1984b; Strickland & Morrow 1989). Gary continued to listen to Ann and his classmates read from class novels, and at times he even volunteered to read orally. We talked with Gary and gave him opportunities to talk, and we continued to encourage him to enter into discussions during sharing time. Ann found additional time to discuss daily incidents with him—what he did before class, what happened after school, an episode of his favorite TV show or activity. When talking about sequenced events, Ann discovered that Gary could not tell time. In fact, it became evident that Gary had no sense of how the day was sequenced; he had no sense of time or at least didn't have the language to describe this concept. Ann decided that she would teach him to tell time while she was working on sequencing concepts—earlier, later, before, after, first, middle, last—and spatial concepts—next to, on top of, in front of, above, and below. This was not done with work sheets but by giving attention to everyday occurrences in Gary's life and in the classroom. Many of the other students began helping Gary, especially as he learned to tell time. For example, when students wished to leave the room to go to the lavatory, one of the classroom rules required that they sign in and out with the time. Since Cole's desk was nearest to the sign-out sheet, he would frequently help Gary; he would not tell him the time, but he would help Gary figure it out. "Now remember," Cole would explain, looking at the analog clock in the room, "count by fives." When Gary succeeded at figuring out the time, Cole would quietly praise him and, once Gary had left, tell Ann and Emily that Gary was "getting it."

Some might see Gary's difficulty in understanding these concepts as confirmation of his "disability" or "handicap." Ann saw this gap in Gary's learning as more the fault of his environment and past experiences than as his fault or lack of ability. Gary simply had not learned these things earlier in his life, owing to difficult family situations and a lack of language modeling. His previous schooling, with its phonics instruction and programmed learning, had done little to fill in what most students acquire naturally in their social environment of home and family.

Ann worked on story schema with Gary by using shared reading strategies similar to those used by parents while reading bedtime stories to their children or by primary teachers reading with young students. Ann would invite Gary to sit with her in the large beanbag chair and ask him to hold one side of the book as they read together. In reality, Ann would read to Gary, but as he became immersed in stories, he displayed more and more reading behaviors—turning pages at appropriate places, tracking with his finger, stopping to comment or to ask questions. Because Gary was such an affectionate child, he loved those times spent with Ann. They shared many stories that Gary had never heard before: popular fairy tales; stories by Tomie dePaola, Eric Carle, and other children's authors; and elementary books usually used in primary grades. Gary loved these books! He would laugh, ask for them to be read over and over, and would always have another book ready to read, even after he and Ann had been reading together for over an hour. Gary had no problem with reading what some students would term "baby books." Levels were not a consideration in Ann's class, and her students saw value in all books. Because Ann would use any book appropriate to the purpose, regardless of level, the students soon lost their concept of "grade level" when using books. In fact, the entire class enjoyed the rhythm of a children's alphabet book called *Chicka Chicka Boom Boom* by Bill Martin, Jr. and John Archambault, as well as Shel Silverstein's funny poems in *Where the Sidewalk Ends* and *The Light in the Attic*. Gary might be reading *If You Give a Mouse a Cookie* independently in the morning and *Bridge to Terabithia* as a shared reading experience in the afternoon. In Ann's class, a book was a book.

For months, either Ann or Emily shared Sustained Silent Reading time with Gary every day (they would go into another room so they would not disturb other readers), and whenever Gary had a few extra minutes, he shared a book with someone. Ann always provided time for Gary to *talk* about the stories he was reading, positing that this activity, along with the other ways she was supporting his oral language development, would help Gary develop a sense of story.

Growing as a Reader

During the period that Ann was working with Gary individually in shared reading activities, he was still participating in the reading of class novels. I noticed that Gary's participation in literature groups was beginning to change. Previously, as Ann or the other students read orally from novels,

Gary's attention would drift away, but in November, I observed a change in Gary. Although he had enjoyed *The Cay* and *Charlie Skeedaddle*, books the class had read earlier in the year, Gary seemed much more involved when the class was reading *Bridge to Terabithia*. As we read in class, Gary actually followed along, sometimes sweeping the line with his finger, often using a bookmark under the lines to help him track, and turning pages at the appropriate time. Even more noticeable was the level of his responses during the discussions of the novel: He seemed to be following the story line; he held his own in discussions; and he was able to retell parts of the story to illustrate points he was trying to make with the class. At the end of the reading of *Bridge to Terabithia*, Gary had tears running down his face, such was his level of involvement and identification with the characters.

The day the students finished *Bridge to Terabithia* they were discussing what they had liked about the novel, what their favorite part was, and who their favorite character was. Gary spoke up during the discussion, "This book reminds me of *Charlie Skeedaddle*." The students in the class glanced around at each other, anticipating one of Gary's "far out" comments, as they could see little similarity between this novel and the one about the Civil War. Gary continued, "When Charlie killed the painter [dialect in the novel for the word *panther*], he did it to get courage to face his fears, and when Jess went back to Terabithia after Leslie died, it was to face his fears."

When Gary finished what was a sophisticated comparison of the two novels—read several weeks apart—everyone in the room was amazed. The students gasped, "Wow, Gary; that's terrific!" Ann and I were dumbfounded, but excited nevertheless. I have to admit that even as I recount this experience today I get chills at the memory of the depth of Gary's thinking. This interpretation was completely Gary's own, and it was one only a reader could make. We praised Gary, telling him that we agreed and had not thought of this comparison before. Gary, proud of himself and grinning ear to ear, concluded by stating, "I thought this was a great book!" Was this the thinking of a "disabled" learner?

Reading Is Stories!

Reading gradually became something very different for Gary. He summed it up very articulately in a group discussion late in the year when he said, "I used to think reading was words, but now I know it's stories."

Reading was no longer decoding and phonics work sheets. Reading had helped Gary develop a sense of story—a story schema—and his reading behaviors and perceptions changed dramatically. Studies by researchers imply that, most probably, simply having many experiences with "well-formed" stories helps a reader develop story schema (Mandler and DeForest 1979; McGee 1982; Whaley 1981). Additionally, a failure to understand story structure could be an important factor in reading disability (Bruce 1978). When the story structures in beginner programmed readers—basals—were examined, it was found that basal selections of readings have a greater emphasis on decoding skills with a higher percentage of plotless stories, often sacrificing story line to teach component skills (Morrow 1982). Research now suggests the importance of providing young readers with well-formed materials and points out that programs that emphasize language and literature employ more stories emphasizing plot structure (Bruce 1978).

Before coming to Ann's class, Gary had been instructed in basal skills programs; more importantly, this programmed approach to reading instruction had not seemed to help him develop an understanding of "story" or story schema. In Ann's class, Gary had opportunities to read stories with an emphasis on plot structure rather than on component skills. Through the use of literature, Gary responded as a reader and began to see reading as constructing meaning. He was beginning to be a "meaning maker," as Gordon Wells (1986) puts it.

Favorite Authors and Useful Information

Although reading *Bridge to Terabithia* seemed to be a turning point for Gary, Ann did not abandon her shared reading time with him. She said he had years of "gaps" to be filled in, so she used Sustained Silent Reading times to try other techniques that would help Gary develop independent reading strategies, especially considering how much his comprehension seemed to be improving. He liked listening to stories on audio tape with headphones and even began to read some books independently. "Short ones," he explained, "not those with thirty or forty thousand pages." A high point for Gary was when he took home Judy Blume's *Freckle Juice* to read over vacation because he had liked her other book, *The Pain and the Great One*, and he was sure *Freckle Juice* would be as funny. He explained that he had "wanted to read this, but [he] hadn't had a chance." Gary was starting to choose books based on favorite authors, another trait typical of readers.

Gary was also beginning to see books as useful tools, a realization made when one joins what Frank Smith (1988b) calls the "literacy club." For example, one day the speech therapist brought her two preschool children to visit the classroom while she picked up some reports. Gary volunteered to show the little boy and girl around the classroom and proudly "introduced" them to the class pets, the hermit crabs the class acquired while reading *The Cay*. Gary proceeded to tell the visiting children all that he remembered about hermit crabs, but being aware that there was much more to know than he could possibly explain, he told the children, "We have lots of books about hermit crabs that tell you all about them. I'm sure Ms. Hunter would let you borrow them if you're real careful and then you could read about crabs."

Comments such as this showed that Gary, who had previously said to anyone who would listen that he hated to read and had never read books, realized that books were useful tools containing information he could access. Furthermore, because the visiting children were very young—only three and four years old—Gary's remarks indicated a realization that reading is still reading even if someone reads the books to you, a very important step for Gary as he redefined for himself what it means to read.

Growing as an Author

Along with changes in Gary's behaviors and attitudes toward reading came similar or at least parallel changes in his writing behaviors and attitudes. When he first came to Ann's class he was, for all intents and purposes, a nonwriter. He could only write his name in printed letters, not in cursive, and anything Gary did attempt to write would only be a few words long. Furthermore, such writing could rarely be deciphered owing to the fact that his spelling was often prephonemic and his text consisted of only a few disjointed words. As is illustrated in Figure 5, although Gary tried, writing was difficult. Common sight words such as *and*, *of*, *she*, and *will*, were legible, but the writing didn't convey any of Gary's thoughts or ideas.

Because writing, which took place every day in Ann's classroom, was such a difficult activity for Gary, Ann decided to use a language experience approach with him, hoping that, even though a teacher was transcribing Gary's ideas for him, it would help him verbalize his thoughts and use writing as a mode of thinking. Figure 6 is an example of Gary's ideas transcribed by Ann while using a language experience approach. Although each sentence was a different thought and not connected by any transition, there were *ideas* expressed in this writing, in contrast to the writing in Figure 5. Ann was also modeling writing for Gary during this experience—the process of writing as well as mechanics such as spelling and punctuation.

FIGURE 5   Sample of Gary's Early Writing

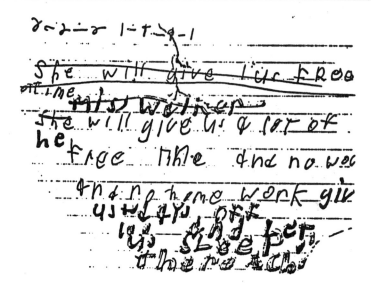

FIGURE 6   Sample of Gary's Writing Using Language Experience

> The ship was torn apart and that
> how I got on a raft.
> I felt scared and upset.
>
> I got tired, sleepy, hungry and thirsty.
>
> The ocean was very smooth and
> calm.
>
> I hoped someone would come for
>
> Then I saw a big sub! It saved
> me! I was happy.

Gary seemed to enjoy this approach. In the beginning, Ann used a questioning technique to help provide direction and offer support, but after a few weeks, she used transcription for drafting purposes. After transcribing his thoughts, Ann would have Gary copy a draft in his own handwriting, so he could share it with the class. Challenged at one point by Shannon, who said that the story Gary had read was Ms. Hunter's, Gary argued that the story contained his thoughts, so it was his story. Shannon agreed with his reasoning, "I guess writing belongs to whoever thinks it up."

Changes in his attitude toward writing came easier for Gary than changes in his writing behavior. Early in the school year he had confided to me that he was "nervous" about writing. He did not know how to do it, he told me. I assured him that we would all work together, and it was all right to learn as he went along. The use of a language experience approach and a great deal of positive reinforcement from teachers and fellow students helped to ease Gary's nervousness. He seemed much more relaxed, and as his sense of story developed, his attitude became more positive and he had more to say.

The most obvious behavioral change came in the amount of text Gary produced. In September, he was writing only a few words, but by late October he could write almost a page. Nevertheless, the writing was still difficult to read, even for Gary, not only because of his misspelling, lack of punctuation, and poor handwriting, but also because, without guidance in the form of questions or other prewriting and drafting support, it had little organization or focus. The following excerpt from his response journal (see Figure 7) was typical:

> dear diere 1863 I am a brumm boy for conFederate. I Just Saw Stowall Jackson die. I fill so ma and sorry for hem and he standed like a stonwell that is how he got his name Lee saide the I flee like I just losed my right Arm and Jackso was bron in Lakecare at Clarksburgva. now West Virginia on Jun

It was possible for Ann and others who were aware of Gary's interest in Stonewall Jackson to confer with him about his writing, using a response from his journal, such as that in Figure 7, and guide him in ways to organize, write, and revise his thoughts so that an audience might read them. But for Gary, even this proved difficult because, when he returned the next day to a response like the one in Figure 7, he often could not remember what he had been trying to say.

Gary's writing behavior changed gradually, as it had with reading, in response to a combination of factors. For one thing, he was writing every day and often in response to reading. As his understanding developed in reading, his responses in writing began to make more sense, at least when he dictated his compositions orally. When Gary's attitude toward writing changed

FIGURE 7   Early Entry from Gary's Response Journal

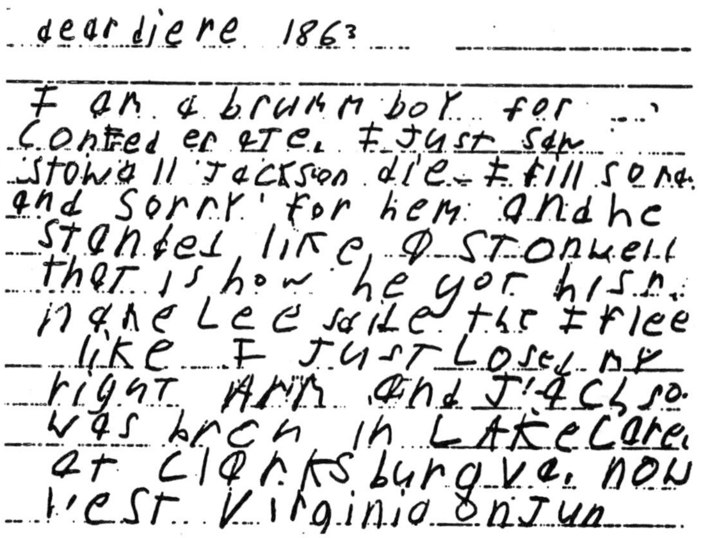

dear diere 1863

I an a brunm boy for
confred er ete. I Just saw
Stowall Jackson die. I fill sene
and sorny for hem and he
stanpel like a Stonwell
that is how he got his n.
name Lee saide thr I flee
like I just losey ny
right Arm and J'4cl so
was brcn in Lakecare
at Clorksburg va. now
west Virginia on Jun

and when he felt less intimidated and less unsure of himself, he began to take more risks. He wrote more in his literature response journal, and he volunteered to read his responses to the class. Often this sharing and answering of his classmates' questions about his writing helped him clarify his thoughts.

Although a stranger looking at Gary's writing at the end of the year would probably be distressed at the presentation and simplicity of the text, I saw startling differences when I compared his writing in the later months to his writing in those first few weeks of the school year. Compare Gary's Civil War diary entry a few months before (Figure 7), with this final draft of his reaction to *Bridge to Terabithia* (Figure 8):

> I think that the book is good for people to read and to write about and to feel good a bout it. This book. is funny and sad. And. the part of the story that I liked best was when Jesse gave Leslie a puppy. The puppy was cute. I was happy here beause it was nice of Jesse to give here a puppy. Jesse was pro und of his gift. I feel proud of of my self lots of times for giveing to other people The characters make this a good, book. The. author made them seem very interesti and realy greate. I think that people would enjoy reading this story, I know I did.

FIGURE 8   Gary's Reaction to *Bridge to Terabithia*

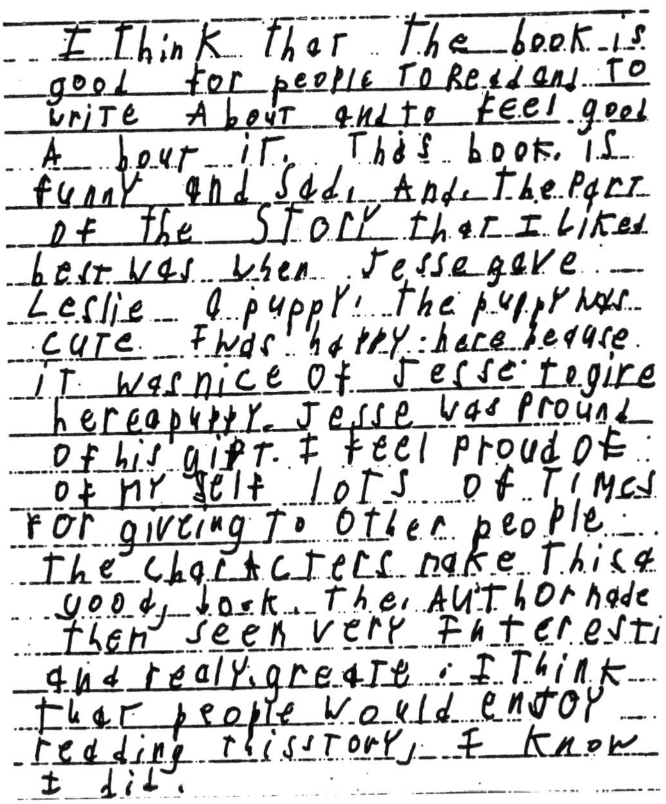

> I Think that the book is
> good for people To Read ans To
> write About and to feel good
> About it. This book is
> funny and sad, And the part
> of the Story that I liked
> best was when Jesse gave
> Leslie a puppy. the puppy was
> cute. I was happy here because.
> It was nice of Jesse to give
> here a puppy. Jesse was proud
> of his gift. I feel proud of
> of my self lots of Times
> for giveing To other people.
> The charcters nake this a
> good book. the Author made
> then seem very Fnteresti
> and realy greate. I Think
> that people would enjoy
> redding this Story, I know
> I did.

This later writing, which was drafted, revised, and edited by Gary, was organized, legible, and made sense. He used mechanical conventions, such as punctuation marks, and in his final copies, after editing, he was using more conventional spelling. At this point, he looked at writing as a process. He talked about his drafts and about publishing his work. Although he required a great deal of assistance during each phase of the process, he was writing more coherent drafts, thus his revising was actual revision instead of merely rewriting.

Growing as a Language User Outside the Classroom

Changes in Gary's attitudes and use of language were observed by other teachers who worked with him outside the classroom. The speech teacher, for example, recalled that when Gary came to the school, his oral language was so disorganized that she had problems carrying on any conversation with him. He had extreme difficulty in "sequencing events," she told me. She said that although they worked on "listener understanding," Gary seemed to first need to be aware that he had a problem with communication and to try to "slow down and think" about what he was going to say. As they worked together, the speech teacher noticed a change in Gary; he began to share with her what was happening in Ann's classroom when he came to her for his weekly sessions. She had to ask numerous questions at first to direct him through a discussion, clarifying points he was trying to make, but Gary wanted to tell her about the stories he was reading in class, the projects he was involved in, and details that he was learning about in content areas. He seemed eager to make his speech teacher understand. The speech teacher said she began to use this enthusiasm and interest to work with Gary on his oral language problems.

"Ann's [whole language] approach made all the difference in the world," she reported. He was very motivated to work on telling a story logically so he could share these experiences with a listener, in this case with his speech teacher. Gary's sequencing improved as he recounted his classroom experiences and those of the characters in his favorite books.

The speech teacher became interested in how Ann was teaching reading and writing and offered to support this language learning during sessions with the students she saw. Subsequently, the speech teacher met regularly with Ann to discuss student progress, compare observations, and decide how they could best work together to help the students. By the end of the year, the speech teacher reported being convinced that classroom teachers and speech therapists must work together. "I've seen an amazing difference in this school," the speech teacher told me. "I'm also seeing it in other schools where children are in whole language situations. It makes sense that I work with the classroom teacher and use the students' classroom experiences to help them with their speech." She told me that though many professionals in her field agree with this cooperative philosophy, it is not the norm in public schools.

By the end of the school year, Gary had made significant progress in his oral language development. The speech teacher reported that he had improved in "sequencing events," and she pledged that if Gary was still at the school next year, she would continue to work with Ann to support Gary's progress.

Gary's literacy behaviors and attitudes did change over a period of time. During discussions he said that he liked to read because "the stories are . . . interesting, or exciting, and now I can picture the stories like when I watch

TV." Also during a group discussion, Gary remarked, "I like to read now because I'm good at it now and it's not hard."

Gary learned that literacy had a place in his life and that reading could be a tool he could use. He learned that language, when events were sequenced into a story, could be used to retell stories of his own. I asked myself, "Why did Gary begin to engage in literacy activities so enthusiastically, and what had happened this year that convinced Gary that reading and writing were enjoyable and worthwhile?" Both Ann and I believe it was because he could see language serving some real, practical purpose. He was not engaged in learning abstractions about language; he was actively using written and oral language to get something done. Gary had redefined reading and had begun to look at himself as a capable reader. Even Gary acknowledged that he "used to think reading was words," but he now "knows it's stories."

4
Tanya
Searching for Truth and Identity

If words seem to disappear and our innermost self begins to laugh and
cry, to sing and dance, and finally to fly—if we are transported in all
that we are to a brand new world, then—only then—can we say that
we can READ!
J. Wayman

Gary and I know that reading is more than words sitting quietly on a
page. I've been a reader all my life. For me, books are an escape, an adventure, a view of the world I both know and have not yet experienced. I want
to help my students to feel the same way about reading; I want to share
being "transported . . . to a brand new world" (Wayman 1980, title page).

Despite these lofty hopes of mine, Tanya taught me that what was right
for me was not necessarily what another wants or needs. Tanya reminded me
how important it is for teachers to get to know students and to help them
meet their needs instead of trying to decide what is "best" for them. I learned
from Tanya that students' reasons for reading and writing are varied and
often hard to define. Tanya's "language story," for all its differences, is similar to Gary's in that Tanya's view of literacy in her life changed over the
period of time I knew her.

A Survivor

When I first met Tanya, her strength immediately impressed me—not
strength in a physical sense, but a strength of character. Tanya was a sur-
vivor. A tall, attractive thirteen-year-old African American girl, Tanya had
lived all her life in an inner city. She had been uprooted from the community she knew and placed in a school whose rural surroundings Tanya rated
as "boring" (though she had to admit that they were "pretty"). Despite its
nonurban locale, Tanya found herself one of four females in a racially mixed
classroom. Tanya emerged as a class leader, earning the respect of both boys
and girls and becoming a role model for the other African American girl in
her class. Her strength made her appear older than her thirteen years and

made her seem self-assured, sometimes to the point of what one middle school teacher regarded as "having an attitude." I saw that "attitude" as one of determination—Tanya had a mind of her own and would not allow anyone, adult or fellow student, to tell her what to do. Although this could be trying at times, especially in our society, in which adults make the rules, Tanya's traits had been what had helped her survive up to this point. Ann knew that although Tanya did not like to work "cooperatively" (since she felt she already knew what was best for her and everyone else), she was articulate and bright. I found her to be honest, even when her opinions were not "teacher pleasing," and quite brave; Tanya was a risk taker.

Her Reaction to the Curriculum

Prior to her placement in Ann's classroom, Tanya had spent all of her time in public school in a regular classroom. Because her IQ was reported to be in the 90s, she had not been labeled learning disabled, but her personal background was such that, up to this point, school apparently had little effect on her life, an observation dutifully reported in the file sent to the institution at the time of her placement. In public school, her standardized test scores were low and her reported absenteeism was high; yet the school, aware of home problems, did little to support Tanya's drift from grade to grade, indicating in her records that she was "capable" but "lazy." Consequently Tanya felt that school was of little value to her, and she planned to bide her time until she was old enough to drop out. School had definitely been a waste of time for Tanya and for others like her; the world outside the school building seemed much more appealing. Tanya was interested in reality and in life, and in her opinion, school was neither useful nor real. I had seen many students like Tanya—those whom the system had failed, but who blamed themselves for the failure. As far as I could determine by looking at her records and from conversations with her, no teacher or administrator had ever talked to Tanya to try to discover her needs, her wants, or her abilities.

Tanya was very honest about the fact that when she first came to Ann's class she did not consider it "real" school. Tanya was unhappy about being placed in this situation, and while she had never found "regular" school very relevant, at least it was a place "where normal kids go." She was also uncertain of Ann's methodologies and curriculum, which she immediately recognized as different. Tanya complained to me in my early days in her class, "She [Ms. Hunter] lets us choose what we want to read. How do I know what I should read?" Tanya disliked any activity that involved thinking. She was used to completing her work by rotely filling in blanks and putting forth as little effort as possible. All Ann's discussion, writing, and thinking was too much work in Tanya's eyes.

Tanya told me that although she liked Ms. Hunter, she didn't see how Ms. Hunter could know if she was really learning, since they didn't do "real school stuff" in this classroom. In her old school Tanya knew that her teacher could tell if she was learning because once she finished one of her "reading books" (basals), she was allowed to go on to the next. There were no "reading books" in Ann's class, so Tanya presumed that Ann was unable to tell how she was progressing.

Reading wasn't the only subject that disturbed Tanya about the curriculum in Ann's classroom. "We used hard books in my old school," Tanya commented suspiciously. As I talked to Tanya, I realized that the "hard books" she referred to were the science and social studies textbooks used in her previous classrooms. "The books we had were like Social books; you know, *thick* books," she explained. For Tanya these books were "real"—they were difficult to read. When I asked her what she liked about textbooks, she replied simply, "I don't know." When I asked her if she read out of reading books or if she read novels, she replied, "No, we'd read like about the heart in science." She admitted that she couldn't read them or make sense of the textbooks, but as with the basals, she was comfortable with them because she believed they were necessary to her learning. Obviously, at this point, the purpose of reading to Tanya was content reading, and she was disturbed that Ann seldom used textbooks in her classroom.

Tanya's reaction is not atypical for middle-school students, according to educators who use literature in an integrated approach to teaching. Tanya was comfortable with what she was used to; school might not be useful or enjoyable, but it was predictable. After eight years, she knew what "real" school was, and because Ann's class was not predictable, she approached its difference with a great deal of skepticism. Though she didn't know why she missed the textbooks, she felt uncomfortable about the fact that they were not the center of instruction. Her reaction is similar to the "disbelief, guarded interest, and uncertainty" that Marie Dionesio (1991, 9) encounters when middle-school remedial reading students discover that, in her class, they will not be using the workbooks and skills exercises that they have had for years.

Experiences with Reading

Early in the school year Tanya told me that reading was something you had to do in school, and although she said she was "okay at it," she freely admitted that doing it was neither something that she enjoyed nor anything that made much sense to do. Tanya did mention one novel that the class had read that seemed to have made an impression on her—S. E. Hinton's *The Outsiders*. She liked that book because "it showed how the world really is." Considering the stories Tanya had recounted of her life, I realized that to an inner-city teenager, who grew up surrounded by gangs, violence, and peer loyalty, *The Outsiders* was indeed a novel to identify with. While the class was reading the book, Tanya was enthralled—she reacted, interacted, and became involved in the characters' lives. In fact, Tanya was so involved in the story that when Johnny, one of the characters, died, Tanya—tough, street-wise Tanya—sat in class crying openly.

She entered discussions about the characters' loyalty to one another and why they needed gangs to "stick together." She liked the fact that the brothers were self-reliant and survived without adults telling them how to live. Tanya was engrossed. She felt she knew these characters, and she wrote furiously in her response journal. Once she had finished the book, she wanted it to continue and even decided to write a sequel.

Ann told me that she was excited about Tanya's reaction to *The Outsiders*; it was a breakthrough, she felt, but only a beginning. Reading *The Outsiders* did not immediately change Tanya's negative attitudes and behaviors toward reading. "Changes in human behavior never happen quickly," warns Marie Dionesio (1991, 14). Teachers who believe that learning cannot be imposed but must be learned through transactions and discovery give students time and opportunity to discover what literacy is and the place it can have in their lives. Working with reluctant readers requires patience, something difficult in an educational system in which teachers have little time to really get to know their students (in intermediate grades and above, many teachers see students for only forty-five minutes a day). Teachers who get to know their students as individuals—their likes, dislikes, experiences, and opinions—can meet students' needs as they listen, talk, read, and write with them. Learning and changes in attitude take time; teachers have to take time to watch for signs, document changes, and support students as they move forward.

A Search for Truth

The day Ann introduced Theodore Taylor's *The Cay* to the class, she mentioned that the novel was fiction. Tanya wondered *why* people read fiction. "If it's not true, then why waste your time reading it?" Tanya asked. Her question led to a discussion of why it is valuable to read fiction.

What a strange question, I thought, since my personal taste in reading runs to both fiction and nonfiction. I began to wonder how Tanya had acquired this notion—if it's not true, why read it? I knew little of Tanya's background, but somehow she had learned that stories should be real, much the way documentaries are "truthful." Tanya's attitude reminded me of the research of Shirley Brice Heath (1983), who studied the language of two communities, Trackton and Roadville. Heath discovered the notion of the truth value of stories when she studied the children in Roadville, who were not allowed to tell stories unless an adult announced that something that had happened to a child made a good story and was worth retelling. When children were asked to retell such events, they were "expected to tell non-fictive stories which 'stick to the truth'" (158). As adults listened to these stories, they corrected any facts that were not retold as the adult remembered them. Fictive stories that were exaggerations of real-life events, modeled on storybook plots or characters, were considered by the adults as "lies," without "a piece of truth" (158).

Tanya's reaction was not unusual; flights of imagination are not always encouraged. From my reading and my experiences teaching students from various backgrounds, I was aware that in some cultures children are taught that all stories fall under two distinct categories—truth and lies (Cazden 1972; Heath 1983). I wondered if someone in Tanya's past, either at home or in school, had taught her that stories must be true or else they were lies. With this possibility in mind, I listened to Ann's explanation of the reasons for reading fiction. For example, she said that "fiction is often based on things that have happened or could happen to people" and that "fiction teaches you about other times and places but does so through the eyes of characters." Although Tanya was trying to make sense of this, trying to find a place in her life for reading fiction, I could tell that she was not convinced at this point. What I took for granted because of my culture and background—that stories using imagination were admired, encouraged, and nurtured—required a big leap for Tanya, one that the culture of American schools demanded that she accept, regardless of her own cultural background. Children whose background is other than white and western European are at a cultural disadvantage attending schools in which the curriculum reflects what the culture of power considers to be "correct" or valuable (Cazden 1988; Cazden & John 1971; John 1972). The validity of this observation is borne out by the disproportionate number of African American children who are labeled as having some sort of learning disability. The schools of the dominant culture neither understand nor value the culture and language of others (Labov 1972).

Heath (1983), underscoring the need for teachers to understand the communities in which children live, illustrated how differences in language use are linked to the systematic relations between education and production for members of a community. Many teachers, myself included, know very little of the cultures of the children they teach. Tanya had been placed in Ann's school—miles away from her home community—and her teacher and I were of a different cultural background. We learned, through Tanya, that we had best be careful not to view the world only through the eyes of our own culture.

A Search for Identity

Tanya would not be easy to convince about the value of fiction. When the class began reading *The Cay*, she acted bored from the start, determined to tune out this story that was not "real." She continued with this attitude until the character of Timothy, an elderly black man, was introduced in the tale. Tanya loved the way Timothy talked (the novel is written so that Timothy speaks with a Jamaican accent). At first Ann herself read these parts aloud so that decoding the dialect did not confuse the students; however, more and more students asked to read orally, including Tanya, and all managed to do very well with the dialect (most using context as a strategy to read).

As the novel progressed, Ann continued to teach about the Caribbean, including the dialect of the people of these islands. Tanya seemed especially interested in this discussion: she asked, "Does everyone in Jamaica talk this way or only the black people?" This question seemed typical of the kinds of questions that Tanya had asked ever since coming to Ann's class; Tanya seemed to be trying to figure out who she was—typical behavior for an adolescent—and she seemed interested in how the issue of ethnicity and race fit into identity.

Since the students were interested in the Jamaican sound, I brought in tapes my husband made for them of reggae music by various Jamaican artists. All the students, including Tanya, seemed to enjoy the rhythm of the music and its language. Her interest in reggae reminded me of her interest in the rhythmic language of *Chicka Chicka Boom Boom*, a book Ann had read to the class one day for fun. Tanya loved that book; although the text was simplistic, she was fascinated with the way language was used. Tanya danced, swayed, and snapped her fingers to the rhythm of the text as the class read the book together. *Chicka Chicka Boom Boom* is "a black book" Tanya told the class, thereby explaining why she felt it worthy of her attention. Although *Chicka Chicka Boom Boom* wasn't written by an African American author,

Ann was able to order an audiotape of the book read by Ray Charles, a rhythm-and-blues musician known variously in the African American community as "Brother Ray" and "The Genius." Nevertheless, Tanya was disappointed, insisting, "He doesn't have the beat right!" She moaned, "I like the way we read it better!"

As the students continued to read *The Cay*, Tanya became engrossed in what they were learning in social studies; the focus of the theme of study was the Caribbean—the geography, people, customs, even the food. In fact, the class had a tasting party one afternoon to experience the foods of the Caribbean, sitting on the floor, eating the foods that the characters in the novel ate. Most of the students had never tasted crab; Tanya said she had never seen a coconut; and none of them could imagine eating seaweed! Ann had found directions for opening a coconut, so David and the teacher's aide took the coconuts to the dining hall to heat them. When they brought them back, Tanya volunteered to "whack" the coconuts with a hammer. Shielding her eyes from flying coconut shell, she hit the coconuts and opened them as the rest of the students watched. All sampled the meat and milk of the coconut, some liking it and asking for more, others deciding they were glad they would not have to eat "this stuff" to survive on an island. Tanya said she thought the coconut meat was sweet and ate Debby's piece as well when Debby decided she didn't want it.

As we continued our tasting party, Gary, having spent a great deal of time living "on the shore," gave directions about cracking shells and eating crab. Not only was it encouraging to see him taking charge, but he was giving directions in correct sequence—a task normally difficult for him. Tanya was one of the first to try everything, and she was very honest and vocal about her feelings. "The coconut's good," she said, "but the crab's disgusting. Uh-uh, not for me."

The students did not use a textbook during their unit on the Caribbean; instead Ann used movies, travel brochures, stories, magazine articles, and maps to teach social studies. The students even had live hermit crabs in the classroom and read about their habits and care. Tanya could often be found reading the crab books and letting the crabs crawl on her hands and desk, and she even volunteered to come to the classroom during the weekends to feed and water them. She had never had a pet and was learning that, while it was fun to have them and play with them, pet owners were also responsible for their care and well-being.

As the days progressed and we continued to read *The Cay*, Tanya seemed caught up in the unit. Although she was involved in the curricular activities, such as learning about the ocean, the coral reefs, the tides, and the

Caribbean islands, she was even more involved in the characters in the novel. She was angry at young, white Philip's feelings about black Timothy, and one day Tanya told the class that Philip learned prejudice from his parents, an idea that was hinted at in the novel but a conclusion Tanya drew on her own from evidence in the text. Tanya loved the character of Timothy; in the book he was smart, resourceful, and patient. Timothy didn't hate Philip; in fact, he won his friendship, but he also would not stand for Philip's bigotry. At one point in the novel, when Timothy "tells off" Philip, who was being racially insulting, Tanya responded, "Yeah, man!" Tanya was visibly upset when Timothy died in the novel. Even though she responded most to Timothy, she felt her favorite part of the book was when Philip was rescued because she "thought he was going to die on that island, and he was too young to die." Tanya explained to the class that she felt that Philip was a different person because of what he learned from Timothy. Although I don't know at this point whether Tanya had changed her mind about the reality or truthfulness of *The Cay*, it was obvious that she was learning from it— reading skills, linguistic awareness, science, and social studies.

To me, the most interesting aspect of Tanya's change in reading attitudes occurred late in the year when Ann mainstreamed Tanya into the public middle school for science classes. Tanya did very well; in fact, she was getting A and B grades. Tanya's description of the class was what I found interesting, and I could not help but compare her views of reading to those she had expressed when she first came to Ann's classroom. When talking about the textbook in her science class, Tanya offered, "Well, my science book doesn't give me much information. They don't write much. They just sum it up." In talking with Tanya about what she meant, I found that she realized textbooks just "sum up" information, whereas in literature, information is included in the story, background, and characters. Tanya confirmed my interpretation in a later group discussion when she said that she had learned more about science from books like *The Cay* than she had from any science textbook because the novels, she reported, "tell you more about science by things in the story." Although I'm not sure that Tanya's definition of truth and untruth had changed (nor do I believe it should), it was obvious that her attitude toward the worth of literature, both fiction and nonfiction, had changed.

After being mainstreamed, Tanya was very pleased with her grades in her science class and was happy that she could now read the textbook. She confided that she still did not do much reading in her free time; she would rather participate in sports, games, or watch TV, but she was proud of the fact that she "reads better."

"I still like reading aloud to myself" [subvocalization], Tanya told me; "I understand it more, but I don't mind reading anymore, especially books like the ones we read with Ms. Hunter." If Tanya ever reads on her own, and she said that she does once in a while, she reads books Ms. Hunter shows her because "she knows what I like."

It is important to note that in a few months time Tanya had not changed all her attitudes toward reading. It was still not something she chose to do on her own very often, but it also did not mean just reading text-books anymore. She saw books—novels as well as textbooks—as tools; she now had a purpose for reading.

Tanya chose books about what she believed to be real life—other S. E. Hinton novels, the Murphy novels written by an author she knew was writing about the adventures of her real children, and books like *The Story of Jackie Joyner Kersee* (Tanya had discovered biographies of black athletes when she began to run track at middle school and Ann bought some for her as a gift). She had found a reason for reading, even reading fiction, because she had found examples of the realities of life in the novels she read.

Attitudes About Writing

Tanya's changes in attitudes toward writing and her writing behaviors were influenced by the literature she was reading in class. Early on, Tanya explained to me that she really did not like to write, although she proudly noted that her writing was getting neater. Tanya's pride in her penmanship, with its emphasis on presentation, lasted throughout the time I knew her, yet other things did change concerning how she approached writing and how she felt about it.

A few months after I started working with Tanya's class, she wrote a story following the class reading of *Charlie Skeedaddle*. Her story concerned a sister and brother who lived on a farm in Virginia at the time of the Civil War. The brother went to fight for the South, and the sister became a nurse for the North. Tanya said that she pretended she was the sister, and she wrote the story with "I" (in the first person), something she had never tried before. After she completed "Home," an eight-page typed "book," she shared the following thoughts about the process:

How do you feel about this piece?

Good!

Do you think webbing [a prewriting strategy involving the cluster-ing of ideas] helped you at all when you were writing this?

Yeah, 'cause it helped me get the point across and organize.

Remember when we first started it [webbing], and you didn't want to do it? You just wanted to write. What changed your mind?

Now I'm glad I did it. It's the longest thing I ever wrote!

How would you compare Tanya the writer now, with Tanya the writer a year ago?

I couldn't write a year ago, but now I'm getting there.

How do you think you've learned to write this well in just a year?

By reading.

What do you mean?

Reading gives me ideas of what to write and tells me things I can put in my writing.

Writing was not your favorite thing to do a few months ago. How do you feel about writing now?

Better.

It was apparent from Tanya's remarks that her feelings about writing were beginning to change. Tanya said, "[Writing] feels good; I like being an author. It feels good to know someone is depending on you to publish or whatever your book, and they say, 'oh yes, I like your book.'" Tanya was beginning to look at herself as a writer. When I asked her how she felt when she wrote "Home," Tanya replied, "Good. I was surprised that I put that much effort into it. It came out pretty good."

Figure 9 is a selection from Tanya's typed copy of her story "Home," which is several pages long. In her fictional account of a young woman's place in history, Tanya weaves in facts that she learned about the Civil War during the thematic unit—from Clara Barton's brown hair to the crackers and molasses—to make her story more authentic.

Peer Responses to Writing

One weekend I took drafts of the students' stories home to respond to them, at their request and Ann's. At the end of each story, I responded as a real

FIGURE 9   Selection from Tanya's Story, "Home"

HOME

It was one of those hot summer days in West Virginia and Zachiarah and I were in the fields picking potatoes and in five minuts the church bell would ring, then it would be time for dinner. Dinner was at 5 oclock but the potatoes wern't done in time so we ate a half hour later. When I was setting the table Zachiarah and I got into an argument over slavery, and I kept telling him that it wasn't fair. He said I know, then I ask then why do you wan't to go down South to fight for slavery. Because this is our state and I am going to fight for it.

I sattled in Pennsylaina where alot of fighting went on and after seeing no one help the wounded. That's when my mind was made up I would become a nurse. When I got home I look in the newspaper that the battle had began, and they needed nurse. The person who I went to go see was Clara Barton, she was short with brown hair, she was very nice. She traind me, and I was on my way to Gettyburgh. When I got there I was happy. I got to meet General Grant he had his soilders give me my supplies and I was out on the battlefield and all I saw was god creation, dead young men. I got really sick that night thinking of all the thing I saw that day. When I went home I ate crackers and molasses for dinner, then I went to bed and tried to sleep.

---

reader by writing a couple of questions and observations. As I had with all the stories, I commented at the beginning and end of Tanya's draft, and this upset her. Tanya explained to me during a conference that she did not want teachers to "mess up" her paper by writing on it (a valid objection, in retrospect). As a teacher I had assumed that she would welcome my feedback, but instead I had insulted her as a writer. Tanya saw her writing as finished rather than a draft in progress. It might have been better if I had simply talked with her about her writing as a reader would.

If looking at writing as a process was not an easy thing for Tanya to accept, it was also difficult for her to participate in peer conferencing. Learning to respond to others' writing requires modeling and practice and is learned gradually, as Donald Graves (1983) points out. Even though Ann used various techniques to help students learn to peer conference, some students, including Tanya, regarded questions or suggestions as criticisms, especially when they came from fellow students. It is no wonder that genuine peer response is difficult to accept at first, considering that students rarely have the opportunity to learn to value others' suggestions. Instead of giving students the opportunity to support each other, schools ask them to "correct" each others' papers. Since Tanya, like other adolescents, would often become defensive when a fellow student made comments or suggestions, Ann, Emily, and I divided the class into three peer groups and each of us sat in with a group to help it move along productively and peaceably. Tanya still regarded response as criticism, and although she did make some progress in this area, she accepted advice somewhat grudgingly.

As the months went by, Ann and I modeled the sharing of responses to our writing for the class. It was about this time that I brought in drafts of my letter to the dean, showing students the finished product as well as several drafts of the letter with comments, cross outs, arrows, insertions, and word changes. Tanya was the one who was incensed that I let my husband "mess up" my letter by marking it up. After this, Tanya seemed more willing to participate in the response part of the revision process. It was still necessary, however, to phrase such response positively and as a suggestion only; Tanya was not about to let anyone "take over" her writing.

Tanya also used her writing to respond to what she was reading. In a journal response, Tanya used writing to sort out her feelings about the first four chapters of *Bridge to Terabithia*.

> Chapter 1-4 I like the parts I read so far because in a way it like my family and friends. Jesse & Leslie are friends just like some of my relationships that I had in my pass. I don't like that part about the book is Jesse hides his feelings (don't share) I like Jesse & Leslie is that they are both athletic and so am I in many ways and I love running to, so that is why I love the book. And I afraid of the dark in many ways only if I watch a scary movie.

Her writing became a vehicle for her thinking and questioning. It still seemed as though Tanya was trying to see a purpose in reading this book— how it was real. She seemed still to be wondering in what ways the book related to her.

Tanya also started to use her writing in ways she had not tried before. I once had asked Tanya if she ever wrote letters, and she answered that she didn't like to write and she would rather use the telephone. Yet, late in the year, after she had been mainstreamed, she wrote Ann the following letter:

> Dear Ms. Hunter,
>
> I would like to thank you for picking out the right teacher for me. She is nice as you. And also thank You for the gum also. Every

once in a while you got to know how I feel about science (Mrs. Green) and also how I feel about you.

Love,

Tanya

P.S. THANK YOU

This letter illustrated that Tanya had something to say and found writing to be an appropriate way to say it.

Literacy in Her Life

Tanya seemed to be changing her attitude toward reading and writing owing to the fact that she was discovering a purpose for literacy in her life. She also felt more trusting of her teacher and now accepted what she at one time felt were not very sound teaching methods. As mentioned earlier, I asked the group during a class discussion, "You all feel you're better readers now. How did you become better readers?" Tanya answered first, "I'm goin' to tell you the honest-to-God [truth]—Ms. Hunter."

I asked what Ms. Hunter had done that made a difference.

"She lets us read more," Tanya explained. "We read more books in here."

As they had with Gary, a whole language philosophy and literature-based instruction had changed the way Tanya viewed reading and writing. Although reading and writing were still neither her favorite activities nor always enjoyable, Tanya had found a purpose for literacy in her life. Her search for truth in texts and her search for her own identity were aided by the characters in novels, and their experiences not only broadened her schema but also reflected her own experiences. She began to see herself as a capable reader and writer—she had found a place in her life for literacy and saw reading and writing as useful tools that she could use as she saw fit.

5
David
Growing as a Reader and Writer

*Stories help us shape our lives and our society because they have the
power to lure us into learning*
Katherine Paterson

$Public$ school teachers often ask how a whole language approach works in
classes with students of varying abilities. I tell them of students in Ann's
class, such as Gary, introduced earlier, and David, the subject of this chapter. These were two very different students, with widely varying intellectual
and social capabilities, who both grew in literacy use as they shared literature and learning together. What they received from the experience was personal, as it is with any learner, but they were also able to contribute a great
deal as members of a literate community. They read, shared, and listened to
others as they interacted personally in response to what was happening in
the novels they read, or during discussions in class, or while researching
answers to real questions. This whole language class met their individual
needs because literacy in Ann's class surpassed skills exercises, literal inter-
pretations, and predictable teacher-questions. David, arguably the highest-
ability student in Ann's class, was able to grow individually, as each student
was encouraged to do. David's "language story" shows his growth: his change
in attitude toward literacy, toward learning, and toward his assessment of his
own abilities as a reader and a writer.

Sullen and Withdrawn

Twelve-year-old David reminded me of so many students I had seen in other
classrooms in public schools. He was bright and capable, full of potential,
yet his school career had been less than stellar. David had been labeled as an
"underachiever" and "troublemaker," although his average to above-average
IQ scores placed him in regular classes in public school. David came to
Ann's classroom with problems, both academic and social, in response to

which he seemed to have developed a type of aloofness and distrust of adults, especially those in authority in the classroom.

When I first met him, David was sullen and withdrawn. He came to the school in the middle of the school year, and it was apparent to me and to others who saw him in the classroom and at the school that he was not happy about the placement. He told his staff counselor that he "hated this place. . . . It was for dummies." He seemed always to have a scowl on his face, spoke only when addressed directly, and even then answered with as few words as possible.

David had been placed at this school for other than academic reasons. He had never been in a special education setting, and I assumed that he entered Ann's classroom with experiences somewhat different from the other students, all of whom had participated in special remedial programs or had been assigned to resource rooms. Having always been in regular classes, David found this classroom quite different from what he was used to—no desks in rows, no teacher's desk, and only ten students in a small room. Understandably, David was unsure of what to expect. David, like Tanya, had let the institution staff know that he did not consider this "real" school. "It's too easy," he told staff members. "We don't even have tests."

During those first few weeks, Ann and I noticed that David was quiet, staying mostly to himself and not seeming to want to become part of the community, even though he participated because it was expected. He rarely smiled, never initiated conversations, kept his chair on the outskirts of any discussion circle, and moved slowly and halfheartedly as if he wanted every-one to realize he was bored with what was going on. Ann worked to find ways to interest him and help him feel a part of the community.

One Sunday afternoon shortly after David came to the school, my hus-band and I attended an open house that the school sponsored. As we walked up the driveway, Tanya ran up to us, eager to give us a tour of her residence hall. Tanya was so pleased to have a visitor that she felt inspired to describe each of the features of the rooms (my husband remarked that she ought to consider a career in real estate). Debby greeted us at the next building and, though not confident enough to perform a house tour, did manage to giggle and chatter as only a thirteen-year-old can. Gary was not only pleased to see us but he attached himself to our side during the rest of the afternoon's activities, chatting continuously with my husband about rap stars, such as Vanilla Ice. In fact, all the students greeted us with smiles and hellos, gen-uinely pleased to see us in the crowd of parents, guardians, and benefactors. All but David, that is. He acted as if he did not know me, avoiding us in a way that was obvious. David was not a happy boy.

An Outsider Comes In

During the first few days in class, it was evident that David was a capable reader; he read what was expected with little or no difficulty. I talked with him casually about reading, and he admitted that he had done little reading either in or outside of school. When I asked him about reading, he said he had never read books, "like stories" (novels), in his old school. There, reading was out of reading books (basals) and he had a workbook and "sheets" to do. When he had done some reading on his own, he seemed especially to like reading scary books, a taste typical of readers his age.

Ann began *The Outsiders* as a class novel a few weeks after David's arrival. From the day she introduced the book, David seemed to "perk up," sitting up in his chair and looking at Ann as she spoke. This was a noticeable transformation since he typically spent most of his time with his head on the desk or staring out the window. Ann read the first couple of chapters aloud to the class, and David seemed totally involved in the novel. When Ann suggested that the students put the books away for the day, David, along with the others in the class, pleaded for her to keep reading. Ann noticed this new interest of David's, so she followed his lead and read one more chapter with the class.

David seemed intrigued as Ann talked about the teenage author, a sixteen-year-old girl who called herself S. E. Hinton. As the days went by, David became more and more involved with the novel and the characters. In his journal and during class discussions, David commented that this was the first time he had ever shared literature with other readers through response and discussion; slowly, during these weeks I watched him begin to become a part of the community. The change was gradual but obvious: When discussing favorite characters, David shared his thoughts and feelings about Darry, who like David, was the oldest brother. *The Outsiders* enabled students to hear how characters they respected and with whom they identified learned to deal honestly with their feelings and emotions. For example, when the character Johnny explains, "nothing gold can stay," all the students, David included, responded with personal experiences and feelings that were similar to those in the novel. For the first time since coming to Ann's class, David was participating—listening and sharing, fully involved with his peers as he and they responded to the novel. David was becoming part of the community, bonding with others while reading and responding to literature.

Having become quite knowledgeable about adolescent literature and reading taste, Ann routinely made suggestions about books she thought students might enjoy reading during daily Sustained Silent Reading. Seeing how much David was enjoying *The Outsiders*, Ann suggested he try other books by the same author. David replied that he already knew this was a good way to select books, having read many books by his favorite author—Stephen King (however, he hadn't ever applied the strategy since he couldn't actually name another author). David took Ann's suggestion and began reading other books by Hinton, such as *That Was Then, This Is Now* and *Tex*. Ann felt this was a first step in broadening David's interests, and his interest in books seemed to be growing. He read daily, asked for book suggestions, and talked with the other students and teachers about what he was reading.

A Journal for Dialogue

David soon began reading more on his own, supplementing the class readings with novels on the same topic. For instance, when the class read *The Sign of the Beaver*, David read a much more sophisticated novel on his own—*A Light in the Forest*. This book, though more difficult, was accessible to him in part because of what he was learning in social studies class through the thematic unit about Native Americans. Ann tried to interact with David as he read, but he was not yet at the point where he would initiate such discussion. If Ann was going to discuss David's independent reading selections with him, she had to find time and she had to remember to pull David aside and share reactions to the novel. This wasn't always possible; Ann found it increasingly difficult to meet David's individual needs as a reader, since he was more advanced than others in the class and needed a person with whom he could share his reading.

At this point I suggested the possibility of using a dialogue journal with David. Dialogue journals use writing to promote reader response in much the same way we use conversation—to negotiate thoughts and ideas through the use of language. Instead of oral conversation, the dialogue takes place in writing.

As with other types of journals, there is no one method for setting up dialogue journals; sometimes students use a spiral notebook with a double margin (or draw in margins, dividing the page in half lengthwise before writing). Typically after reading or discussion, students respond by writing on one side of the page in their journals, expressing their ideas, concerns, reactions, and connections as they would for other journal experiences. Then students share their opinions and ideas by exchanging dialogue journals with another student. The teacher provides time for the paired students to read each other's entries and the responder, be it teacher or student, must actually attend to what the writer has to say. After reading, the responder writes back in the journal, using the other side of the double margin page, building on what the writer has said, intent upon carrying on a conversation. The journal's owner is then free to write a further reply. The purpose is to open up a dialogue, not to make a judgment about the thought or idea.

Ann was unsure of the procedure, so I volunteered to approach David with the idea. At the time I hoped to interest David in a dialogue journal, the class was discussing award-winning authors and titles; many of the students were choosing novels to read that had won Newbery or Children's Choice Awards. David had decided to read Jerry Spinelli's *Maniac Magee*. I took David aside one afternoon to discuss his choice. I told him that, although I had not yet read the novel, I had heard terrific things about it and I had it on my list of books to read soon. I suggested that we both read *Maniac Magee* at the same time, and we could talk about it as we read. I proposed to David that one way to read together was to write down our thoughts, feelings, and reactions as we read and then share them with another reader, who subsequently "writes back" a response. I explained that this was called a dialogue journal. To give the activity more credibility, I showed him a dialogue journal that I had kept in graduate school and told him why I felt that keeping a dialogue journal had been a valuable and enjoyable activity for me as a reader. David seemed interested, especially in the fact that I had used a dialogue journal at the university. He looked through mine and was impressed by the amount of writing back and forth. "Will we do this?" he asked as he pointed to responses to my ideas written by my friends and classmates. I assured him that we would, and he seemed truly anxious to get started. I gave him a spiral notebook, explained how to set up the journal, and invited him to begin whenever he felt he wanted to. He had already started *Maniac Magee* and asked if he should write from the beginning; I told him to start from where he was, and I would catch up in the reading.

Two days later I returned to the classroom. David immediately grabbed his journal, jumped out of his chair, and came toward me with an excited but tentative look on his face. "Want to read my journal?" he asked.

"Terrific," I responded, "I'll read it this afternoon and get it back to you before I leave."

While the students were in art class, I went into Ann's office to read and respond to David's journal. I was excited not only about his responses to what he had read but also by his obvious enthusiasm in sharing his reactions through writing in a journal.

David's reactions were short but powerful. Unlike many students who are new to keeping a journal, David did not summarize what he had read. Reacting much as a reader would when verbally engaged with another reader, David responded in writing to the part of each chapter that was most significant to him, either because he could identify with what was happening in the story or because he wanted to analyze the characters' actions. In the following example from his dialogue journal, David reacts in his entry to Maniac's early-morning runs and draws a profound conclusion about the character's actions:

> Maniac has no where to go. He goes to the zoo, sleeps there a couple of nights. In the mornings he walks around town. He called these times his special time with the town. He looks everywhere except the P&W trolley in which his parents died on. I feel that he loves the morning so much because there is no division, no barriers between whites and blacks. I feel sorry for Jeffrey Lionel Magee.

When I read this entry, I was struck by the depth of David's thinking. In the novel, there is an underlying theme of racial tension and prejudice. However, when I read the novel I saw Maniac's morning runs as either a means of personal escape or a way for Maniac to feel the exhilaration that runners say they feel. When I read David's interpretation, I knew he had entered the novel, reacting to and interpreting the story based on inferences made. I didn't remember reading that Maniac's running was a time to see the town as a whole, free of the racial tension that separated it, yet David saw this as a reader. I was impressed and excited, and in my response to David, I reacted to his entry as a fellow reader:

> Wow, David, very insightful! You know, I never thought of it that way before, but I see what you mean. When I think of it this way, I think that Maniac is lonely, not only because he has no home but because people being cruel to other people makes him sad. I feel sorry for him too.

David also used his journal to sort out what was happening in the novel. For example, when he wrote the following, it was evident that he was using writing as a mode of thinking:

> I don't really understand the first part. I think that Magee runs in the morning and Mars Barr knew that so he decided to run into Magee. In the second part I feel that Magee didn't realize what he

was on [the tracks] and when he did, he remembered his parents and just couldn't handle being there so he ran away from his feelings and down the street. I sorda know how he feels because my friend died in a car wreck and my parents had to force me to ride in a car when I didn't want to.

Over the next few months, David's actions showed how much he enjoyed writing entries in his dialogue journal. He had the journal ready every day, and when I arrived, he brought it to me immediately. After I responded and returned it to him, he quickly opened it, read my responses, and started to react in writing to what I had written. We were engaged in a dialogue, sharing a novel as two readers.

David and I continued to share other literature through his dialogue journal. David had mentioned that one of his fondest memories was coon hunting with his grandfather, so Ann suggested reading *Where the Red Fern Grows*, a novel about a boy, his grandfather, and hunting raccoons. David's background experiences formed a personal basis for interest and understanding. I have known other children, some from the inner city and even some from the suburbs, who were uninterested in reading *Where the Red Fern Grows* (regardless of its standing in the children's literature canon), but David was eager to read it independently and to write about it in his journal.

As David read *Where the Red Fern Grows*, he frequently connected the novel to his own experiences, reading the novel from cover to cover in just a few days. Figure 10 shows a typical response from David's dialogue journal. David became so involved in the book that his journal responses became less frequent. This was because he only wrote when he stopped reading, which occurred only after he had consumed several chapters at a sitting. At first David apologized to me for not writing as often as he had before, but I assured him that it was best to write when he felt he wanted to, not when he thought he had to. David continued his journaling throughout the year—first with me, then with Ann—and Ann planned to try peer dialoguing in the near future after observing how several other students became caught up in David's enthusiasm for the activity.

The Patience for Writing

David's feelings about Ann's class in general seemed to change as a result of his experiences—particularly his experience with literature. Several months after David came to Ann's class, I asked him how this school compared to his old school. David responded that "she [Ms. Hunter] doesn't put the high people with the high people. She puts everyone together in a group." This was a reference to homogeneous grouping as compared to heterogeneous grouping. David said he liked being grouped this way, heterogeneously, because he could work on things he was interested in with other students who had similar interests. He commented further that reading was more fun in Ann's class and he felt that he was learning more. As he came to this realization, David's entire attitude toward school changed. He had become interested, attentive, and involved with what was going on in class, a different boy from the one I first met.

FIGURE 10   Entry from David's Dialogue Journal

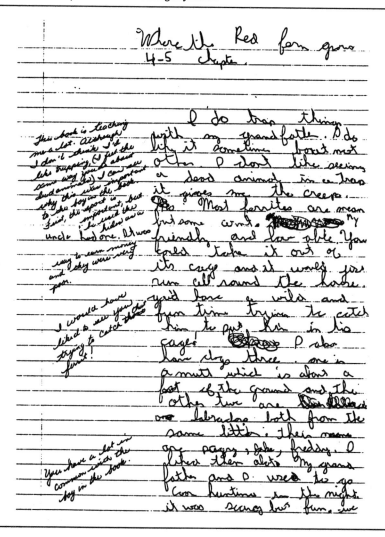

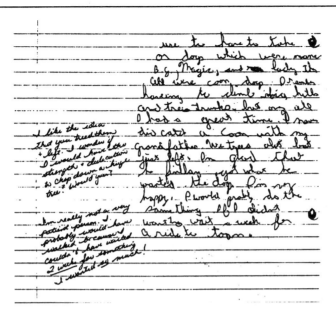

FIGURE 10   Entry from David's Dialogue Journal, continued

This change was evident from David's growth not only as a reader but also as a writer. David told me that prior to his coming to Ann's class, writing consisted of grammar work sheets and penmanship exercises, which he called "practicing cursive writing."

Although David might have been aware that writing took time, I noticed that early in the year he wrote quickly, as though he were trying to get it over with. "I don't like being patient," he explained. David had little tolerance for the process approach to writing and at first thought prewriting was a waste of time. "Let's just write it," he would say. David told me that he got all his "feelings, like [his] whole story down too quick"; he still did not enjoy writing.

As the year progressed, Ann worked rigorously with the students on prewriting strategies, techniques that would help them organize and plan before they wrote. Gradually David became interested in how these strategies, especially webbing, could help him.

David used webbing to brainstorm ideas for his Civil War story about Johnny, the older brother mentioned in the book *Charlie Skeedaddle* (see Figure 11). David was fascinated by this character, who had died before the story line began but who, like Darry, the eldest brother in *The Outsiders*, was looked up to by his younger brother. In his web, which was drawn on eleven-by-seventeen-inch white art paper, David began with broad topics for his story about Johnny—such as "How he lived," "New York," and "How the war

FIGURE 11 David's Brainstorming Web

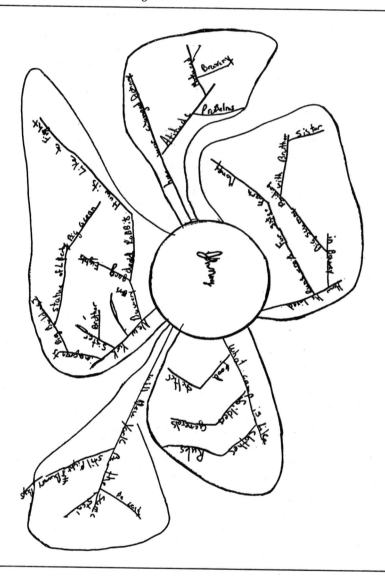

changed Johnny." He thought of these as topics a reader might be interested in, and ones the original book did not address. David then brainstormed possible ideas to write about under each major topic. For instance, under "What the camp was like," David thought of things such as food, shelter, soldiers, general's clothes, and rules. Under "How the war changed Johnny," he thought of writing about attitudes, problems, maturity, and bravery.

After completing his web, David used the ideas he had brainstormed to outline a plan for his story (see Figure 12). He first used heading and subtopics and then arranged the topics in a sequence that made sense to him (see the organizing numbers subsequently changed on the side of the list).

Such prewriting strategies help writers like David to organize their thoughts before writing. David felt so confident about this story (which was over thirty pages long!) that he wrote it as a mininovel containing several chapters. Obviously, this was a labor of love, which progressed over many weeks. When I asked David how he felt about this experience, he said his Civil War story was much better than anything else he had ever written, and that it was organized and longer because he had thought about it before he

FIGURE 12   David's Outline

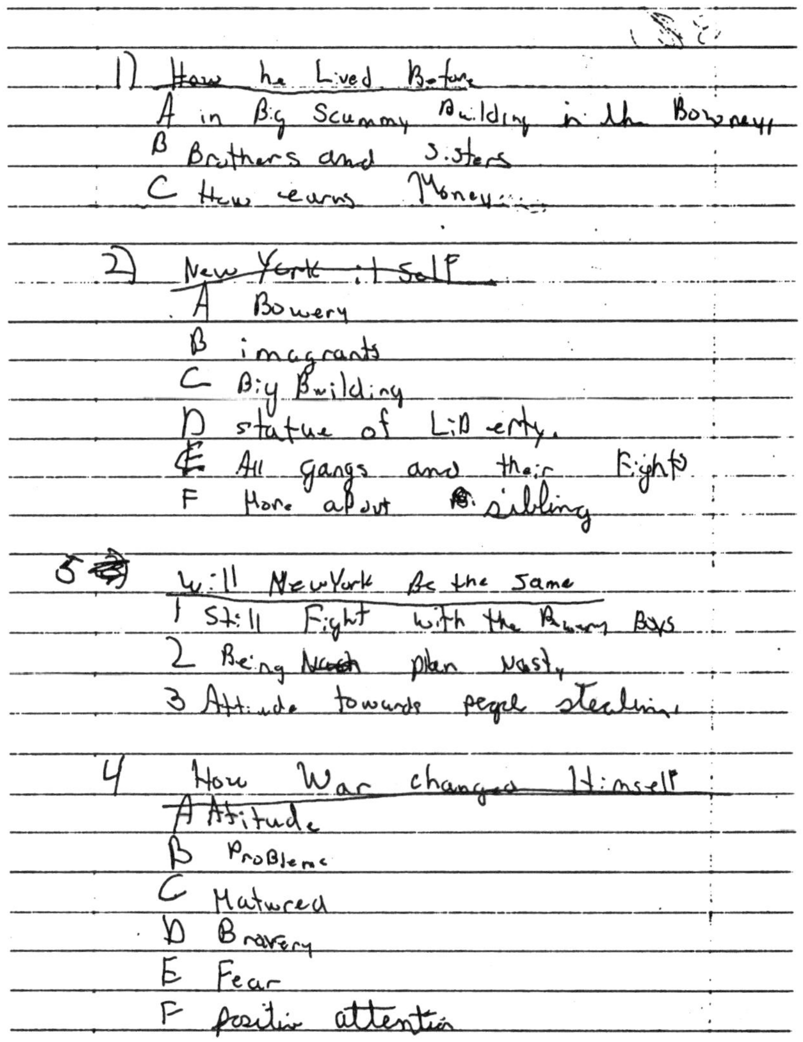

1) How he Lived Before
   A in Big Scummy Building in the Bowery
   B Brithers and Sisters
   C How earns Money

2) New York itself
   A Bowery
   B imagrants
   C Big Building
   D statue of Liberty.
   E All gangs and their Fights
   F Hope about sibling

5 3) Will New York Be the Same
   1 Still Fight with the Bowery Boys
   2 Being North plan Nasty
   3 Attiude towards people stealing

4 How War changed Himself
   A Attitude
   B Problems
   C Matured
   D Bravery
   E Fear
   F positive attention

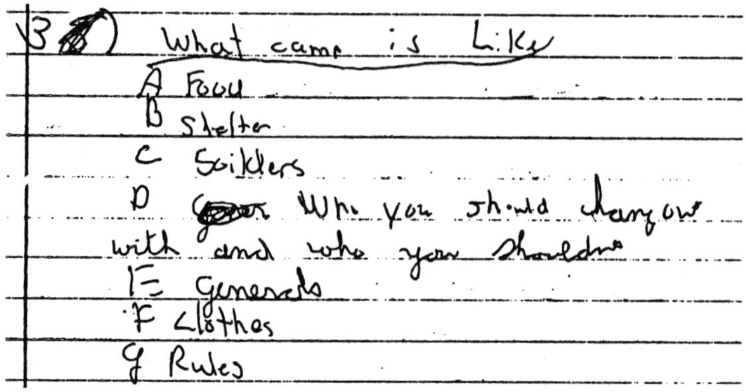

FIGURE 12   David's Outline, continued

started to write. He said that he "never had a plan" when he wrote before, but this time he "didn't want to rush through it." When I asked him what he felt helped him the most with his writing, he replied, "I read a whole bunch of books here [in Ann's class], and that's what's helped me write my story. The way they [the authors] write sentences and stuff. I look at the way they write and try to write like that."

David was growing as a writer by paying attention to the style of the authors he read, and he was able to articulate that idea, first because he was a reader and a writer, and second because he had been thinking about how someone becomes a writer. David had learned that writers are also readers and that writers often assume a style modeled after an author they have read. After he read his Civil War story to me, I asked David how he felt about writing. "Well, it depends," he answered honestly. "This is the biggest thing I ever wrote and it makes me feel good inside."

A Changed Outlook

Teachers continually wonder how to meet the needs of students with a wide range of developmental abilities and interests. I watched Ann do this so logically—in David's case, encouraging independent reading of books that were challenging but of interest to him, ones he could discuss or comment on in journal entries as he read. The same was true for students like Gary, who was confidently reading books related to the central theme under study, ones that he could read independently. Although the students had choice, they also valued Ann's opinions and advice. She wouldn't tell them what to read, but made suggestions based on ability, interest, past readings, relation to theme, and favorite authors. (Once again, knowing one's students is a pre-

requisite to meeting their individual needs.) Ann also let the students follow up on their reading in ways that were appropriate for them. For example, sometimes they would dialogue in a journal, write a story or ending,
work on a project, draw illustrations for the book, or create a bulletin board.
All these activities would reinforce the central theme and complement what
others in the class were working on, but they would also afford the students
time, choice, structure, and support—the elements all students need to pursue learning.

David's literacy behaviors and attitudes had certainly changed—in fact,
his entire outlook toward school had seemed to change. Not only Ann and
I, but others who worked with David noticed that he seemed happier and
more self-assured. During class time, he responded to activities enthusiastically and willingly joined in class discussion. Often he would smile or laugh
aloud during class as he reacted to literature or worked with his peers. Reading had not only proved to be valuable to David, but it was also something
he had learned to enjoy. He had opportunities to share insights and ideas
with other readers, and through dialogue journals he had transacted with
text through writing. By the end of the school year, David viewed himself as
a reader and writer and seemed to have an idea of how literacy had affected
him as a learner. During a class sharing time late in the school year, David
expressed his goal as a reader and a writer:

> I like to read now to try to understand an author and try to figure
> out where she's coming from. . . . In writing, I want to keep writ-
> ing down my ideas and thoughts. I have to learn to listen to criti-
> cism, though. Taking criticism from other people about my writ-
> ing is hard. I wrote it and it's my feelings, so it's hard.

David was also asked about other goals for his future.

> I'd like to learn to write movies, but first I have to learn whether
> something is good or not. You know, I have to learn to be a criti-
> cal reader and a critical watcher. I still don't read or write enough
> to tell what's really good to other people. I'm learning that by see-
> ing how authors write and doing it the way they do it.

In the spring, David was mainstreamed in the middle school for math
and social studies. It was interesting to watch the progress David was making. Ann told me he was doing well, getting A's and B's, and I had several
opportunities to watch and listen to him when he returned to Ann's classroom with reports of what was happening in the public school. No longer
did he look at Ann's classroom as easy. In fact, he often turned to her and

his classmates for advice and help on his middle-school class assignments. He knew how to approach a project—how to research a subject, use references, and write expository pieces—all things he had learned in Ann's class during thematic study. He proudly but shyly shared his successes with his classmates as Ann read aloud the glowing progress reports that he brought back. "Way to go, David!" his classmates cheered. As David thanked them I remembered that sullen, withdrawn boy I had seen a year before, and I compared him to the David I now saw as part of a community of learners who support each other. As a learner, David had a better idea of who he was and where he was going.

Leaving Ann's classroom was difficult for David in many ways, as it is for many students who learn and grow in a supportive whole language classroom and then, in subsequent years, find themselves back in traditional, behaviorist classrooms. Such was the case with David.

When David left the institution and was placed in a wonderful, supportive foster home, he kept in touch with Ann by telephone and by letter. His new school proved to be very difficult, especially English class, where the ninth-grade curriculum consisted of Wariner's grammar and spelling and vocabulary tests. David, who was used to real reading and writing in Ann's class, became angry and refused to do the grammar exercises in his new class. He told Ann it was "stupid," and he was angry that they were "wasting his time" with this "junk." Ann tried to convince him that he should just do his work, try his best, and continue to read and write in his free time.

David's grades began to fall; the A's and B's he was getting in middle school dropped to D's and F's, and he was in danger of being dropped from the football squad. His love of sports was what finally convinced him that he had to "play the game" in school too; he had to do all the work even if he felt it was not worthwhile and even if he didn't have an opportunity to read or write for pleasure. Although it was a rocky year, David survived. He pulled C's in his courses (one D in English) but was able to play football. It's a shame that students must learn to survive in school. I remembered the young man who read voraciously in Ann's class and wanted to learn more about evaluating good writing so he could become a screenwriter. Could others take away what Ann, his classmates, and David himself had given David in the time he spent in Ann's whole language classroom? I hope not, but I know there will probably be setbacks and frustrations, especially in classrooms that don't support learners. Once a person becomes a reader and a writer, in the sense that they see a place for literacy in their lives and recognize the power of literacy, can that person be robbed of membership in the "literacy club?"

During his high school years, David continued to write and call Ann. With the help of his foster parents, and some good high school teachers, David's academic performance improved. His grades went up to A's and B's, and he told Ann that some of his teachers encouraged reading and writing (at least he had fewer "exercises" to contend with). David now talks about going to college and seems to feel that learning has a place in his life.

But I continue to worry about David: Can others take away what David acquired during his time in a whole language classroom? I see too many college students who are not readers and writers. They *can* read, but they don't. They tell me that they have so much required reading that reading is not something they would choose to do "for pleasure." For them, reading is work and what they are reading is textbook material. Most educators would agree that our goal is to help students become lifelong readers, but the system does little to support this goal. When students spend most of their lives in classrooms where reading is a subject rather than an act, they are robbed of an opportunity to learn in a literate community of readers. Although a year or two of whole language experiences may help to start students on their way, I'm not sure all of them will keep what they started to build in whole language classrooms. Good luck, David.

6
Debby
Raising Her Standards

A book is a cooperative venture. The writer can write a story down, but
the book will never be complete until a reader of whatever age takes
that book and brings it to his own story. . . . It is only when the deepest
sound going forth from my heart meets the deepest sound coming forth
from yours—it is only in this encounter that the true music begins.
Katherine Paterson

Teachers who work with "at risk" readers and writers, in special classrooms or mainstreamed in regular classes, yearn for a formula, a key, or a
method that will transform these learners. Ken Goodman (1991) suggests
that it is the students themselves who must come to revalue the process of
reading as a construction of meaning rather than a completion of skills
before they can make advances in their literacy learning. Students must
come to appreciate their own strengths, to recognize productive strategies
they use already, and to build positively on those. Of course, none of those
conditions will occur unless students are exposed to a wide variety of reading materials and are given opportunities to discover these things about
reading and about themselves as readers.

Before coming to her classroom, Ann's students were, like Mike Rose's
(1989) students who were living their *Lives on the Boundary*, in jeopardy of
being lost in the system—a system that expected students to fit the mold
and was prepared to remediate any differences detected. Fortunately, differences were celebrated in Ann's classroom. For Debby, as for Gary, Tanya,
David, and all the other students in Ann's class, reading and writing became
an important part of life, but in a different way and for a different purpose.
Debby, of all the students in the class, displayed the most obvious change in
self-concept as a learner. Literature gave her a vehicle by which to discover
a purpose for reading and writing, and she proceeded to use language to grow
and learn in a community where such learning is natural and purposeful.
Debby's "language story," like those of the other three students, illustrates
the personal effect that literacy had on one life.

My First Book

Debby, a very likable twelve-year-old, had been in Ann's classroom longer than any of the other students. When I first began visiting, Debby had already been there for a full year and was beginning her second year in the class. Ann told me that during her first year at the school, Debby appeared very unsure of herself. Although shy, Debby craved individual attention from the teacher and seemed content when she received it. During her first weeks in the classroom, it wasn't unusual to hear Debby repeatedly saying, "Ms. Hunter, I don't know how to do this," or "I don't understand this." In response to these pleas, usually made in a whiny, sing-song voice, Ann, or Emily the aide, would often help Debby with whatever she was doing. Debby would then work diligently and would seem pleased when Ann or Emily praised her, even when they pointed out to her afterward that she *could*, in fact, do the assignment.

Some of the students whom I spoke with when I first began visiting Ann's classroom had left the school by the time I became a regular member of the class, but I remember those early visits with Debby. I was struck by how enthused she seemed about the books she was reading, often showing them to me when I came to class. *Amelia Bedelia* seemed to be a favorite, and since that particular book usually appeals to readers who are much younger, I was curious about her choice. Her interest became clearer when she told me, "I never used to like to read. *Amelia Bedelia* is so funny—do you know her? This is my first book that I ever read myself."

I assume that most readers do not remember the first book they ever read independently, probably because this event normally occurs when we are young and happens gradually as we are learning to read. However, when Debby told me about *Amelia Bedelia* she was twelve years old, and apparently she looked at reading this book as a milestone in her life.

While I was getting to know Debby, we would talk about her interests and about school. Debby told me that before coming to Ms. Hunter's class she did not know how to read. She told me of past experiences in special education classes. She had never read a book by herself during those years, and in her old school, writing consisted of copying things off the board or out of books. Asked if she went to reading class in her old school, she said she had but never learned to read out of those reading books. From her description I assumed that "those reading books" were basals. Asked about reading in Ms. Hunter's class, she told me how she learned to read:

When I first came here I couldn't read by myself and Ms. Hunter would read to us every day. Sometimes I'd come in here [the supply room] with Ms. Rowe [Emily the aide] and we'd read together. Things are better now; I read by myself.

Saying What You Mean

Debby, like Gary, seemed to have difficulty expressing ideas orally. The speech teacher at the school told me that she believed much of Debby's speech problem was due to a lack of experience with oral language. Debby's vocabulary was that of a much younger child; she had absolutely no knowledge of figurative language or idioms, and she seemed to have a difficult time retaining any of the exercises the speech teacher used in her sessions. It was necessary to speak very literally to Debby; expressions such as "time flies" or "the last straw" were just not part of her past language experiences and, as is the case with some students for whom English is a second language, such expressions proved to be very confusing to Debby. Instead of using exercises to meet Debby's needs, Ann talked with Debby about language and read books like Fred Gwynne's *Chocolate Moose for Dinner*. *Amelia Bedelia* helped Debby think about language, and the series became one of her favorites. Debby became more interested in idiomatic expressions, and although she didn't seem to use them in her own speech, which was still marked by simple and direct verbal constructions, she didn't seem as bothered when they were included in others' conversations or in novels the class was reading.

A Step in Writing

Debby insisted that she could not write and would not even attempt it at first. Ann used a language experience approach with Debby during her first year in Ann's classroom, because of Debby's problem with verbal expression and her virtual inexperience with writing. Since Debby seemed to do better when she was getting individual attention, Ann or Emily began by transcribing ideas that Debby dictated orally. Later that first year, Debby did begin to write by herself, and this seemed to happen more frequently as she began to read independently. Her writing at this point was very much like that of all beginning writers—short, simple sentences and text so brief that it was difficult for a reader to comprehend fully what Debby was trying to say. Figure 13 is an example of an early piece of Debby's writing—a response

FIGURE 13   Debby's Reaction to *How to Eat Fried Worms*

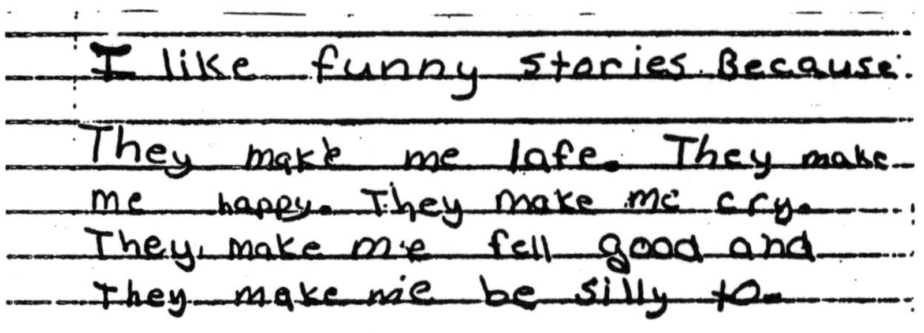

> I like funny stories Because.
> They make me lafe. They make
> me happy. They make me cry.
> They make me fell good and
> They make me be silly to.

to a prompt asking why Debby had liked *How to Eat Fried Worms*, a book the class was reading at the time.

> I like funny stories Because They make me lafe. They make me happy. They make me cry. They make me fell good and They make me be silly to.

Although the syntax of this writing is simple, it is important to note that Debby wrote it by herself. It was printed and looks similar to the writing of a much younger child, but it was a positive step toward Debby's realization that she was a writer. Debby, writing on her own, was beginning to take risks.

Teacher as a Catalyst

By the time I started to work with Ann on a regular basis, Debby was a reader and a writer, and I had the opportunity to watch her grow. She worked more independently at this point, and although she still asked how to spell many words and asked for directions to be repeated two or three times, she was, nevertheless, working on her own more often. She read independently during daily Sustained Silent Reading time and volunteered to read orally during shared reading. Ann still supported Debby in her oral reading, but Debby seemed pleased to be part of the group, smiling broadly after reading and looking at Ann for approval. She would beam when Ann responded with, "Great job, Debby," or "Nice reading." Ann was working hard to build Debby's self-esteem, letting Debby know that she recognized her abilities.

How had Debby become a reader? What elements had caused the change, not only in Debby's attitude toward literacy but also toward her perception of herself as a capable learner? Perhaps it was a matter of revaluing reading and self, something that does not happen simply, easily, or quickly, as Ken Goodman (1991) points out. Revaluing requires great patience and gentle support from teachers helping students in a long, slow rebuilding of their sense of self and sense of reading. Students like Debby need to place proper value on themselves as readers, understanding that no one can read everything easily and allowing that perhaps some texts may be difficult either because they contain new and complex ideas or because they are poorly written. Goodman stresses that "a revaluing program involves getting readers to read real, meaningful texts, to strengthen and gain new appreciation of the productive strategies that lead to comprehension, and to drop the nonproductive strategies" (130). As readers, students like Debby need to understand that the books they have the most interest in and the most background for will be the easiest for them to read and will give them the most pleasure.

It was apparent from talking to Debby that she saw her teacher as an important reason for her progress in reading, a catalyst for her growth, though it was difficult for her to express *why* this was true. Debby said, "Ms. Hunter's a really nice teacher—she helped me. She brought me a really long way. She talks to me. If I have something to talk about she lets me right there. Ms. Hunter brought me a long way in reading."

Debby explained that Ms. Hunter lets her talk and that Ms. Hunter listens. In a transactional classroom, a teacher learns about a student by interacting with the student as they read together and discuss what has been read, not through diagnostic tests that tell little about the student as a person. In this way, the teacher learns who the student is and what the student is interested in. The teacher moves slowly and supportively to overcome fear and despair. Often, as students relax, they reveal themselves to be much more capable than either they or the teacher had imagined.

When Ann started working with Debby, she did not assume that Debby was devoid of reading ability. Wary of test scores that indicated a "below normal" IQ and reading scores on the primary level, Ann began with what she knew about Debby and worked from there. Debby loved to be read to, and Ann wanted to begin with a reading situation that was completely nonthreatening. Thus, she began by reading aloud to Debby as Debby followed along. Ann tried to read books that Debby would enjoy, and those often

FIGURE 14 Early Draft of Debby's Civil War Story

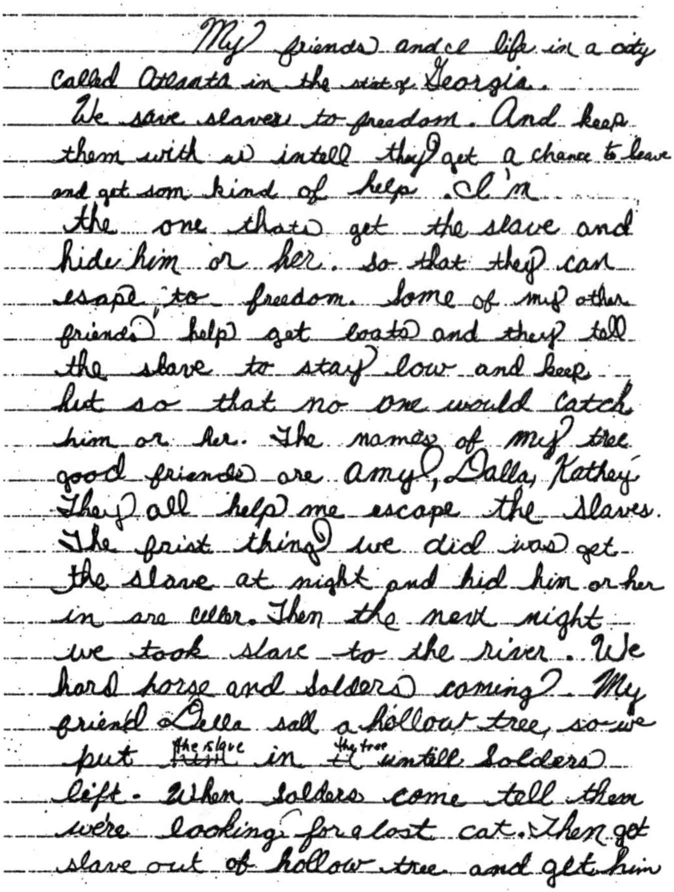

My friends and I life in a city called Atlanta in the sit of Georgia. We save slaves to freedom. And keep them with us intell they get a chance to leave and get som kind of help. I'm the one thats get the slave and hide him or her. so that they can esape to freedom. Some of my other friends help get coats and they tell the slave to stay low and keep hid so that no one would catch him or her. The names of my tree good friends are Amy, Dalla, Kathey. They all help me escape the slaves. The frist thing we did was get the slave at night and hid him or her in are celler. Then the next night we took slave to the river. We hard horse and solders coming. My friend Dalla sall a hollow tree, so we put the slave in the tree untill solders left. When solders come tell them were looking for a lost cat. Then get slave out of hollow tree and get him

included light, funny books that would cause Debby to laugh aloud. As Ann learned more about Debby's interests—animals, for instance—she was able to include or recommend literature that Debby would be interested in, and therefore, that Debby would have an easier time reading.

As I watched Ann with Debby, I was aware that Ann often took the lead from Debby. Ann monitored Debby, letting Debby set the pace and direction while she offered the right help at the right time, much the way parents do when supporting young children's language development. Ann did not push her, but she did encourage Debby to take risks. This type of support cannot be prescribed because it depends upon individual students

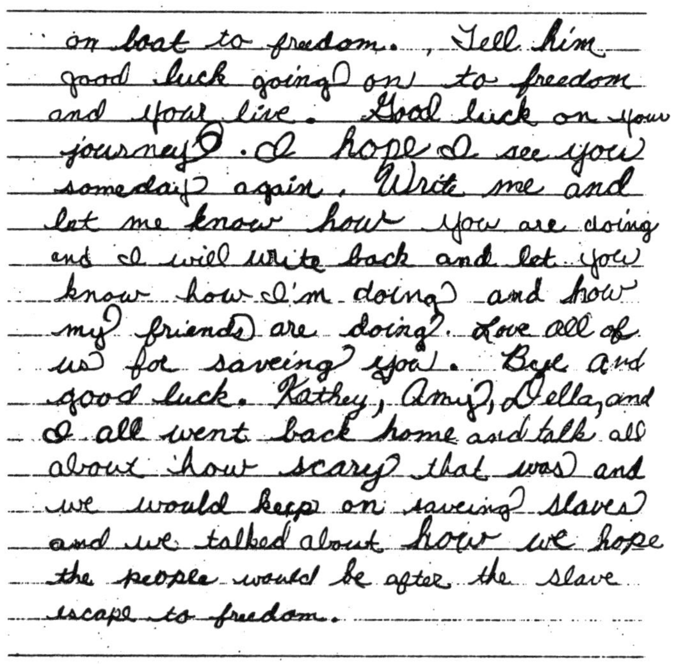

FIGURE 14   Early Draft of Debby's Civil War Story, continued

and their development. An example of this is the way in which Ann supported Debby as she worked to become a writer. At first, Debby was afraid to put anything on paper because she saw misspelled words as a weakness and knew she had trouble with spelling. Although Ann wanted Debby to take risks and use invented spelling in her drafts, this was difficult for Debby because she felt writing had to be perfect. Recognizing this, Ann spelled words for Debby as she asked, even though Ann would have preferred that Debby just keep writing, trying to spell as best she could phonetically.

Debby eventually came to use invented spelling, but it happened over a period of time; it was not something that Ann imposed. She took her direction from Debby, supporting her in the ways that made writing more comfortable to move Debby to the point of taking risks in spelling. Ann worked hard to convince Debby that when writing, it was most important to get ideas down on paper and that drafts could be "sloppy," with misspelled words and less than meticulous penmanship. This was difficult for Debby to accept, but later in the year, Debby began to take risks and, when possible, worry less about spelling, especially when drafting. She gradually began to look at writing as a process and realized that she had the time and opportunity to go back and fix the spelling before publishing it in her finest handwriting. Figure 14 is an early draft of Debby's Civil War story, which she had previously webbed as a prewriting activity. Although there are many misspelled words, the text is very long for Debby, and she was able to get her ideas down on paper in a logical sequence without worrying about lower-level concerns such as spelling, punctuation, and handwriting, which she attended to later.

Peer Support

Ann worked to help Debby gain self-confidence, to "revalue" herself. As Debby began to read and write independently, Ann moved Debby's desk away from the conferencing table, the space where Ann usually sat, to the other side of the room next to David. Ann was aware that students who have little faith in themselves often become overreliant on their teachers because they are afraid to make mistakes and afraid to take risks (Goodman 1991). Debby admired David's abilities, and since peer support was encouraged in Ann's classroom, Debby began to turn to David for assistance, although she still seemed somewhat nervous about being moved away from the teacher. David responded by turning around to help Debby, and he was very encouraging, repeating the same sort of positive remarks that Ann modeled for her students. "That's good, Debby," David would assure her, "but you might want to add more here." After discussing possibilities, David would add, "Remember, Debby, use your words, not mine. They're your ideas."

This collaboration between David and Debby helped Debby take another step toward self-confidence. She was learning that it was okay to rely on her peers, the members of her learning community, and she even began to offer suggestions and advice to David. Although it was still difficult for Debby to be verbally explicit, she was beginning to respond as a reader and to have enough confidence in her ability as a reader to react to another's writing. It began as simple, positive comments—for example, saying, "That's good, David"—and progressed to questioning, such as "I don't get this part" or "this part is confusing." David, whose needs were different from Debby's, actually learned to value Debby's input as a reader, even though in some classrooms David and Debby would never have had a chance to support each other owing to their vast differences in academic development.

Crossing the Bridge

A real turning point came for Debby during the class reading of the novel *Bridge to Terabithia*. Debby became very involved in this story of friendship, a theme important to her personally. Most of the entries she wrote every day in her literature response journal emphasized the developing relationship of Jess and Leslie, two adolescents who were somewhat lonely before their friendship. Debby was so involved in the book that she joined in class discussions about *Bridge to Terabithia* and even read parts of the novel a second time because she enjoyed them so.

A startling example of Debby's involvement in *Bridge to Terabithia* came when Ann showed the movie version of this novel. Debby was an avid movie fan; in fact, so much so that she believed, like so many adolescents, that watching a movie was more fun and more entertaining than reading a book. However, Debby seemed uncomfortable during the viewing of this movie. In fact, in the middle of the movie she announced that the movie was "lousy" and put her head on her desk. After the movie was over, Ann asked for reactions, and Debby was the first to respond.

"I hated it," she began. "Those people were nothing like Jess and Leslie in the book. I liked the way I pictured them in my head better."

"Wow," David responded, "I'd never have thought I'd live to hear Debby say that she liked a book better than a movie." The rest of the class agreed, and Debby again emphasized that the book was *much* better.

Debby had responded as a reader. While reading the novel, she "pictured" the characters in her head. She was not merely reading words; she was lost in a story and was able to personally respond and react to the literature. To Debby this novel was "an event in time. It [was] not an object or an ideal entity. It happened during a coming together, a compenetration, of a reader and a text," as Louise Rosenblatt (1978) explains it.

As Debby improved as a reader, her confidence grew as a writer. Debby told me, "Back when I was younger and I first came here, I didn't know what I was doin' and I didn't know how to write good and now I do." I asked her how she thought this happened, and she said that she thought that reading more made her a better writer. When I asked how reading had helped her writing, she replied, "Because like when you read, it gives you the words you need mostly to write." As discussed earlier, Debby's writing gradually changed over a period of time. Debby was writing every day in Ann's class, and as her reading improved, she became much more expressive in her literature journal. She was able to express herself in writing in ways she had not

FIGURE 15   Debby's Response to Her Favorite Novel, *Bridge to Terabithia*

been able to a year before. Maybe, as Debby herself said, reading gave her the words. Less than one year after reading and responding to *How to Eat Fried Worms* (Figure 13), Debby independently wrote a response to her favorite novel, *Bridge to Terabithia* (see Figure 15). It was difficult to believe this was the same writer who less than a year ago was just beginning to write a sentence. Even her presentation was different. Her earlier response, to *How to Eat Fried Worms*, was printed in oversized manuscript letters and contained short, simple sentences typical of a much younger writer. Her response to *Bridge to Terabithia* was more representative of an adolescent: she wrote in cursive, with fancy curls on beginning and ending letters, a handwriting trait typical of middle school girls, and indicative, I would think, of a writer with some degree of confidence who is aware of presentation and wishes to use it to influence a reader. At this point, she was writing more complex sentences and even using punctuation marks such as commas. Debby's entry was as follows:

Bridge to Terabithia

I liked the book Bridge to Terabithia, because I could relate to Leslie. I'm like her. I'm loving, caring, sharing, and a helping hand. I like to have good friendships with other people in my class. I'm good at the things that I do. I talk to people when they're upset. I also talk to people when they're felling lonely, angre, and very scared. I'm a very good friend when others get mad or something like that. I try to calm people down when they're felling upset. I also try to calm people down when they're crying and when they're crying over somebody eles.

The best part I really liked in the book Bridge to Terabithia is when Jess and Leslie start to be friends. When they were going thow the woods and when they start to have a relationship with each other. I think alot more people will like this book. I really like Bridge to Terabithia a whole lot!

Second Readings

Debby was the only student in Ann's classroom that year who had been there the previous year. The students told Ann they wanted to read *How to Eat Fried Worms* as a shared reading in class, since Debby had mentioned it so often and had highly recommended it. Ann hesitated because she had used the book the year before and Debby had already read and responded to it; Ann was afraid that a rereading might bore Debby or might not be fair to her. Many teachers have this same concern. If they find that several students have previously read a book they had hoped would be a good class experience, they are afraid to use that book. In fact, one of the biggest problems in schools working toward a literature-based approach to literacy is "turf protection"—the third-grade teacher can't use *Charlotte's Web* because the second-grade teachers have claimed it as a second-grade book. This attitude results from the idea that students should only be asked to read a book once, instead of recognizing that many books deserve several readings. If children love a book and want to read it a second or third time, teachers should look at subsequent readings as literacy experiences rather than as "repeating material." In *Side by Side*, Nancie Atwell (1991) reveals that her love of reading leads her to reread novels she loves, yet she confesses that for years she practiced a double standard, forbidding her students to choose books they had already read. She somehow felt it "was cheating." She credits Frank Smith (1983) with helping her to adopt a more informed approach to teaching reading: "Respond to what the child is trying to do" (Smith 1983, 24). Atwell explains:

> When eighth graders chose to reread, I began to respond to their reasons for rereading. They wanted the sense of security they derived from familiar characters in familiar situations and wanted to be with these friends once more. They wanted to notice how the author had written, something readers seldom do their first time through a good story. They wanted their emotions touched, to cry again or feel happy or scared again. They wanted to relax for a few days. Or they didn't know what else to read that they might like. My job was to understand the reader's response and offer help if I thought the reader needed it. Most often, students who reread did not need my help. They were helping themselves by returning to ground they had already covered. Rereading provided an important opportunity to practice fluent reading, to pick up speed through familiar territory and get better at what good readers do (117-118).

Ann decided that since Debby was eager to reread *How to Eat Fried Worms* with this class, the class would use the novel as a shared reading experience. Not only did Debby enjoy the experience, but she also relished the fact that she had read it before and that she was the one who was able to confidently assure those who hadn't read it yet that they would love it. Such a position made Debby feel important and part of the "literacy club," in which readers make recommendations of what to read by sharing their reading selections with others. Debby also had a different experience with a second reading of *How to Eat Fried Worms*, her abilities in reading and writing having improved so dramatically in a year's time. Compare the written response during her first reading (Figure 13) with a response she wrote a year later after her second reading (Figure 16). In Debby's "My Life as a Worm" piece she chose to write from another's point of view and used the content knowledge she had learned when the class did research about worms while reading the novel.

A Different Light

Gradually Debby began to see herself and her abilities in a different light, a change that was apparent not only to her teacher and to me but also to

My life as a worm.

    I love being a slimy worm, but I wish people and things wouldn't go around killing me, and making me bait for fish. My name is Alferd. I live live in a greenish house, with My family. My Mother's name is Vanna White. My father's name is Alen. He and My Mother give me anything I want, because I'm the only child and I'm also spoiledrotten. My parents would never do anything to hurt me. Well, now I'm going to tell you about myself. I have these neat segments that protect me. The kinds of things that eat me and kill me are lird's, and molds. Human's kill me by stepping on me, and eating me, and fring me, and thing's like that, but I always stay in the dark so that I stay safe sound. I don't know why people kill me, because I'm important to them. I help them with their farmlands, and I eat their soil layers. Oh, I almost forgot to tell you that I have five harts, and I'm good for eating dirt, and dried up leaves. I can sense light from dark too.

    All of you Adult's and children if you were a worm, How would you like to be stepped on, and fried, and things like that? I know you wouldn't like it one lit. So don't go around killing worm's for fun. Thank You.

other people who worked with Debby. Her speech teacher was amazed at the change not only in her ability but also in her self-concept. Toward the end of the school year, the speech teacher told me about Debby's progress:

> [Debby] began to have a much different perception of her abilities. She wanted to talk about books and movies all the time. She still had some difficulties explaining movies because she did not seem to understand much of what was going on, but it was better with the books. She was still shy, but now she willingly showed me things she had written in class and seemed proud to share her opinions about books and which ones were her favorites. She was even able to explain what they were about.

Debby's staff counselor, the person in this institutional setting who most closely parallels a primary care giver, also noticed a change in Debby as she observed her in the residence halls, surroundings clearly outside the world of the classroom:

> I was here when [Debby] first came here, and I've seen a huge improvement—it's incredible. Her attitude is amazing. Before it would be, "I'm not doin' this," but now it's different. When Debby first came, it was "I'm dumb, I can't read, I'm not even going to try." And just the other day in one of her journal entries [in a therapy journal], she was to name six good qualities about herself and explain why they were good. One of them was "I'm smart; I do well in school and I know I can try hard." It's a complete change.

Debby's perception of herself as a learner had changed; she now saw herself as capable. Over a period of time, with the support of her teachers and her learning community, Debby came to realize what she *could* do. In fact, even I had to be amazed when I looked at the size and range of the list of "Books I've read by myself" that Debby compiled (see Figure 17). Debby was a reader because reading and writing were used daily for real purposes, and no one told Debby she was unable to do anything. Just the opposite was true. Ann and others in the class supported Debby by having faith that she could be a reader and a writer.

Donald Graves (1985) reminds us that not only do testing practices set standards too low in schools, but standards for "learning disabled" or "at risk" students such as Debby are set even lower. Debby could represent all those in public schools today who have been convinced by the system that they are "stupid." Trapping students in the remediation cycle, giving them more and more of what they have failed at previously, is not the key to helping those like Debby, whom Nancie Atwell (1988) has called "ghosts"—students who were never in class because they always seemed to be in the resource room "being remediated." The key is to pay attention to connecting students' lives with their language. When Atwell began to include her

FIGURE 17   Debby's List of "Books I've read by myself"

Books I've read by myself

① I've read. 1. Baby siter.
   I've read the 4. from loox car
② Children.
③ I've read A..B.
④ I've read Fish race.
⑤ I've read poor little rich girl.
⑥ I've read the price and the pee.
⑦ I've read Honey I shruk the Kids.
⑧ I've read something of the Boys friend.
⑨ I've read Nate the Great.
   I've read a Hippopotamus ate the
⑩ Teacher.
⑪ I've read The Stupids
⑫ I've read Pee wee scouts
   ~~Peanut - Butter Pilgrims~~
⑬ I've read the Cut ups.
⑭ I've read Judy Blume.
⑮ I've read one of those days.
⑯ I've read Encyclopedia Brown.
⑰ I've read In a dark, dark room.
⑱ I've read George and Martha rise and shine
⑲ I've read The Golly Sisters
   go West.

"ghosts" in the bustling, connected literacy of her classroom, they set their own standards—higher standards—independently, in their own time, with the help of a concerned community.

In Ann's classroom, students like Debby were given an opportunity to have a voice, by reading literature that had a connection to their lives and by writing about what was important to them. They were given the time, support, and encouragement to discover what they *could* do; and, once they believed in themselves, they did it!

7

Thematic Teaching and Learning
Literacy Across the Curriculum

> In the ideal interactive classroom the curriculum would move by
> experiences, not by objectives. The teacher and the students, not the
> school board or a committee, would be the curriculum designers,
> deciding what experiences were appropriate at any particular time.
> *Louann Reid and Jeff Golub*

It was a beautiful September afternoon, very warm in the classroom, much more like summer than like fall, and the students in Ann Hunter's class were anxious to go outside. Ann had decided that she would take the students outdoors to do tree "rubbings." The students were in the midst of a science unit on trees—learning, for example, how trees affect the environment, what products come from trees, and what types of trees there are. Explaining the experience she had planned, Ann reviewed appropriate behavior for an out-of-classroom activity, a measure necessary for her students, who in the past had had trouble when placed in loosely structured situations unlike typical school activities.

We all left the classroom with our tree books, white computer paper to be used for the rubbings, and several pencils. We moved to the back and side of the school building, and the students scattered to different trees while Ann, Emily the aide, and I helped the students choose and identify "their tree." The activity was not only an important educational experience in and of itself but also because the school was located in a rural setting and was so different for those students who had lived in crowded urban areas. The students seemed involved in the activity as they ran from tree to tree; there was a great deal of chatter and laughter.

Gary was thrilled when he found an empty bird's nest on the ground, and he carried it around with the idea that he would put it on the science table upon returning to the classroom. The discovery prompted a discussion about birds and their nests. "How did the nest get on the ground? What birds build that kind of nest? Will they use it again if we leave it here?" Gary asked. Gary had many more questions, but he decided to leave the nest where he found it, to be on the safe side, just in case the birds returned. After all, he lamented, the poor things had lost their home.

A Spider's Web: Learning Through Reading

While Gary was asking questions and deciding what to do about the nest he found, Debby and Shannon were picking wildflowers to give to their teachers and the other students were finishing their tree rubbings. In the midst of all this activity, we heard Cole shout, "Hey, come over here, quick!"

"What's up?" asked Ann.

"It's a, you know . . . a, a, a, well you know, a, . . . come here; you'll like it!" Cole pleaded.

Cole, like so many of Ann's students, often had a difficult time expressing himself verbally, especially when excited, and it was obvious at this moment that Cole was excited.

Ann, Emily, the students, and I ran over to see what had gotten Cole so worked up. We found him standing near the gym, a brick building located across the drive from the classroom building; as we got within several yards of him, we saw Cole—a student who had lived all his life in an inner-city neighborhood—pointing frantically at an evergreen bush. There in the bush was a huge yellow and black spider in a web.

"Charlotte!" cried Shannon, referring to the spider in E. B. White's novel, *Charlotte's Web*, a book many of the students had read with Ann the previous spring.

"No, it's not," replied Cole knowingly. "Charlotte wasn't anything like this spider. It's much bigger. But look at the web. This is definitely an orb spider. By the way, I think it's a banana spider."

"How do you know?" asked Shannon.

"I saw it here yesterday, and I looked it up in our spider books," Cole explained.

As we all gathered around, one of the students picked up a daddy longlegs, and threw it into the web; the yellow spider jumped but didn't attack the other spider. "It said they first paralyze their victims and attack when the victim moves," Shannon declared. "That daddy longlegs isn't going to move at all." The "it" in her explanation referred to a book on spiders, one the students had read as part of the science unit that Ann taught while they were reading *Charlotte's Web*.

Jeffrey then picked up a small moth and threw it against the web, but it fell right off. Cole explained that if Jeffrey wanted it to stick, he should throw it on the other side of the web. "Remember," Cole reminded Jeffrey and the others, "the web's only sticky on one side so the spider can walk around." Jeffrey picked up the small moth again and threw it against the other side of the web. The moth stuck and then tried to move, and just as

Shannon had explained, the yellow spider paralyzed it and began feeding, or "sucking out the juice" as the students described it so graphically.

As we stood there, fascinated, a small beetle flew into the web and stuck. The yellow spider immediately moved in and wrapped up the beetle with silk. "Look at his spinnerets!" Debby shouted. "He must not be hungry after the moth. He's saving that guy for later." We all watched as the spider finished spinning and began to use its spinnerets to repair its web.

"Boy, that was cool," Cole said as we started back to the classroom. On the walk back, the topic of conversation was spiders. Robb said that he had a wolf spider living outside his dorm room window. He went on to discuss the spider's size, the fact that it was a hunter, and that it was not an orb spider like the one we had just seen. In fact, wolf spiders live on the ground, he explained to me and others who were not as well-informed about the world of spiders.

As the students entered the classroom, they ran to the book cases and began pulling out spider books. We all sat in a circle, looking at the spider pictures, gathering more information about what we had just seen. Although Ann was part of the discussion and asked real questions that she did not know the answers to, in point of fact, the students conducted the discussion. At the end, almost 3 P.M., the students had to decide who would get to take the spider books home that night.

As the students left for the day, and I sat reflecting on what had happened that afternoon, I could not help but compare what I had just seen to the science classes I typically see when observing other classrooms. I had just witnessed a science lesson conducted by the students for a very real purpose. Even more amazing than Ann's students' obvious interest in spiders (they certainly knew more about them than I ever did!) was the fact that their curriculum unit on spiders had taken place several months earlier, before summer vacation! There were no textbooks visible, no work sheets, and yet these students knew what they were talking about and knew how to find answers to their questions by asking each other and looking in books for needed information. Was this just a fluke, an isolated incident? I came to understand over the next few months that occurrences such as the spider incident were the norm in Ann Hunter's classroom, everyday examples of whole language teaching and learning.

How does something like this happen? Because Ann teaches using literature, she affords students an opportunity to read and write about characters their own age, about their feelings as they read, and about the world around them as it pertains to the novel. Several months before the spider incident, many of these students had read together *Charlotte's Web*, a novel that broadened schemata for those who had no previous knowledge of farm life. *Charlotte's Web* helped students express feelings for a character in literature as they wrote about how they felt when Charlotte died; it also served as a stimulus to learn about nature—spiders in particular. It was logical for the students to study spiders while reading this novel since it weaves so much about nature into the story of Charlotte, Wilber, and the Zuckermans.

What was evident to me that September day was that real learning took place in this classroom—not facts that are memorized, regurgitated, and soon forgotten, as is so often the case in schools, but learning that connects to other things, is used, and becomes part of who the learner is (Smith 1988a; 1988b). This type of learning has its foundation in literacy; as these students used reading and writing in Ann's classroom, they were reading for real purposes, finding answers to real questions.

Thematic Teaching: Uses and Definitions

While in Ann's classroom, I was interested in how literature-based instruction affected her students as learners, how students—*all students*—learned social studies, science, and other content subjects when taught in a classroom using "thematic teaching" with literature as the "core" of the instruction. The term *thematic teaching* is currently in fashion in education circles and is quickly becoming educational jargon. The term itself is used freely by textbook publishers and classroom teachers alike as though they were in perfect agreement about what the term meant in practice. Unfortunately, as with most fashionable ideas, there's a world of difference in the application.

Constance Weaver (1994), in the latest edition of *Reading Process and Practice: From Socio-psycholinguistics to Whole Language*, differentiates among theme units, theme exploration, and theme cycles—practices that move along a continuum from a teacher-directed transmission model to a student-centered transactional one. Figure 18, taken from Weaver's book, provides a helpful overview of what thematic teaching includes, depending on the paradigm that informs the teaching.

The theme unit, the first category, includes prepackaged materials marketed by publishers for "thematic teaching." These thematic units are thoroughly structured from objectives to daily lesson plans to means of evaluation. True, they do in fact connect the content areas by presenting several subjects clustered around a central theme, but all the activities are teacher directed and few choices are made by students. Theme units preclude the possibility of students bringing themselves, their experiences, and their interests to the units. Since the teacher (or the persons who developed the

FIGURE 18   Constance Weaver's Explication of Theme Unit, Theme Exploration, and
Theme Cycles

TRANSMISSION			TRANSACTIONAL
skills across the curriculum →	meaningful, teacher-directed → activities on a topic of study	broad, teacher-chosen topic initiates subsequent student choices -→	students and teacher together determine topic and questions to pursue
Theme unit		Theme exploration	Theme cycles

unit) does most of the problem solving in this type of thematic unit, the teacher, not the students, does most of the learning, as Edelsky, Altwerger, and Flores (1991) point out.

At the other end of the paradigmatic spectrum are theme cycles, the category of thematic teaching that puts whole language principles into action. In this transactional experience, the teacher and students work together to identify areas of interest and brainstorm possible areas of study. Theme cycles "consist of a chain—one task grows out of questions raised in the preceding tasks, all connected to an original theme or initiating question" (Edelsky, Altwerger & Flores 1991, 64). In theme cycles, students don't "do activities," they engage in real research and look for answers to real questions. (For further information, see Harste and Short, with Burke 1988; Short & Burke 1991; "Theme Cycles," *Primary Voices K-6*, January 1994.)

Somewhere between theme unit and theme cycles is theme exploration, the category of thematic teaching that goes a step further than theme units in terms of student involvement. Although the topic of study for theme exploration is chosen by the teacher (or the district curriculum), it is broad enough that the teacher can facilitate student choice and provide for individual interests and personal or collaborative research, giving the students opportunities to answer *their* questions.

Ann Hunter's thematic teaching was an example of theme exploration. Although Ann usually chose the theme and the core literature experience for the area of study, the students were involved in decision making and research of their choice. There was no predetermined plan of study and no prepackaged materials; the theme emerged as the students and Ann read and worked together. Ann planned possible activities ahead of time but used them as springboards when appropriate, not as daily lesson plans. She gathered material in advance and shared all the material with the students for their use when they needed it. She taught skills as their need emerged throughout the unit—as the students read and wrote in real situations and as they demonstrated a need for certain skills to accomplish their goals.

Another Web: Writing in the Classroom

Janet Emig (1977) found in her research with student writers that writing represents a unique mode of learning. When we write, we manipulate our thoughts and make our thoughts visible. Unlike speech, writing is an act of discovery that allows us to see our thoughts and ideas; as Vygotsky (1978) put it, the deliberate structure that writing provides produces a "web of meaning." When these thoughts become visible, we can interact with them, altering them if we so choose.

Although many school curricula do not seem to value writing-to-learn (Britton 1975; Applebee 1981), I found that Ann spent a great deal of time providing opportunities to use writing as a mode of thinking and learning. When I first came to Ann's classroom, she expressed her concerns about writing. Like so many other teachers in American schools, she had had little formal training in the teaching of writing. Her training in college had been, for the most part, in the teaching of language skills, and while she was aware of the writing-as-a-process paradigm through professional workshops and from her reading, she felt insecure about how to use writing in the classroom, as I mentioned in Chapter 5. Ann realized that she could not merely "give information" to the students that would help them become better writers; she needed to act as a coach to help them develop. Ann's classroom was already a positive environment for writing, but she confided to me that she wanted to improve her teaching in this area.

In Chapter 5 I told how Ann and I used dialogue journals with one student, but she wanted to make writing a more integral part of the daily routine for the whole class. Ann's students, like so many students in American schools, had been led to believe that writing was a matter of form—handwriting, spelling, punctuation—rather than a means to express inner thoughts and feelings. To use writing as a tool, they had to see a value to writing without concern for form. To this end, Ann began to informally introduce in-class written responses to literature.

While reading and discussing a novel, Ann gave the students the opportunity to write in their journals about what they had read that day, and she discussed with them some possible ways to do this. Sometimes the students decided to write about a favorite part in a novel, as they did after reading *Bridge to Terabithia*, or about some aspect that had come up in a class discussion, as they did after reading *The Cay*. Other times Ann asked them a question as a prompt for writing. For example, during the reading of *Charlie Skeedaddle*, she asked them to think about how they would feel if they were drummer boys in the Civil War. They first talked about Charlie and then responded in their journals about what they, like Charlie, might be thinking if they were about to go into battle.

Ann wanted her students to use writing for real purposes; she decided that a first step to achieving this goal would be to have the students discover its place in their lives. Ann did this with three very different theme explorations, all focusing on language arts, on science, and on social studies.

The Raft Simulation

Ann and I agreed that writing might be incorporated into her classroom in a variety of ways that would be natural outgrowths of the reading. One way was to use writing to respond to other activities that tied into the class reading, such as role-playing and creative dramatics. Ann did this early in the year when the class was reading Theodore Taylor's *The Cay*.

Early in the reading, the students participated in a simulation activity that paralleled what was happening to the characters in the novel. Around each student, Ann outlined the shape of a "raft" on the floor with masking tape. She directed the students to sit cross-legged on the floor inside the outlined squares and to pretend that they were alone on a life raft, just as Timothy and Philip had been in *The Cay*. They were instructed to sit silent and still for twenty minutes while listening to the sounds of the ocean playing on a tape cassette. Ann sat on her own raft on the floor, sharing the experience of the sea with her students. She asked them to pay attention to their thoughts and feelings as they imagined themselves afloat in the middle of the ocean. At intervals, Ann would quietly remind them of details in the novel—the height of the waves, the temperature, and what they might be able to see as they looked from their rafts. The students seemed mesmerized by this role-playing activity; all were attentive and involved. The classroom was quiet except for the sound of the ocean coming from the tape recorder. This was all the more remarkable to observe considering that many of these students had previously had difficulty attending to assigned school tasks; many had even been labeled as having Attention Deficit Disorder (ADD) or Attention Deficit Hyperactive Disorder (ADHD). On this day all were involved, and their energy was being channeled into an activity that they were interested in.

When the time was up, Ann asked the students how they felt while they were on their rafts. They brainstormed a list of feelings they had experienced, and Ann recorded them on the chalkboard. Ann invited them to write a paragraph or two in their reading journals about their experiences on the raft. She told them that this would be a twenty-minute freewriting activity, emphasizing that it was more important to share the experience than to worry about spelling and neatness. Ann told them, "Right now, just write about how you felt when you were adrift on your raft; there will be time later to copy it over and 'fix it up' if anyone wants to turn this freewriting into a finished piece."

All the students stayed at their desks to write except Gary, who went to the supply room to dictate his experience to Emily the aide. It became obvious that this exercise was easier for some than for others, or at least that some were more comfortable about it than others. Tim sat chewing on his pencil and looking around; Debby told Ann that she didn't "know how to write it"; and Shannon glanced around the room with a puzzled look on her face. The others, however—Robb, Cole, Tanya, Jeffrey, Loretta, and David—were writing furiously. Ann walked around the room, talking to those students who seemed confused or reluctant to begin, and before long everyone was writing.

Robb usually had a difficult time sharing his writing. His inability to organize his thoughts when writing seemed to hold him back even more than his slight speech impediment. Robb's thoughts in this piece, however, were much more organized than usual. Perhaps it was the activity, or the brainstorming, or the fact that he had been given time to think before he wrote, but whatever the reason, after writing, Robb proudly shared his raft experience with the class. Although difficult to read on paper in this draft stage, Robb read the following aloud during sharing time (see Figure 19):

I had a long journey. It was hours away. I got up at 1:00 A.M., headed for the ghetto, got a boat and was sailing on the sea and it was great at first then it started to get cramped, bored, terrified and then I started to think of how I had to accomplish it. I said to myself, "Think calm. Be calm. You'll make it." Sharks were snapping. My mouth was watering. Then the fish started jumping. I started to get scared and lonesome. The waves were splashing. I felt wet and salty. I was thinking like I was going to die. Then I started getting paranoid and stopped having confidence so I started to cry. I was mad that I was the chosen one. I think I can, and I kept saying it and then I said "I know I can. I know I can" and "I know I can" and I did make it! I saw land and got excited. I got closer and closer. I screamed for joy then I realized I was seeing things and I turned back and said, I quit," but no, I can do it. I kept rowing and ate crumbs the people left. Then I looked ahead. I saw shore and I was impatient. I made it at last.

Robb had freewritten for twenty minutes. Although some parts of this story only Robb can understand, he did weave in a familiar setting, the ghetto, the scene of many of his narratives. The story was still difficult for a reader to understand, but it was one of the most organized pieces Robb had ever written. Free of constraints such as spelling, Robb took risks and used words such as *paranoid, cramped, confidence,* and *impatient.* His sentence structure at times paralleled literary text rather than oral language. For instance, consider the passage "I said to myself, 'Think calm. Be calm. You'll make it.' Sharks were snapping. My mouth was watering. Then the fish started jumping." This passage has a print-literate quality to it. Robb also wove in references to familiar stories Ann had told the students in the classroom, such as "I think I can" from *The Little Engine That Could* and the bread crumbs from *Hansel and Gretel.* (Although stories such as these are usually told to primary- or elementary-school children, Ann's students hadn't experienced them in their early years, so at the ages of twelve and thirteen they enjoyed hearing these stories for the first time.) Robb wrote using what he knew about and what he was familiar with. His classmates were impressed and complimented Robb; during the class analysis they chose to mention organization and vocabulary as two strengths of his piece.

Shannon had found it difficult to get started. Like most of the students in the class she had done little writing before this, and her writing was often disjointed and almost impossible to follow. Shannon's piece was still simple and short, but this time it was organized. Shannon proudly volunteered to read it aloud, knowing I think, that this piece was different from her usual writing (see Figure 20):

> I went on a boat ride by myself and it was boring. I thought to myself, "this is going to be great," but it wasn't so good after all. I was so terrified that I couldn't wait until I got off the boat. But then I saw something. It was land and I was so surprised that what I saw and I even seen my friends and I got off the boat. I was safe.

Other students read their stories aloud, and the overwhelming strength of these pieces seemed to be their organization. Writing in her personal log about her perceptions of the activity, Ann noted that this had been the first time she had given her students time to think before writing and concluded

FIGURE 20 Shannon's Written Response to Raft Simulation Activity

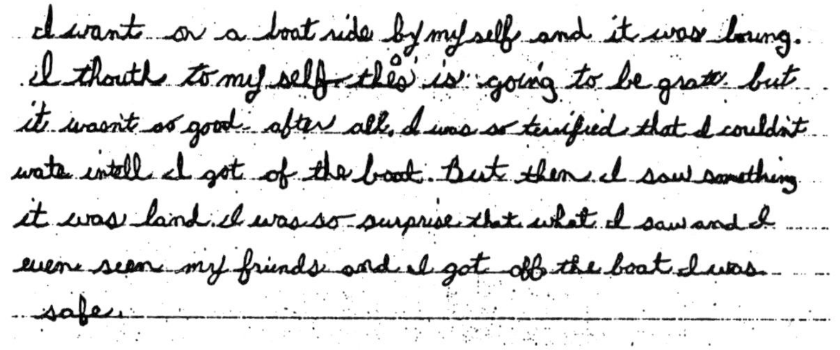
I want on a boat ride by my self and it was boring.
I thouth to my self this is going to be grate but
it wasn't so good after all. I was so terified that I couldn't
wate intell I got of the boat. But then I saw something
it was land I was so surprise that what I saw and I
even seen my friends and I got off the boat I was
safe.

that this prewriting time had been instrumental in their success with the freewriting. Steven Zemelman and Harvey Daniels (1988) agree that teachers must provide the time that such prewriting strategies demand for students to think about what they will write and to organize their thoughts.

This raft simulation activity was an example of writing as a response to literature. It was not a regurgitation of what a teacher had said or even what the author of the novel had said. The students wrote about their own feelings and thoughts, connected to what they had learned from the novel and to what they had experienced in the simulation. The students were allowed, even encouraged, to write about what they had experienced, and they began to make connections between their lives and the literature they were reading; such writing promotes thinking and discovery. The students used a technique that Mayher, Lester, and Pradl (1983) call "percolating," a combination of prewriting activities that take into account writers' accumulated experiences and all their memories of them as well as feelings and ideas. When looking at percolating as part of the composing process, which includes talking, brainstorming, and free associating, the student can "no longer be viewed as an empty vessel whose mind must be filled with knowledge and information supplied by an outside expert before starting to write" (Mayher, Lester & Pradl, 1983, 38). Writers are experts in the matter of personal events and memories, as the students discovered when they thought and wrote about their experiences on the "raft."

One of the most difficult tasks for any writer is to begin, and yet we know that when writing to learn, there is not necessarily a beginning as such. Freewriting activities such as the raft exercise help to generate thought; meaning is discovered as thoughts are put into writing. The raft simulation writing was free of any evaluation on Ann's part; Ann let the students write to discover how writing can be used as a mode of thinking and a way to react to what they had read.

The Shark Report

It has been argued that writing-to-learn can be used in all content areas to teach all subjects (Moffett & Wagner 1992). Ann was interested in helping her students learn by writing expository pieces that were outgrowths of what they were studying. Like many teachers of middle school students, Ann found that her students' previous conception of expository writing was a report more or less copied out of an encyclopedia, provided "you change some of the words so you don't get in trouble," as David explained. Ann frequently taught social studies and science through an integrated theme approach using a novel as the focus for such study. For example, *The Cay* provided more than reading for a language arts lesson; the students learned about the Caribbean in social studies and about oceans and marine life in science. Their readings included sources such as trade books, travel brochures, and magazines. They looked forward to reading reports on "whale sightings" and marine conservation issues in the bimonthly newsletter they received as a result of "adopting" a whale through a contribution to a wildlife organization.

Since the students were reading about issues that were of personal interest to them from a variety of sources, Ann encouraged them to write expository pieces, using writing as a way to share factual material that they learned. In the raft simulation, the students used writing as a vehicle to express thoughts and feelings. Ann wanted to help the students see another use for writing; she began to teach the students to use expository writing that was a composite of their ideas about a subject, formed from the reading and research that they had done, and written in their own voices. Ann felt more comfortable supporting her students this way after reading Nancie Atwell's (1990) *Coming to Know: Writing to Learn in the Intermediate Grades*.

Since this type of writing was new to her students, Ann decided to use a common topic for their first expository piece. The students wanted to write about sharks, a topic they had been interested in and had researched extensively while reading *The Cay*. The students as a class made a list on the board of the "facts" they had discovered about sharks, framing the facts in their own words but returning to the original sources if information needed to be checked or clarified. Once they had assembled their facts, Ann asked the students how they could best share what they knew about sharks with a reader. The students concluded that before writing, they needed to organize the facts into categories. Ann decided to make the categorizing a collaborative activity. She divided the class into groups of three or four students, instructing each group to develop categories for organization and to assign the facts written on the board to their appropriate category headings. Her students worked on this activity for about fifteen minutes and then compared their lists. They were pleased at how much agreement there was from group to group concerning category headings. In cases where the categories differed, or the subsequent assignment of facts to categories differed, they discussed the strengths and weaknesses of each choice.

The following day the students began to write their shark reports. All wrote drafts; all had an individual conference with one of the teachers. All decided to write final copies, which Ann promised would be hung in the hall, along with the other projects they had completed on marine life.

The students seemed to take great pride in their shark reports. The fact that they had learned so much about sharks made the reports "not hard to write." Several students who said they had never written a "real report" before were pleased with Ann's organizational approach. "It helped me get my ideas together," explained Shannon. When I asked Tim why he liked this activity, he explained (using phrasings reminiscent of his teacher, yet sounding very sincere nonetheless), "I learned a lot about sharks and doing these reports helped me organize my ideas and tell my reader what I learned."

The students had successfully shared what they had learned about a subject—sharks—through writing, a new experience for some of them. This collaboration gave them confidence and support as beginning writers. Many of the shark reports were similar because much of the prewriting had been done as a whole-class activity, yet all the students looked at these pieces proudly as their own.

Tim's report (Figure 21) was the longest he had ever written, and was arranged by categories, as was Tanya's (Figure 22), but both pieces were written in the student's own voice. Tanya seemed to be talking to her reader when she asked, "Did you ever see a shark's eye? Well . . . ." She wrote this to interest a reader and to share information as she would orally, which made it quite different from the voice typically found in reports copied from encyclopedias.

Debby's piece was written independently, without her teacher transcribing her thoughts, and because presentation was always an important factor to Debby, she said she made her final piece "fancy," pointing to the curls on her cursive letters (see Figure 23). A few spelling errors remained in Debby's piece—phonetically accurate spellings of words such as "dangrus" for *dangerous* and "fexsible" for *flexible*, a type of error made by risk takers.

David's report contained more description than some of the others and went into more depth (see Figure 24). Like most of the reports done by his classmates, David's final piece was extremely neat, and he was proud to display it. The day the reports were hung, I walked into the room, and David told me immediately that the shark reports were up in the hall, a less than subtle hint that he wanted me to look at his report.

Ann's classroom was not so much a writing or reading workshop, where a novel is read and written about during certain time periods each day; rather, it was a place where language was being used throughout the day as a tool for learning across the curriculum. Though a novel formed the central core or theme of study, Ann did not isolate language study as a separate subject, any more than she did natural science or social studies. Instead of spending time studying vocabulary and spelling in isolation, Ann's students,

FIGURE 21 Tim's Shark Report

A shark is a very interesting fish. Sharks arent very smart. Sharks range in sizes very small to very large. Sharks swim nonstop. There are three hundred and fifty types of sharks in the ocean.

A sharks body is very unique. Sharks have no bones. They have cartilage. Sharks have thousands of teeth arranged in rows. If one falls out, its replaced by another. Sharks skin is very rough, if it rubes up against you, youll get cut. Sharks depend on their senses to find food.

The shark is an amazing hunter. The great white is the most dangerous. Sharks can smell blood from one half mile away. Sharks eat anything. Sharks worst enemy is man and dolphins. Shark are hunted by man because man needs the food to eat and live. Man also hunts sharks because they think theyre dangerous. When dolphins are attacked by a shark a dolphin will poke it to death, at its heart.

by writing across the curriculum, were using words in context as they explained sharks and their habits. For instance, instead of memorizing lists of technical words, her students used such vocabulary as they wrote when it was needed in context. The terms they used in their reports, such as *superoxygenated*, *cartilage*, *camouflage*, and *prey*, came from information they learned in the course of study; it was vocabulary learned in real contexts for real purposes. Language arts—reading, writing, listening, and speaking— were all-day subjects, woven through all other subject areas and used as

FIGURE 22   Tanya's Shark Report

> A shark is a very interesting fish. A shark doesn't have any bones. It has cartilage so it could be more flexible. In a shark's mouth a shark has over six thousand teeth. If one falls out, another tooth will replace it. Under a shark's belly is their heart, and if it gets bumped or hit hard enough you can stun or kill the shark.
>
> A shark is very unique, because as you know sharks breathe through its gill slits. Its skin is thick and very rough, and it feels like teeth. If you rub up against it, it will scratch you, and rip your skin. Did you ever see a shark's eyes? Well, when a shark kills its prey, its eyes close in a special way, he or she blinks from the bottom of the eye, and the eyeball rolls back, so the eye is not hurt.
>
> The shark is an amazing hunter. It can sense blood from 1/2 mile away. Sharks have few enemies. Man and dolphins are among them. Man kills shark for food, cosmetics, medicine, and leather goods. Dolphins kills shark because they are afraid to be eaten or killed by shark.

appropriate and necessary. It was as if Ann's class was a "learning workshop," where literacy was used in the richest of contexts and reading and writing were tools to learn about the world.

The Civil War Story

One of the difficulties in teaching social studies is that adolescents often feel, sometimes rightly so, that historical events, events that happened long

FIGURE 23   Debby's Shark Report

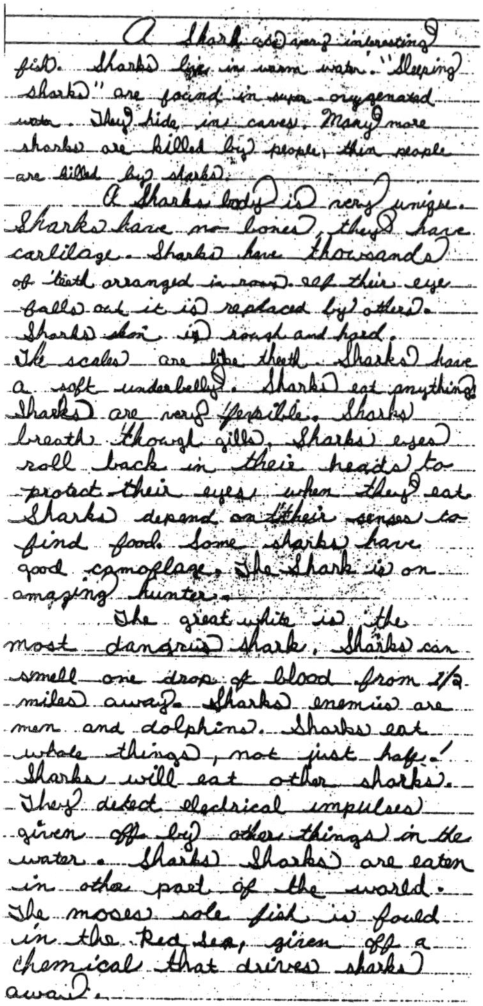

ago, are not real in the sense of being relevant or important in their lives. As Tanya liked to say, "If it's not real, why read it?" It is no wonder that students lose interest in history when it is taught out of a textbook as little more than a recitation of names, dates, places, and facts. Charlotte Crabtree (1988) suggests that "literature would help make these things real" (B10). Ann found this to be true when she used literature to teach a month-long unit on the Civil War.

FIGURE 24   Excerpt from David's Shark Report

> Sharks are very interesting fish. It isn't very smart but might range from 4 inches to 60 feet long. They swim nonstop all their lives except the exotic "sleeping shark" which is only found in super-oxygenated water. Sharks maybe found in cold water, but most of them swim in warm water. People are scared of sharks and are afraid that they might attacks. But did you know that about five time of the amount of sharks killed by man than man by sharks.
>
> A sharks body is very unique. The weird thing is that a shark has no bones. They have cartilage, and are very flexable. They have very rough skin, and just a brush against them will injure you very bad. Sharks breath through their gill slits which is on their side. The sharks protects itself very well by closeing its eyes while attacking. Theyre hiding ability is very good.

The history and social studies lessons embedded in literature are surprisingly complex. As I mentioned in an earlier chapter, Ann chose a novel called *Charlie Skeedaddle* by Patricia Beatty as a focus for her students' study of the Civil War. The plot concerns a twelve-year-old boy from the bowery in New York City, an Irish immigrant who faces prejudice and then loneliness when his older brother dies in battle during the early years of the Civil War. The book, which is historically accurate, describes the reasons for the war, famous battles, generals, prisons, and so forth, and more importantly does so as a backdrop for the human factors of war—hatred, bigotry, ignorance, and fear. Initially, Ann's students had little understanding of the concepts of the North and the South or the Union and the Confederate armies, and what previous exposure they had often glamorized war and fighting. They were certainly uninterested in dates and battle strategies. Instead, Ann knew that they were interested in reading about people their own age, adolescents searching for their identity and learning how to face the realities of life.

As the tale begins, Charlie has rushed off to war to avenge the death of his brother and become a drummer boy for the Union Army. As he prepares for battle, Charlie is arrogant and sure of himself, yet when faced with the horrors of war, he "skeedaddles," running to save his life. Later in the story, Charlie hides with an old woman in the Blue Ridge Mountains and while waiting for the war to end, he learns about mountain people, their customs, their language, and simple human dignity. As the novel ends, Charlie finally learns what it means to be brave.

Ann prepared the students for the novel by constructing a scenario for them. "How would you feel," she asked, "if you turned on your TV this morning and there was a special news bulletin?" She began her hypothetical story by explaining that the state they live in has broken away from the United States because their state wants to make its own laws about abortion, an issue that had been in the news a great deal at the time. As a result, she continued, other states seem to be following Pennsylvania's lead and doing the same thing. The president of the United States is worried that this might mean an end to the United States as we know it and has called out the National Guard, afraid that this could mean war. The people of Pennsylvania are prepared to fight for their rights, and the state's citizens, who had voted to leave the United States, are being asked to prepare to fight. Ann, a wonderful storyteller, dramatic and serious, continued to explain that since only a few states were opposing the huge United States, all men thirteen years of age and older would probably have to be prepared to fight. The students became caught up in this scenario, firing questions at her and one another: "What rights do we want?" "Who will be fighting?" "What if we don't want to go?" Robb immediately responded that he could not fight because all his cousins lived in Florida, a state that might be his enemy. Ann then gave the students a few minutes to write in their journals about how they would feel about going to war under such circumstances. David responded in his journal:

> I feel mad, angry, somewhat excited, but untell [until] I realized I will be watching my friends die in my own arms and I couldn't do nothing about it. I felt terrified and very scared. I would feel sorry for my family on the other side and if I did meet my family in a battle I would probably kill myself instead of killing them.

Tim was worried about how a war would affect his dreams for the future.

> I felt like there goes my future as a ball player. I felt mad, angry,
> upset, nervous, scared, worried, uptight, confused. I also felt could
> we talk about it instead of fighting.

Cole, like others, wrote of his initial excitement at the prospect of fighting, but how, when he thought about it, his feelings changed.

> I was uptight when I heard the news. I thought my brother couldn't
> see me anymore so my excitement slowly drained. . . .

Ann used these reactions to introduce the story of *Charlie Skeedaddle* and the theme of the Civil War. In the weeks that followed, the students as a class read the novel as well as another book, *The Boys' War*, a nonfiction work written in the style of a periodical of the time and employing many reproductions of tintype photographs taken during the war. *The Boys' War* presented the realities of the war from a young person's perspective, paralleling much of what was happening at the same time in the novel but in more historical detail. In addition, Ann showed a videotape of the PBS documentary "The Civil War" for about twenty minutes at the end of each day. Since the documentary was chronological, it gave the students a clearer idea of how the war progressed over time and helped them sequence events. As the reading progressed, the students waited for certain historic events or people to appear in the documentary.

Ann continued to use many of the writing strategies she had employed earlier in the year. She asked the students to write daily in their literature logs about the readings and activities. After noticing how interested students were in the famous people they were reading and learning about, Ann suggested that each student research a famous Civil War hero or heroine—someone the student wanted to learn more about. Each of the students chose someone different to research: Tanya, for example, read everything she could find about Harriet Tubman and the Underground Railroad; Shannon was so caught up in Clara Barton's life that she told me that she had decided to become a nurse; Stonewall Jackson became Gary's hero. Gary even knew the name of Stonewall Jackson's horse, and he became visibly upset when he told me how General Jackson died. Ann was thrilled with his excitement, encouraging Gary to write on and on as he continued to read about Jackson. Gary wrote pages and pages about his hero, sometimes in text so confused that no one else could comprehend it, but remarkable in that he wrote enthusiastically for weeks.

The students were so caught up in their research that they were aware of who each person in the class was researching. One day Tanya brought a book to class about Clara Barton that she had found in the library because she thought Shannon would like it. Although the students wrote research papers on their Civil War personality as a culminating activity, it did not signal an end to their reading. Months later, when Ann gave Gary a biography of Stonewall Jackson for Christmas, he was thrilled. He carried it around for weeks, showing everyone he met, and when reading it, he turned the pages carefully, almost reverently, so they would stay crisp. Stonewall Jackson was "his" topic—something he knew more about than most people—and he was proud of his expertise.

Many of the students used their knowledge of Civil War events as a backdrop in their own fiction. Some even used the historical figures as the basis for fictional characters in their narrative stories. The students wrote, revised, and edited for weeks. Some, such as Shannon, Debby, and Tim, wrote two or three pages, but others, such as Cole, Jeffrey, David, and Tanya, wrote several chapters. For Cole, the Civil War story became an ongoing task, and after writing more than forty pages, he told me that he had decided to end his story, although he could have written more. Cole's writing, which was historically accurate, was also quite literary. He used a great deal of dialogue, and in the second chapter of his story, he told about going off to war and signing up to be a soldier.

> "James go enlist over there" he pointed toward a tent. I went over and a person in a hood was the enlister. "Excuse me." I said. "I'm suppose to enlist here." "Whats your name" said the person that had a gentle voice. Just then a gust of wind came over the camp and the enlisters hood came off. It was a girl! She had beautiful eyes. She looked up at me and stared at me for a minute. Then she smiled in a shy way. Her eyes was green and looks was gentle and kind. I smiled. "My name is James. I'm only 15, but in two weeks I will be 16, please, don't tell anyone" I said. "OK but don't tell who I am" she said. "Whats your name" I asked. "Erin Jackson" she said as she smacked away a brown Recluse spider. . . .

Cole's story was written with a reader's perspective. He used description, dialogue, and even worked in a place to mention spiders, his favorite topic since reading *Charlotte's Web* months before.

As mentioned earlier, David's story told of a character named Johnny, Charlie's brother in the novel *Charlie Skeedaddle*. This character was mentioned but not developed in the novel, yet David was able to write an eight-chapter, thirty-page story about Johnny, New York City, the gangs of young immigrant boys, and eventually the war. David used information in his story that he had learned in Ann's class about immigration, Ellis Island, and the difficult life of Irish immigrants in the nineteenth century. Some of his information he gathered from listening to Ann read another novel to the class every day after lunch, *Orphan for Nebraska*.

Debby's Civil War story, included in Chapter 6 (Figure 14), was a major accomplishment because she wrote it independently. During a writing conference, I helped her construct a web to graphically represent her ideas, and although the concept was difficult for her to understand, the ideas that were produced were all hers and resulted in a finished story that was two pages long. Debby's story was personal, telling how she and two friends hid a run-away slave in their basement, took him to the river, and hid him in a hollow tree when they heard Confederate troops approaching. In the story, Debby's character told the soldiers that they were out looking for their lost dog. When the soldiers rode away, they put the slave into a boat that would take him north to freedom. "Good luck going on to freedom and your life," Debby wrote. "Good luck on your journey. I hope I see you someday again."

These students' stories demonstrated how much they had learned about the Civil War. In fact, a substitute teacher mentioned one day how amazed she was by their knowledge about the Civil War; they, in turn, commented nonchalantly that "we read so much in here, we learn a lot about a lot of things." The students were not only proud of their knowledge, they enjoyed having it; in fact, they played a sort of Civil War trivia game in the evenings with members of their supervising staff, a game that they themselves created (and always won!).

Through thematic teaching, these students had learned more than just facts and dates about a topic; they had learned about the human element of history, that which makes it real and connects it to contemporary life. As they were reading and writing, these students were thinking and learning, a belief that Ann Berthoff (1981) shares, that writing is the essence of thinking: "The work of the mind is making meaning. When we write, we do, in a particular sense what we do when we make sense of the world. We compose by virtue of being human" (16).

In the months that I watched Ann teach about social studies, science, and even mathematics using literature as a core, I repeatedly saw how language could be used as a tool for discovery, how literature-based instruction influenced learning across the curriculum. The students used reading and writing to think and learn about content areas, and as their worlds enlarged, they had more to read and write about. They were learning not merely about a subject but about life and people, and learning was helping them grow as human beings.

Different Routes and Multiple Opportunities

Literature-based theme exploration seems to provide depth and breadth over and above textbook units, as can be seen in Ann's students' study of the Civil War. While a novel provides the central theme or "core" of study, there are multiple opportunities for the students to explore specific topics or domains during the unit, just as Ann's students did when they researched their Civil War heroes and historical events of interest, such as the Underground Railroad and immigration. The students made many more discoveries because their individual and group projects had a purpose and a connection as related to the central theme of the Civil War; their learning had a richness and significance rarely seen when basals and textbooks determine the course of study (Gamberg, Kwak, Hutchings & Altheim 1988).

Unlike traditional teachers who believe that their job is to transmit "packaged" programs and to "cover" the curriculum, Ann Hunter, as a whole language teacher, sees herself as a professional who owns and develops her programs with input from her own students. Using a literature-based theme unit provides choices and provided enough sustained time for the students to pursue their areas of interest. Having time for systematic inquiry and topics of their choice led the students to reflective thinking, evidenced for me in the students' own versions of the war in their Civil War narratives. Students in classes such as these operate from their own schemata and consequently travel different routes to learning. Their teachers view learning in an integrated language classroom as an active reconstruction of knowledge that is constantly being negotiated. What happens in the classroom, therefore, must be done in a cooperative way (Hyde & Bizar 1989). Through Ann's use of thematic teaching and the students' use of literature, reading and writing became vehicles to learning in all content areas.

8

Inclusion versus Equality
The Politics of Labeling

*If Dewey and the pragmatic philosophers are correct, if indeed we learn
what we experience, then the only way to guarantee a reservoir of
democratic sentiment in the culture is to make public schooling a
center of democratic experience.*
George H. Wood

Sometimes, in a desire to help, educators make life extremely difficult for
learners. When I read the following poem by Karen Morrow Durica, published
in *The Reading Teacher*, I breathed a silent "amen" to her prayer for all children.

THE LABELED CHILD

I pray for the labeled child;
That child who is gifted and talented.
No longer can she be lazy and idle
Or a daydreamer.
So much more is expected
Of those as gifted and talented as she.

I pray for the labeled child;
That child who is learning disabled.
No longer will the world expect brilliance
No longer will someone tell him to reach for the stars
Because that is where greatness will be found.

I pray for the labeled child;
That child who is dyslexic.
Reading—oh, the joy of reading!
Will always be hard for her to find.
No matter that she can recite—no sing
Mary Had a Little Lamb,
She won't be able to read it,
At least not without difficulty.
She will learn that all her friends
Who laugh and cry and wonder about books
Can do so because they are not dyslexic.

I pray for the labeled child;
That child who is A.D.D.
An unorganized bubble of hyperactivity.

No longer will someone teach him to cope in a world
That values compliance.
No longer will someone say, "You can do this;
Oh, it may be hard, but it is within you to do this."
A dose of medicine now replaces the need for that inner effort
And eliminates the possible victory.

I pray for the labeled child;
That child who is emotionally handicapped.
That child who rebels
Because she should rebel.
The child who acts out
Because there is nowhere else
For the hurt and anxiety and fear to go.
The child who is diagnosed "sick,"
When perhaps her actions are the one true sign of sanity
In the demented world in which she is forced to live.

I pray for the child of no label.
In a system which marks so many special,
This child neither shines nor demands.
For this child life has been neither harsh nor generous.
This is the one who "makes" the teacher's day
Because there are so many children who need real attention.

I pray most of all for some magic day
When the tests, the labels, and the names
Will disappear—will be forgotten.
When each child who enters a classroom
Will be an apprentice of learning.
When each classroom will be a safe place
To discover—on your own—
What will be the struggles of your life,
And the victories.
When the feeble and the bright,
The gregarious and the shy
Will all find their place
In the great adventure of education.
When the only label that will be attached to anyone is
    LEARNER.

Karen Morrow Durica

If Only: Teaching for the Future

If only teachers and parents and administrators could put aside all labels and look at children as learners, each with her own strengths, own needs, own view of the world, own experiences.

If only "regular" classroom teachers and "special ed" teachers could work together as team members with the shared goal of aiding all children as each child reaches toward his own personal goal.

If only the government would get out of the way and let teachers educate children without worrying about collecting test scores to categorize students under labels and without requiring the artificial guidelines of these tests scores as a basis for allocating the resources necessary for schools to teach everyone.

If only schools could be places where children learned to work cooperatively and not competitively; where children only compete against themselves, striving for their "personal best" the way runners do, working to reach the next goal that they set with their teachers and classmates.

If only children could believe in themselves because teachers and parents believed in them first.

Am I idealistic? Certainly many would say so, as they try to explain to me why these things can't be. However, I truly believe that my "if onlys" are realistic goals—maybe not ones I'll see achieved in the American educational system, but certainly ones that many individual teachers are striving for in their classrooms today. These aren't fantasies. They are what must be realities if all children are going to be afforded equal opportunities to learn and to achieve everything they are capable of achieving.

I am the first to admit that all children aren't the same—they don't look the same, act the same, speak the same, or learn the same. "Viva la difference!" Unfortunately, for over one hundred years American schools have used classrooms to try to produce look-alike, act-alike citizens, ones who would fit an assembly-line adult world where they do as they are told, do not question, and complete an isolated skill on the assembly line of life without ever knowing or caring about the completed product. "Now, what I want is Facts," begins the opening address given by Mr. Gradgrind to the school teacher of his model school in Charles Dickens' *Hard Times*. "Teach these boys and girls nothing but Facts. Facts alone are wanted in life. Plant nothing else, and root out everything else. You can only form the minds of reasoning animals upon Facts: nothing else will ever be of any service to them. This is the principle on which I bring up my own children, and this is the principle on which I bring up these children. Stick to the Facts, sir!" A government official visiting Gradgrind's school concurs, "You are to be in all things regulated and governed . . . by fact. We hope to have, before long, a board of fact, composed of commissioners of fact, who will force the people to be a people of fact, and nothing but fact." Wouldn't Mr. Gradgrind be delighted to learn of the success of the standardized testing industry, applying his principles to every facet of twentieth-century education? It should come as no surprise that Dickens titled the chapter in which Gradgrind puts forth his curricular program, "Murdering the Innocents."

Even less surprising is the fact that a century later every publication, every politician, every parent, and every teacher who criticizes today's educational system talks about a model program of education preparing students for the next millennium. What I see in schools across the country are educators tripping over themselves trying to be "helpful" to all learners. They've categorized and labeled children for so long, and made the process so complicated that parents, teachers, and even the children themselves actually believe that the labels are real and definable. In the year 2000, America will need citizens from diverse cultures who are able to work in a diverse world; America will need citizens who are able to think, to question, to problem solve. Citizens must know who they are, what they can contribute, and how they can work together to move the world forward. To do this, schools are going to have to prepare students for such an adult role. Schools will have to prepare students to understand and respect the worth and contributions of others' cultures. It will not be enough to know the facts to pass the latest cultural literacy test. Schools will have to teach people to think, to problem solve, to communicate orally in face-to-face transactions and electronically across computer networks. They will have to help students to take risks, to experiment, to realize that one answer isn't enough. Some teachers "may believe that useful knowledge can come . . . only in the form of a textbook series or a kit, ready for immediate application with no prior training"; but "knowledge, however valid, can usefully influence reading instruction only if teachers have grasped its nature. When teachers understand the relevance of psycholinguistic theory and research, they will see reading materials in their true perspective" (Smith & Goodman 1973, 307). Before schools can teach children to think and then to learn, educators must first educate themselves to think and to problem solve and to respect and understand all their students.

Teacher Preparation

For many years teacher education programs have worked to help prospective teachers learn to teach. Based on the most up-to-date research, the programs teach strategies, methodologies, and sometimes (hopefully) philosophy. These teacher education programs are preparing students to be "regular" classroom teachers. (I've always wondered what a "regular" classroom is. I've certainly never had the privilege of teaching in one, since every class I've ever taught has been different, populated with students who were all different in many ways, but who had one thing in common—they were in my class-room to learn, even if they didn't realize it).

Students who are being prepared to work with learners who may have special needs (what learner doesn't), learners who are different from those in a "regular" classroom, are usually enrolled in special education programs, often housed in separate buildings at the university, taught by separate faculty with training and philosophies different from their colleagues in elementary/secondary education. These future teachers are taught that their students will undoubtedly fall into categories of populations with specialized needs, including those who are physically challenged, those who are mentally retarded, and those who have had emotional and learning difficulties (for example, learning disabled, which is now called "learning support"). In recent times, special educators have even been trained to work with those with another specialized need, the group of learners commonly labeled "gifted." Obviously these categories are vague; most teachers and administrators would have a tough time defining them, though they are quite adept at assigning them to students. (The only people excluded from these categories, I guess, are those who by default we call "normal," based on a series of test scores, physical diagnoses, social behavior that fits an accepted norm, background, and past performances in learning situations.)

I have the utmost respect for those in the field of special education. As I've shared throughout this book, much of my research has been with special education teachers, Ann Hunter in particular, and my daughter is studying to become certified in special education. Most special education programs prepare future teachers in management techniques, diagnosis, and life management. A weakness of many programs is the lack of training in academic learning, training based on current research in the fields of literacy, mathematics, sciences, and the arts.

In far too many teacher education programs, students are taught by professors whose philosophies of learning are fundamentally behaviorist. Such a stance is not limited to special education departments, although this discipline has been slower to change its position on learning philosophies than have elementary education programs across the country. Students who are dual majors, those pursuing certification in special education and elementary education, are often confused by the conflicting philosophies that these two education programs present. Even more disturbing is the fact that there is often little communication and a great deal of "turf" protecting among departments, a situation that encourages colleges and universities to present conflicting philosophies rather than to encourage dialogue, combined research, and team teaching (some justify it as nothing more than presenting both points of view).

Inclusion: An Exclusionary Term

The separatist mentality in teacher education programs, under which the special education program is housed in separate buildings, taught by separate faculty, and governed by separate philosophies, is not limited to colleges and universities; it exists at the classroom level in school districts as well. However, recent "inclusion" regulations have thrown these educational factions into a quandary. Under state laws, many children who in the past had been taught by special education teachers in pull-out or separate classes are now being mainstreamed, returned to the "regular" classroom. The legislation provides the opportunity for students who have been variously labeled as in need of special programs to be included as part of a regular classroom, taught by a "regular" teacher with elementary or secondary certification, and supported by a teacher with special education certification who works within the classroom, supposedly as a partner with the classroom teacher. The return of the special students to the regular classroom has made more clear the gulf that exists between the special education and the elementary/secondary education disciplines. Many of the regular classroom teachers are frightened, unprepared, and angry about this change, one that has as much to do with budget concerns as with educational philosophy. Many of the "special ed" teachers have never been taught or encouraged to work as a team with classroom teachers. Both groups have separate agendas and often different educational backgrounds. In the past, "special ed" has been down the hall, not in the classroom, and "those" kids were always taken care of by someone else.

The ironic thing about the term *inclusion* is that it is exclusionary. For a learner to be "included" in the regular class, she must first be labeled as different from the group that will now be including her. When classroom teachers are told that they have several students who must be included in their class, these students already enter with a label. A typical conversation in a faculty room reveals how labels become who the students are: "I have three ADD's and one in a wheelchair. Most of my children are from dysfunctional families and now they tell me I'm getting one with a speech impediment. What a year. I don't know how they expect me to teach."

Comments like these aren't unusual, they're just sad. This teacher believes that the labels these students have been assigned are descriptions of who these children are, and the teacher feels that these students are obstacles to her teaching. The problem with the term *inclusion* is that by accepting such a concept, educators are in turn accepting the fact that students must be labeled. The label comes before the inclusion, and consequently the teachers of these students view them as "different" or perceive them as problems.

Concerning physically challenged students, it is true that the teacher who is upset with including these labeled students in her class may have had little training in working with students with special physical needs, such as those in wheelchairs, but such training should be part of all teachers' professional development. This teacher and the other students should not only accept physically challenged students in their class, but they should also recognize that such challenges can help all members of the educational community learn to support one another as they do in writing, reading, and academic subjects in which they learn from one another. The goal is not inclusion but equality, such that all students are respected and seen as capable of learning.

The Russians Are Coming

Many teachers, however, welcome the diversity of culture and development into their classrooms. Rhonda McKissock, a first-grade teacher in Pennsylvania, sees students as individuals. Rhonda works hard to know her students and to identify their strengths so she can use those strengths to meet their needs. I had the privilege of team teaching with Rhonda for several months, and during that time came to know twenty-seven individuals who saw themselves as part of a larger community. Developmentally, the students were all different, as is the case in every first-grade class; but such differences in Rhonda's class are not only accepted, they are appreciated. I know there were students in her class with labels, but those labels were not in evidence, and Rhonda didn't use the labels as an excuse not to teach. I asked Rhonda to share the story of what transpired when one "special" student was included in her classroom.

> When my principal first approached me in November, he began by saying, "Even though you have the largest class size, I have a favor to ask . . . ."
> Assuming that I was getting a new student, I quickly said, "Sure, no problem."
> He smiled and responded, "You say 'yes' too quickly. You need to learn to listen before you answer." And he finished telling me that a six-year-old girl from Russia, who didn't speak a word of English, would be enrolling at our school and that she would be placed in my classroom.
> Fear and excitement seized me at the same time. I had never had an ESL student before, but I welcomed the enormous learning opportunity this would provide for my students and myself. The first graders in my room were also excited, and they kept asking, "Is Sveta coming today?"

It occurred to me on Sveta's first day that I would be witnessing language development through her learning experiences. As I reflect back now, I realize the gift she provided. She allowed me to step back and witness my teaching philosophy in action. I believe that learning is social and active, and that we learn through examples modeled for us. I also believe in providing an inviting learning environment in which children feel safe to experiment with their new knowledge during extended blocks of time. I also believe that students are effective teachers and can make important decisions in their learning. I believe this is accomplished when a teacher celebrates an individual's abilities and uses a child's deficiencies as a guide for learning, rather than an evaluation.

We devoted Sveta's first day to introducing ourselves, building friendships, learning classroom routines and different areas of the classroom. My motive was to make her as independent as possible, showing her that the class was student centered and that she could make decisions about her learning needs. Realizing that a lot of teacher talk was not going to accomplish this, I let the children immerse her in their learning activities. I was amazed at how quickly Sveta adapted.

The class' favorite area in the room was the writing center. This center promoted social interaction while students were reading pieces of writing, coaching one another in spelling, exchanging writing ideas, and sharing personal stories and experiences. It soon became Sveta's favorite area also. It was incredible watching her writing in a language that she couldn't speak or read yet. On her first day in our classroom, Sveta chose to go to the writing center as most of the class did. The first graders quickly showed her where she could find the materials and made room for her to sit at the writing table. Others who could not sit at the table, gathered around on the floor. The children began drawing pictures and talking about what they were writing. Sveta watched with great interest and began drawing her own pictures as well. Two girls began reading Sveta their stories, and she listened attentively. She then wanted to write on her paper too. The girls quickly asked me, "How does Sveta spell her name?" But before I could begin telling them, the class began collaboratively stretch-spelling her name [what Rhonda calls their "invented spellings" or sounding out when spelling]. The *s* and *v* came very naturally, but then the debate began whether the next letter was an *e* or an *a*. I confirmed the *e* and the class finished the rest of her name with the *t* and the *a*. One child wrote Sveta's name for her on the top of her paper, which Sveta began copying several times. Sveta then had her own writing to share, and she began reading her name to the children at the table. She beamed with her success, and the children smiled and applauded. This began our celebration of Sveta's successes to come.

Sveta's journal was also evidence of her literacy development. She began by drawing pictures and writing her name at the top. When she shared, we applauded her, and when others shared, she noticed their writing on their pictures. Soon she began writing strings of letters along with her name and pictures. The children noticed this when Sveta shared her work and continued to encourage her. Soon she began drawing pictures of houses, girls, flowers, dogs, cats, suns, hearts, and rainbows. When I would conference with her, I would point to different pictures and ask, "What's that?" She would answer, "Dog, cat, house, . . ." I began writing these words for her, and immediately she began copying them. Now when she shared, she would read her labels and show her pictures.

At this point, her literacy development exploded. She began copying print from around the room. She would copy the class schedule, the language experience stories from that morning, texts from books, chart stories and poems, and other children's writing. She was devouring print and experimenting with it as much as she could.

She began drawing pictures of classmates, and during our conferences she would dictate, "I like Kristen" or "I like Bryan," which I would then write for her. She would recopy, and then read it to the class when it came time for her to share. Noticing her pattern in writing, "I like . . . ," one of the children at her table showed her how she could refer back to other writing in her journal to find the words that she needed. She seized this independence.

As Sveta's conversation developed so did her writing ideas. Much of what she wanted to say, she could now stretch-spell on her own. Beginning and ending sounds appeared first. Next she began placing vowel markers in the middle, and by the end of the year, many of her vowel markers were correct. Many of the sight words that she now recognized were also written conventionally.

At the same time she also began asking to help pass out papers. Sometimes she would ask, "Is this Ashley or Alex?" or "Derek or Drew?" It was evident that she was using initial sounds to help her identify names of her classmates. The children picked up on this and began quizzing her on their names. She really enjoyed this, and beamed with pride at her accomplishments.

Sveta also surprised us one day during our daily morning news. When she raised her hand to volunteer, she was immediately chosen by her classmates. She reported the date, "Today is Tuesday, March 14, 1994," echoing a child who was assisting her. Soon after this she began reporting the weather or our special classes for the day using an echo technique. Then one day, she did it independently. The class roared with excitement and shouted praises.

Sveta flourished in our community. She took control of her learning, realizing that we were focusing on what she could do rather than what she couldn't. She worked cooperatively with others and learned from their modeling. Aware of what her needs were, the children guided her toward satisfying those needs. By doing this, the children became more aware of their own learning as they explained to Sveta how to do something.

The children also modeled their love for reading and writing, as well as the ability to experiment with language. These children knew that their successes were celebrated, and if Sveta was to learn, her successes needed to be celebrated also. The children never commented on what she couldn't do; they viewed her as extremely capable.

It is no accident that the similarities between Rhonda's classroom and Ann's are striking. Both have similar philosophies of learning, and their students respond similarly, regardless of age, in spite of labels or categories. Their students share a belief that they have talents and strengths and can count on the support of their classroom teacher and peers in areas that are difficult or new to them.

Learning Disabled—Vague, But Dangerous

I'm convinced that labels, however vague, can significantly influence learning situations, but more importantly, they have a tremendous effect on the people being labeled. I remember being asked to review Denny Taylor's book *Learning Denied* for a professional journal (Strickland 1991b). I agreed because I had read other things by Taylor, and I knew she had very strong views about the politics of education, including the effects of labeling students and the consequences of such labeling. I started reading the book and found that I couldn't put it down—what Taylor was describing was what I myself had seen for years as a Chapter I reading teacher and later while working with classroom teachers as a consultant. Patrick, the child Taylor described, was not much different from students I worked with when I taught in Tonawanda, New York. Rob, Theresa, Mike—they had all acquired labels like "disabled," and by the time I worked with them in middle school and high school, they had pretty much accepted what they had been told about themselves. All shared common beliefs: they hated school; they hated reading and writing; and they would all tell you that they weren't "very smart." I remember realizing early in my teaching career that first I had to change the attitudes of these children, not just about school and about literacy, but about who they were. All were capable and intelligent, but even their parents were convinced that they were "different"; they had trouble learning and couldn't be held responsible for what they didn't know. Their parents had attended Committee For the Handicapped meetings at which they were told their children were "minimally brain-injured" (a term that preceded learning disabled and learning support) and to receive the services they needed from public school, they would have to be labeled as such. Many parents, like Patrick's parents in Denny Taylor's book, were not in agreement with such a diagnosis, but they usually gave in to pressure from the district so their children could receive the services they hoped would help them.

These were the hopes that Theresa's mother had for her daughter. I had worked with Theresa for two years in middle school, and I was pleased with her effort and a turn-around, however slow, in her attitude toward her own abilities. Mary, the resource room teacher in our building, was a wonderful teacher and very supportive of the students with whom she worked. As is the case in many districts, this special education teacher worked as a support teacher during what would be study hall periods. She assisted students with content subjects, such as science, math, social studies, and English, usually by helping them complete assignments or study for tests. The content area teachers saw Mary as little more than a tutor and sent along assignment sheets for the students to complete in Mary's class. What Mary did, however, was much more important; she helped the students change their attitudes about themselves. Because she believed in them, and let them know this, she was often able to accomplish a great deal in just those forty-five minutes a day. I felt that with Mary's assistance, Theresa would be able to continue to move forward. But to work with Mary, who was paid by the government, Theresa would have to be labeled "learning disabled," based on standardized test results and the school psychiatrist's recommendation.

I remember my first meeting with Theresa's mother. She had never completed high school and neither had any of Theresa's older siblings, but she was pleased that Theresa seemed to like school more than she had before and that she had begun to talk about maybe graduating and going to business school. Theresa's mother expressed her surprise at this development since all of Theresa's previous teachers pointed out in great detail Theresa's difficulties in school; in fact, her mother believed that Theresa would drop out by her sixteenth birthday. When I told her that I felt Mary could be of help to Theresa, she was encouraged and asked when Theresa could start working in Mary's class. I remember trying to broach the need to classify Theresa as "learning disabled." As diplomatically as possible, I began to explain the procedure to this mother and saw the look of disappointment and failure in her eyes. "So Theresa is slow then," she replied softly. I remember feeling tongue-tied and tried to think of a logical way to explain to this mother the complications of the system. There was no way, and so I stumbled through a jargon-filled explanation, feeling like a hypocrite all the while.

I remember my feelings of helplessness in this situation; now, years later, I would handle the situation differently. I'd feel confident saying, "Of course not! Theresa's very capable. This is just red tape, and ridiculous, but until we can change things, this is the only way we can get Theresa into Mary's class." Still, I know even now this is not reason enough to put a label on a person—a label that tells parents, teachers, other institutions of learning, and more importantly the student herself what she can't do. Once applied, the label stays with a person forever, and when one is formally labeled by a committee of professionals who are all certified as knowledgeable in their judgment, it becomes pretty official. I knew in Theresa's case that this was a no-win situation. Students like Theresa would suffer until the system changed, and so far we haven't done a very good job of changing it. When I have this discussion with my students and in-service teachers, so many ask, "Why?" It's a question of politics, not education, I tell them.

The Politics of Labeling

To understand what is happening in schools today, it is important to understand the history of terms such as *learning disabled*. It is used so easily and so widely that it has become part of school jargon. Yet it is used without a real definition, or at least without a definition that is theoretically accurate.

During the 1960s the term *learning disability* became a category of educational abnormality that was applied to over one million American schoolchildren (U.S. Office of Education 1973, 2). This directly resulted from recognition of a theory that a disability was a "condition" affecting learners. This condition was explained as a "disordering of a child's basic thought processes brought about by neurological malfunction" (Carrier 1983, 948). Hence the classification "minimally brain damaged." Such a disorder was diagnosed through testing and symptoms, including underachievement in school, perceptual or conceptual abnormality, and hyperactivity. Researchers such as Cruickshank (1971), Barsch (1965), and Frostig and Horne (1973) supported the theory that learning disability was a neurological condition. Although early researchers referred to "brain injury," later research gave way to terms that were much more vague, such as *disorder* and *dysfunction*. This research, which was behavioral and psychological, was based on testing situations in which children gave answers to problems or situations that differed from "the norm." For instance, in the early research of Strauss and Werner (1942) children were shown pictures and were asked to group objects. As with many of today's standardized tests, researchers were looking for "right" answers based on what most respondents answered. If children's responses varied from the norm, Strauss and Werner and subsequent researchers concluded first, that the variations were caused by an "abnormality of thought which occurred because of faulty perception and second, that faulty perception occurred from a neurological disorder" (Carrier 1983, 957). What wasn't taken into account by these behavioral researchers, and by later researchers who continued the belief that variations in learning style and ways of looking at the world stemmed from a neurological disorder, was that the abnormality was defined by socially based educational values and practices, not by something within the brain of the child. The values, structures, and practices of American education and educational psychology determined this label, not the ability or intelligence of the child. James Carrier (1983), in his article "Masking the Social in Educational Knowledge: The Case of Learning Disability Theory," explains that "learning disabled children . . . do not exist independently of the communities of people who produce, define, and study them. Thus these children and the learning disability they are supposed to manifest do not exist in some nonsocial objective realm" (952). This is a perspective that Carrier credits to the work in science and paradigms of thought by Thomas Kuhn (1963).

Mike Rose's (1989) book *Lives on the Boundary* describes it so well—the frustration I have felt for years about what he calls the "educational underclass" (xi). This book moves me, makes me feel angry, hopeful, and reinforced. Rose says his book is about

> what happens as people who have failed begin to participate in the educational system that has seemed so harsh and distant to them. We are a nation obsessed with evaluating our children, with calibrating their exact distance from some ideal benchmark. In the name of excellence, we test and measure them—as individuals, as a group—and we rejoice or despair over the results. The sad thing is that though we strain to see, we miss so much. All students cringe under the scrutiny, but those most harshly affected, least successful in the competition, possess some of our greatest unperceived riches. (xi)

Traditionally our schools have worked to point out to students what they don't know. Our tests are usually constructed to evaluate not what students know, but what they have memorized and regurgitated. We seem to think that there is only one way for students to demonstrate what they know and one answer that is correct. Last year, while in Rhonda's first-grade classroom, I was involved in "testing week." This is the week in April when all children, grades one through five, take the Iowa Achievement Tests. The politics of these tests is obvious—parents are made aware of their importance by a letter in the mail that announces the tests and asks them to make sure their children get plenty of rest and eat a healthy breakfast. Since this advice is given only once during the year, parents conclude that this is the most important thing their children will do all year. The teachers too are aware of the tests' importance—after all, they will be judged on how well they teach, regardless of the fact that the test may not be an appropriate measure of many of the goals for their class. And finally, the children know how important these tests are. Even in classrooms where teachers are supportive and where cooperative learning is encouraged, everything is different during test week. For hours these little people must sit without a word, ask no questions (even if the problem is ambiguous or confusing), and refrain from looking for any help from their teacher or peers. One little boy in Rhonda's first-grade room put it so simply, "But you're the teacher. Aren't you supposed to help us?" Not this time, Ryan, I thought.

The worst part of these tests is not the boredom, or the fear, or the ambiguity, but the results. The tests are used to classify and label. All children are judged by the same criteria, which are set not by those who work with the children but by a test company whose job it is to pigeonhole all children into categories (commonly called stanines). These categories will determine who receives special help, who will work with the Chapter I reading teacher, who will be placed in a transitional first grade. More importantly, the tests will dictate to teachers and parents the ability of an individual child, and the results will be accepted with little question.

Such labeling most often looks to neurological or biological explanations for a child's difficulty in school. Even the terminology is scientific sounding. We "diagnose," "prescribe," and "remediate," and children attend reading "clinics" where we hope they receive the right amount of medication—skills work sheets, SRA kits, and workbooks. And in fact, these treatments may help students score better on the next standardized test, since most of them test isolated skills and are formatted like many popular basal reading programs. But do they help students learn?

Good teachers do question and try to fight the results with more authentic assessments—data that has been collected over a period of time in authentic learning situations. But such data doesn't carry as much weight as standardized test results, and the child still must bear the burden of their classification in permanent records and be judged by it in years to come. I know many students who do much better in the day-to-day activities of reading and writing and mathematics in the classroom but who score poorly on standardized tests. Does the school district throw out the test results as inaccurate or an inadequate measure of the child's true ability? Sometimes, to an extent. Schools whose administrators respect the ability and judgments of classroom teachers sometimes use other data the teacher has collected and use the test scores as only one piece of the puzzle. Others, however, religiously subscribe to the test scores. If a student does better in class than predicted by the test score, the child is said to be an "overachiever." What a ridiculous term—what in the world is an overachiever? I've come to realize that this label is a good way to continue blaming the child for not fitting the system. In other words, the test is correct in its assessment of what the child cannot do, and when a child somehow manages to do the impossible, then he is "overachieving."

Is Disruptive Behavior a Learning Disability?

Many behaviors that are often attributed to a learning disability can be explained equally well as student resistance to school culture (Christensen,

Gerber & Everhart 1986). It is not uncommon for learning disability theory to cite disruptive behavior in school as evidence of a neurological disorder. We now have labels for this behavior—ADHD (Attention Deficit Hyperactive Disorder), as well as hyperactivity, hyperkinesis, and other terms that are medical in nature but are applied to children whose behaviors irritate teachers and others in the class. When these disruptive behaviors are accompanied by low achievement in school they are often cited as the cause of the low achievement. Bryan and Bryan (1975) reported that the most frequently defined behavior of learning-disabled children was hyperactivity, short attention span, and distractibility. Although I haven't seen current research to support it, I would say this has changed little in the last twenty years, except we now use the term *ADHD* to define the behavior. For example, hyperactivity was defined by Bryan and Bryan (1975) as "behavior which was disruptive to the group" (34) and short attention span as a disorder that "reflects the child's interests in things other than those on which he should be concentrating" (35).

Is this disruptive behavior due to neurological problems or to resistance to a school system that is not meeting students' needs? My nephew Ben, who is a bright, active boy, has done well in school, but school has not always met his needs. Though polite, Ben is always busy, always engaged, and not able to sit and do nothing. One day while in first grade, soon after Christmas vacation, Ben was in school during a morning math lesson. The teacher was explaining something on the board and looked back to see Ben playing quietly at his desk with his two new Pound-Puppies® (a popular family of stuffed animals). She asked Ben to put the toys away and pay attention; Ben complied. Several minutes later, she looked back and again the puppies were prancing around his desk, one in each of Ben's hands. She demanded more sternly that Ben put them away, and he slid them into his desk. Not five minutes later the puppies were out again, moving around Ben's desk for the third time. The teacher, understandably peeved, asked Ben if he had heard her the first two times she had told him to put the puppies away. "Yes," Ben answered, and continued his reply by asking innocently, "but when are you going to teach me something I don't already know?" Ben's behavior, which to his teacher must have been seen as disruptive, didn't result from a learning disability or an attention deficit disorder. Ben's question wasn't asked to be rude or elicit a laugh from the class. Ben was asking an honest question. The teacher had been teaching the same lesson to twenty-five learners, some of whom, like Ben, had no need for the direct instruction. Unfortunately for Ben, most of his classmates were good at "playing school"—sitting quietly even when bored to death. Ben can't do that; he must always be busy. The fact is, playing with his Pound-Puppies® made more sense than sitting and doing nothing. (Ben's parents, teachers themselves, did give him a lecture on the importance of following his teacher's directions, and thereafter "frisked" him each morning for contraband Pound-Puppies®.) Nevertheless, the question remains whether Ben's disruptive behavior resulted from a problem that he had or from the curriculum not meeting his needs.

Ben's standing in the school community—the child of white, middle-class, educated parents—saved him from being labeled. But research indicates that a disproportionate number of minority students are identified as learning disabled (Tucker 1980), a statistic that suggests low socioeconomic status may be a factor in the labeling. Willis (1977) and Everhart (1983) have suggested that the low academic achievement of many students may be the result of "their resistance to instruction rather than an innate or biological deficiency within the student" (Christensen, Gerber & Everhart 1986, 325). In 1983, Malmstad, Ginsburg, and Croft conducted an ethnographic study of a summer remedial program for learning-disabled students. They found that the students engaged in covert and overt forms of resistance in response to teaching and learning strategies that were inadequate in remediating their learning problems. Some students acted out in defiance, others tuned out, still others daydreamed, and most probably hoped it was almost time to go home and play in the sunshine. As Karen Morrow Durica (1994) wrote, sometimes a child "rebels / because she should rebel, . . . acts out / because there is nowhere else / for the hurt and anxiety and fear to go, . . . is diagnosed "sick," / when perhaps her actions are the one true sign of sanity / in the demented world in which she is forced to live" (503).

What the students in the 1983 study were really doing was understandable. I have observed many such summer programs and have seen students as young as six or seven being drilled, studying huge stacks of flash cards, and filling in workbook pages—the same activities that gave them trouble during the school year and precipitated their placement in the summer program. How frustrating it must have been for these learners to have to do more of what they couldn't do, thereby perpetuating the "scenario for failure," as Ken Goodman (1991) calls it.

When parents of children who are not succeeding in school reading programs ask me about a summer remedial program, I ask them to first look into what that program will entail. Will children be reading real literature of their own choice or will they be doing reading exercises such as word lists and flash cards? Will they be a part of a literate community that shares responses to literature or will they sit alone quietly at a desk and fill in one-answer questions in a workbook? Is the goal of the program to help children look at themselves as capable readers and at reading as a pleasant activity or is it to "remediate" them so they can "catch up" to others at their grade level? If the program is not the former in each of the questions, I encourage the parents to let the children enjoy their summer by playing with other children and to spend time reading to and with their children daily, enjoying books together. Not real school, you say? You bet it isn't, but it will do more good than many remedial reading programs.

Getting Ready for Readiness

In summary, behavioral psychologists and educators have used the entity of "learning disability" to explain what they feel are deviations from the norm, but it is a norm that has been defined by them, created by them. It always amazed me that children never seem learning disabled before they come to school. As soon as they deviate from the "traditional" norm in the classroom, they are "at risk." In fact, children can be labeled "at risk" before they've even begun school, diagnosed according to kindergarten readiness tests, measures of isolated skills based on what test makers consider to be the "right" answer (Martin 1988; Taylor 1991).

Anne Martin (1988) tells the story of one child's encounter with readiness tests. It seems that "before Laurie even entered my kindergarten," Martin says, "I was told to look for serious difficulties." Martin managed to postpone the meeting with remedial services to discuss the supposed learning deficiencies, hoping to get to know Laurie as a person first. What Martin discovered was a "girl who loved books and language, who played with other children, who separated from her mother easily and followed routines well, who was clearly interested in discussions, in topics of study, in written symbols, and the world around her" (491). Most teachers would agree that Laurie was more than ready for kindergarten and formal schooling. Martin found the following diagnosis in the report that recommended remediation in the learning center three times a week:

> Laurie's best performance, which was advanced for her age, was her recall of story details which require memory for extensive, meaningful verbal information. Notably, when recall required verbal information that did not have a context—verbal and number series—she was less skilled. . . . It appears at this time that Laurie's memory is enhanced when the information is verbal and meaningful. This has implications for Laurie's "listening" skill. (491)

Teachers like Anne Martin and Ann Hunter would have read the report and said, "That's what we've been saying. Learning is enhanced when information is meaningful and presented in context." Instead, the professionals whom Martin met with were convinced by the test results that "if Laurie didn't have special services now, she might suffer 'in the third grade' and then it would have been our neglect in kindergarten that caused the problem" (491). Martin wasn't cynical enough to suggest that they were more concerned about possible litigation than the child's welfare. She merely says that she felt that "instead of making self-fulfilling predictions of failure in the third grade, we should respond to problems if and when they arose" (491). Laurie's parents were ultimately faced with the dilemma of whom to trust with their daughter's education.

The most frightening part of all of this, of course, is how it affects children. Many teachers have problems with the tests and labels, but teacher observations and professional judgments do not carry as much weight as test scores and the recommendations of "support service" personnel who sometimes have never even met the child prior to the testing situation, much less worked with her. Nevertheless, caring teachers do what they can. I remember that my daughter had a new, dedicated, and very caring teacher in kindergarten, Mrs. West. Laura loved her teacher and had a wonderful, productive year. In the spring, I received a call from a hesitant and somewhat nervous Mrs. West. She explained to me that having worked with Laura for several months, she was delighted with Laura's progress and was pleased that she was now reading. She had adjusted well socially and seemed to love school. The problem? Well, Laura was not much of an artist (genetic, I'm sure), and she drew people as round blobs with arms; their legs came directly out of the circle; and they had two dots for eyes, a "nose" dot in the middle, and a big smile. She told me that within a few weeks her students would be tested to determine next year's first-grade placement and that in some cases that test could even be a factor in determining retention for some children. One test to be given was the Goodenough "Draw-A-Person" test, and the district weighed this test very heavily. Mrs. West was concerned that Laura might be placed in a "lower group" in first grade based on this test. I thanked Mrs. West for the information and did what any concerned parent would do. Every night for the next few days Laura and I sat at the dining room table and drew people. We had a lot of fun and made a game out of seeing how many parts we could put on our characters—eyebrows, ears, hands, fingers. Laura even decided that she liked to include knees, elbows, and toes because they looked so funny. Obviously Laura was prepared to take the test, and Mrs. West was delighted with the results. Was Laura smarter or more prepared for first grade after being coached by her mother? Of course not—I had simply played the game. Mrs. West helped me by warning me of a potential danger to my daughter, and I reacted in a way that best helped my child. It was ridiculous that I had to do it, but having been a public school teacher for so many years, I was aware of the power of the tests and I knew that the opinion of Mrs. West, a first-year teacher, would be of little consequence when weighed against the standardized test.

Laura's good fortune was having a new teacher who was willing to take a risk and a mother who knew the system. What about all the other children who aren't as lucky as Laura? How many children are labeled when they are seven or eight years old because they don't fit a system that has determined the "normal" way children should think, learn, and develop?

Hope

As discouraging as all this sounds, I am an optimist. At my age, I don't worry anymore about changing the system; I now understand that schools are a mirror of our society and basically political in nature. But I am encouraged about what I see in classrooms. That is the purpose of this book. Good teachers do make a difference—teachers who believe in children and what they can do, and who can look past labels and politics into the heart of the learner. This book tells the story of one classroom, classified as a special education classroom and taught by a teacher who knows and believes in all children, even those who are different or unique. Is teaching according to a transactional philosophy difficult? You bet it is. After spending over two years in this classroom I was exhausted and emotionally drained, but what I saw will keep me moving ahead for years. In fact, it is the reason for this book. If it can happen in Ann Hunter's classroom, for these children, it can happen for the thousands of children all over the country who have been labeled and think they can't learn. It *has* to happen—it is the right of all students to learn.

Appendix

Summary of the developmentally appropriate practices recommended in "Guidelines for Appropriate Curriculum Content and Assessment in Programs Serving Children Ages 3 Through 8: A Position Statement of the National Association for the Education of Young Children and the National Association of Early Childhood Specialists in State Departments of Education (adopted November 1990)," published in *Young Children*, March 1991, 21–38.

Teaching-learning is . . . an interactive process. [The] following is a summary of the basic assumptions about learning and teaching as an interactive process that inform [the Guidelines]. [The basic assumptions are:]

- Children learn best when their physical needs are met and they feel psychologically safe and secure.
- Children construct knowledge.
- Children learn through social interaction with adults and other children.
- Children's learning reflects a recurring cycle that begins in awareness, and moves to exploration, to inquiry, and finally, to utilization.
- Children learn through play.
- Children's interests and "need to know" motivate learning.
- Human development and learning are characterized by individual variation.

Guidelines for curriculum content.
Guidelines are standards or principles by which to make a judgment or determine a course of action. The following statements are guidelines to use in making decisions about developing and/or selecting curriculum content for young children (what children are expected to know and be able to do).

1. The curriculum has an articulated description of its theoretical base that is consistent with prevailing professional opinion and research on how children learn.
2. Curriculum content is designed to achieve long-range goals for children in all domains—social, emotional, cognitive, and physical—and to prepare children to function as fully contributing members of a democratic society.
3. Curriculum addresses the development of knowledge and understanding, processes and skills, dispositions and attitudes.

4. Curriculum addresses a broad range of content that is relevant, engaging, and meaningful to children.
5. Curriculum goals are realistic and attainable for most children in the designated age range for which they were designed.
6. Curriculum content reflects and is generated by the needs and interests of individual children within the group. Curriculum incorporates a wide variety of learning experiences, materials and equipment, and instructional strategies, to accommodate a broad range of children's individual differences in prior experience, maturation rates, styles of learning, needs, and interests.
7. Curriculum respects and supports individual, cultural, and linguistic diversity. Curriculum supports and encourages positive relationships with children's families.
8. Curriculum builds upon what children already know and are able to do (activating prior knowledge) to consolidate their learning and to foster their acquisition of new concepts and skills.
9. The curriculum provides conceptual frameworks for children so that their mental constructions based on prior knowledge and experience become more complex over time.
10. Curriculum allows for focus on a particular topic or content, while allowing for integration across traditional subject-matter divisions by planning around themes and/or learning experiences that provide opportunities for rich conceptual development.
11. The curriculum content has intellectual integrity; content meets the recognized standards of the relevant subject-matter disciplines.
12. The content of the curriculum is worth knowing; curriculum respects children's intelligence and does not waste their time.
13. Curriculum engages children actively, not passively, in the learning process. Children have opportunities to make meaningful choices.
14. Curriculum values children's constructive errors and does not prematurely limit exploration and experimentation for the sake of ensuring "right" answers.
15. Curriculum emphasizes the development of children's thinking, reasoning, decision-making, and problem-solving abilities.
16. Curriculum emphasizes the value of social interaction to learning in all domains and provides opportunities to learn from peers.
17. Curriculum is supportive of children's physiological needs for activity, sensory stimulation, fresh air, rest, hygiene, and nourishment/ elimination.

18. Curriculum protects children's psychological safety, that is, children feel happy, relaxed, and comfortable rather than disengaged, frightened, worried, or stressed.

19. The curriculum strengthens children's sense of competence and enjoyment of learning by providing experiences for children to succeed from their point of view.

20. The curriculum is flexible so teachers can adapt to individual children or groups.

Guidelines for appropriate assessment.

Assessment is the process of observing, recording and otherwise documenting the work children do and how they do it, as a basis for a variety of educational decisions that affect the child. . . . The following guidelines first address the primary use of assessment: for planning instruction and communicating with parents. Guidelines for screening and program evaluation follow.

The following principles should guide assessment procedures . . .

1. Curriculum and assessment are integrated throughout the program; assessment is congruent with and relevant to the goals, objectives, and content of the program.

2. Assessment results in benefits to the child such as needed adjustments in the curriculum or more individualized instruction and improvements in the program.

3. Children's development and learning in all the domains—physical, social, emotional, and cognitive—and their dispositions and feelings are informally and routinely assessed by teachers' observing children's activities and interactions, listening to them as they talk, and using children's constructive errors to understand their learning.

4. Assessment provides teachers with useful information to successfully fulfill their responsibilities: to support children's learning and development, to plan for individuals and groups, and to communicate with parents.

5. Assessment involves regular and periodic observation of the child in a wide variety of circumstances that are representative of the child's behavior in the program over time.

6. Assessment relies primarily on procedures that reflect the ongoing life of the classroom and typical activities of the children. Assessment avoids approaches that place children in artificial situations, impede the usual learning and developmental experiences in the classroom, or divert children from their natural learning processes.

7. Assessment relies on demonstrated performance, during real, not contrived activities, for example, real reading and writing activities rather than only skills testing.

8. Assessment utilizes an array of tools and a variety of processes including but not limited to collections of representative work by children (artwork, stories they write, tape recordings of their reading), records of systematic observations by teachers, records of conversations and interviews with children, teachers' summaries of children's progress as individuals and as groups.

9. Assessment recognizes individual diversity of learners and allows for differences in styles and rates of learning. Assessment takes into consideration children's ability in English, their stage of language acquisition, and whether they have been given the time and opportunity to develop proficiency in their native language as well as in English.

10. Assessment supports children's development and learning; it does not threaten children's psychological safety or feelings of self-esteem.

11. Assessment supports parents' relationships with their children and does not undermine parents' confidence in their children's or their own ability, nor does it devalue the language and culture of the family.

12. Assessment demonstrates children's overall strengths and progress, what children can do, not just their wrong answers or what they cannot do or do not know.

13. Assessment is an essential component of the teacher's role. Since teachers can make maximal use of assessment results, the teacher is the primary assessor.

14. Assessment is a collaborative process involving children and teachers, teachers and parents, school and community. Information from parents about each child's experiences at home is used in planning instruction and evaluating children's learning. Information obtained from assessment is shared with parents in language they can understand.

15. Assessment encourages children to participate in self-evaluation.

16. Assessment addresses what children can do independently and what they can demonstrate with assistance, since the latter shows the direction of their growth.

17. Information about each child's growth, development, and learning is systematically collected and recorded at regular intervals. Information such as samples of children's work, descriptions of their performance, and anecdotal records is used for planning instruction and communicating with parents.

18. A regular process exists for periodic information sharing between teachers and parents about children's growth and development and performance. The method of reporting to parents does not rely on letter or numerical grades, but rather provides more meaningful, descriptive information in narrative form.

Guidelines for identifying children with special needs. . . .
The following principles . . . should guide assessment procedures used to identify children's special needs:

1. Results of screening tests are not used to make decisions about entrance to school or as the single criterion for placement in a special program, but rather are used as part of a thorough process of diagnosis designed to ensure that children receive the individual services they need.

2. Any standardized screening or diagnostic test that is administered to a child is valid and reliable in terms of the background characteristics of the child being tested and the test's intended purposes. This is determined by a careful review of the reliability and validity information that is provided in the technical manual that accompanies the test and of independent reviews of tests such as those available in Buros' Mental Measurement Yearbook.

3. When a child is formally tested, the procedures conform with all regulations contained in P.L. 94-142. Parents are informed in advance, and information about the test and test results are shared with the child's parents. Any interpretation of test scores describes, in nontechnical language, what the test covered, what the scores do and do not mean (common misinterpretations of the test scores) and how the results will be used. Allowances are made for parents to remain with the child during screening, if desired.

4. The screener approaches all interactions with children in a positive manner. The screener has knowledge of and prior experience with young children in order to score the measure accurately and support the validity of the results.

5. The younger the child, the more critical it is that the screening activities involve the manipulation of toys and materials rather than pictures and paper/pencil tasks.

6. If the results of the screening indicate that a child has not performed within an average developmental range, the child is seen individually by an experienced diagnostician who is also an expert in child development.

7. If a comprehensive diagnostic process is recommended after screening, key conditions warranting the implementation of this process should be delineated and documented for the parents in writing in non-technical language they can understand. Throughout the assessment process, parents must be informed in writing about diagnostic resources, parent rights and reasons for referral, as well as rights of refusal.

Guidelines for program evaluation and accountability. . . .
It is essential that [a] program be evaluated regularly to ensure that it is meeting its goals and that children and families are benefitting from participation. . . . The following guidelines are designed to guide program evaluation efforts:

1. In constructing assessment procedures related to evaluating programs or determining program accountability, no other stated principles of curriculum or assessment are violated.
2. Performance data of children collected by teachers to plan instruction are summarized and quantified by teachers and administrators to use in evaluating how well the program is meeting its goals for children and families.
3. The program uses multiple indicators of progress in all developmental domains to evaluate the effect of the program on children's development and learning. Group-administered, standardized, multiple-choice achievement tests are prohibited before third grade, preferably fourth.
4. All components of the program are evaluated to judge program effectiveness within the overall context of opportunities provided for children and families, including staff development and evaluation, parent satisfaction and feelings about how well the program serves their children and their opportunities for involvement, administration, physical environment, and health and safety. Results of outside independent evaluation such as that obtained from program accreditation is useful in program evaluation.
5. Programs which are mandated to use a standardized test of children's progress for program evaluation or accountability purposes employ a sampling method whenever feasible. This approach eliminates the need to subject all children to a testing procedure which can consume large blocks of time, cause undue stress, and produce results which are used for unwarranted decisions about individual children.

Contemporary Classroom
Literature Cited

Amelia Bedelia by Peggy Parish. New York: Harper, 1963.

The Boys' War by Paxton Davis. Winston-Salem, NC: John F. Blair, 1990.

Bridge to Terabithia by Katherine Paterson. New York: Crowell Publishing, 1977.

The Cay by Theodore Taylor. New York: Doubleday, 1969.

Charlie Skeedaddle by Patricia Beatty. New York: William Morrow, 1987.

Charlotte's Web by E. B. White. New York: Harper & Row, 1980.

Chicka Chicka Boom Boom by Bill Martin, Jr. and John Archambault. New York: Simon and Schuster, 1989.

Chocolate Moose for Dinner by Fred Gwynne. New York: Simon and Schuster, 1988.

Freckle Juice by Judy Blume. New York: Four Winds Press, 1971.

How to Eat Fried Worms by Thomas Rockwell. New York: Watts, 1973.

If You Give a Mouse a Cookie by Laura Joffe Numeroff. New York: Harper & Row, 1985.

The Light in the Attic by Shel Silverstein. New York: Harper Collins, 1981.

A Light in the Forest by Conrad Richter. New York: Bantam, 1990.

Maniac Magee by Jerry Spinelli. New York: Little, Brown, 1990.

Orphan for Nebraska by C. Talbot. New York: Atheneum, 1979.

The Outsiders by S. E. Hinton. New York: Viking Press, 1967.

The Pain and the Great One by Judy Blume. New York: Bradbury Publishers, 1984.

The Sign of the Beaver by Elizabeth Speare. New York: Dell, 1983.

The Snowman by R. L. Stine. New York: Scholastic, 1991.

The Story of Jackie Joyner Kersee by K. Dillon. New York: Sports Illustrated, 1991.

Tex by S. E. Hinton. New York: Delacorte Publishing, 1977.

That Was Then, This Is Now by S. E. Hinton. New York: Viking Press, 1971.

Where the Red Fern Grows by Wilson Rawls. New York: Doubleday Publishers, 1961.

Where the Sidewalk Ends by Shel Silverstein. New York: Dell, 1986.

REFERENCES

Applebee, A. 1981. *Writing in the Secondary School: English and the Content Areas.* Urbana, IL: National Council of Teachers of English.

Atwell, N. 1987. *In the Middle: Writing, Reading and Learning with Adolescents.* Portsmouth, NH: Boynton/Cook.

———. 1988. "A Special Writer at Work." In *Understanding Writing: Ways of Observing, Learning, and Teaching K–8,* ed. T. Newkirk and N. Atwell, Portsmouth, NH: Heinemann.

———. 1990. *Coming to Know: Writing to Learn in the Intermediate Grades.* Portsmouth, NH: Heinemann.

———. 1991. *Side by Side: Essays on Teaching to Learn.* Portsmouth, NH: Heinemann.

Barsch, R. 1965. *A Movigenic Curriculum.* Madison, WI: Bureau for Handicapped Children.

Berthoff, A. 1981. *The Making of Meaning.* Portsmouth, NH: Boynton/Cook.

Bissex, G. 1980. *GNYS AT WRK: A Child Learns to Write and Read.* Cambridge, MA: Harvard University Press.

Bloom, B. 1956. *Taxonomy of Educational Objectives: Handbook I: Cognitive Domain.* New York: McKay.

Britton, J., et al. 1975. *The Development of Writing Abilities 11–18.* New York: Macmillan.

Bruce, B. 1978. "What Makes a Good Story?" *Language Arts* 55: 460–66.

Bryan, T. H., & J. H. Bryan. 1975. *Understanding Learning Disabilities.* Sherman Oaks, CA: Alfred Publishing.

Calkins, L. 1986. *The Art of Teaching Writing.* Portsmouth, NH: Heinemann.

———. 1991. *Living Between the Lines.* Portsmouth, NH: Heinemann.

Cambourne, B. 1989. *The Whole Story.* Sydney, Australia: Ashton-Scholastic.

Carrier, J. G. 1983. "Masking the Social in Educational Knowledge: The Case of Learning Disability Theory." *American Journal of Sociology* 88: 948–74.

Cazden, C. 1972. *Child Language and Education.* New York: Holt Rinehart and Winston.

———. 1988. *Classroom Discourse: The Language of Teaching and Learning.* Portsmouth, NH: Heinemann.

Cazden, C. B. & V. P. John. 1971. "Learning in American Indian Children."
In *Anthropological Perspectives on Education*, ed. M. Wax, S. Diamond
& F. Goering, New York: Basic Books.

Chall, J. [1967] 1983. *Learning to Read: The Great Debate*. New York:
McGraw-Hill.

Chomsky, N. 1957. *Syntactic Structures*. The Hague: Mouton.

Christensen, C., M. Gerber & R. Everhart. 1986. "Toward a Sociological
Perspective on Learning Disabilities." *Educational Theory* 36: 317–31.

Clay, M. 1967. "The Reading Behavior of Five Year Old Children: A
Research Report." *New Zealand Journal of Education Studies* 2: 11–31.

Crabtree, C. 1988. "National Center Set to Improve History Teaching."
New York Times March 23: B10.

Cruickshank, W. 1971. *The Brain Injured Child in Home, School, and Community*. London: Pitman.

D'Alessandro, M. 1990. "Accomodating Emotionally Handicapped Children Through a Literature-Based Reading Program." *The Reading
Teacher* 44: 288–93.

Dewey, J. 1916. *Democracy in Education*. New York: Macmillan.

Dionesio, M. 1991. "A Journey to Meaning." In *With Promise: Redefining
Reading and Writing for "Special" Students*, ed. S. Stires, Portsmouth,
NH: Heinemann.

Durica, K. 1994. "The Labeled Child." *The Reading Teacher* 47: 503.

Edelsky, C., B. Altwerger & B. Flores. 1991. *Whole Language: What's the
Difference?* Portsmouth, NH: Heinemann.

Emig, J. 1971. *The Composing Process of Twelfth Graders*. Urbana, IL:
National Council of Teachers of English.

———. 1977. "Writing as a Mode of Learning." *College Composition and
Communication* 28: 122–28.

Everhart, R. B. 1983. *Reading, Writing and Resistance: Adolescence and Labor
in a Junior High School*. Boston: Routledge and Kegan Paul.

Flower, L. & J. Hayes. 1980. "Identifying the Organization of the Writing
Process." In *Cognitive Processes in Writing*, ed. L. Gregg and
E. Steinberg, Hillsdale, NJ: Lawrence Erlbaum.

Frostig, M. & D. Horne. 1973. *The Frostig Program for the Development of
Visual Perception*. Rev. ed. Chicago: Follett.

Gamberg, R., W. Kwak, M. Hutchings & J. Altheim. 1988. *Learning and
Loving It: Theme Studies in the Classroom*. Portsmouth, NH: Heinemann.

Goodman, K. S. 1986. *What's Whole in Whole Language?* Portsmouth, NH:
Heinemann.

———. 1987. "Reading and Writing: A Psycholinguistic View." In *Language and Thinking in School: A Whole-language Curriculum*, ed. K. S. Goodman, E. B. Smith, R. Meredith, & Y. Goodman, Katonah, NY: Richard Owen.

———. 1991 "Revaluing Readers and Reading." In *Redefining Reading and Writing for "Special" Students*, ed. S. Stires, Portsmouth, NH: Heinemann.

Goodman, K. S., Y. M. Goodman & W. J. Hood. 1989. *The Whole Language Evaluation Book*. Portsmouth, NH: Heinemann.

Goodman, K. S., P. Shannon, Y. Freeman & S. Murphy. 1988. *Report Card on Basal Readers*. Katonah, NY: Richard C. Owen.

Goodman, Y. M. 1978. "Kid Watching: An Alternative to Testing." *National Elementary Principals Journal* 57: 41–45.

———. 1986. "Children Come to Know Literacy." In *New Perspectives in Comprehension*, ed. W. H. Teale & E. Sulzby, Bloomington, IN: Indiana University School of Education.

Graves, D. 1983. *Writing: Teachers and Children at Work*. Portsmouth, NH: Heinemann.

———. 1985. "All Children Can Write." *LD Focus* 1(1): 36–43.

Hairston, M. 1982. "The Winds of Change: Thomas Kuhn and the Revolution in the Teaching of Writing." *College Composition and Communication* 33: 76–88.

Hall, W. 1987. *The Emergence of Literacy*. Portsmouth, NH: Heinemann.

Halliday, M. A. K. 1975. *Learning How to Mean: Exploration in the Development of Language*. London: Edward Arnold.

Harp, B. 1991. *Assessment and Evaluation in Whole Language Classrooms*. Norwood, MA: Christopher-Gordon Publishers.

Harste, J. & K. Short, with C. Burke. 1988. *Creating Classrooms for Authors: The Reading-Writing Connection*. Portsmouth, NH: Heinemann.

Harste, J., V. Woodward & C. Burke. 1984a. "Examining Our Assumptions: A Transactional View of Literacy and Learning." *Research in the Teaching of English* 18: 84–108.

———. 1984b. *Language Stories and Literacy Lessons*. Portsmouth, NH: Heinemann.

Heath, S. B. 1983. *Ways with Words: Language, Life, and Work in Communities and Classrooms*. New York: Cambridge University Press.

Hickman, J. & B. Cullinan. 1989. *Children's Literature in the Classroom: Weaving Charlotte's Web*. Norwood, MA: Christopher–Gordon Publishers.

Hilgard, E. 1956. *Theories of Learning*. Englewood Cliffs, NJ: Prentice–Hall.

Holdaway, D. 1979. *Foundations of Literacy*. Portsmouth, NH: Heinemann.

Hollingsworth, P. & D. R. Reutzel. 1988. "Whole Language with LD Children." *Academic Therapy* 23: 477–88.

Huck, C. 1977. "Literature as the Content of Reading." *Theory into Practice* 16: 363–71.

Hulme, C. 1981. *Reading Retardation and Multi-Sensory Teaching.* London: Routledge and Kegan Paul.

Hyde, A. & M. Bizar. 1989. *Thinking in Context: Teaching Cognitive Processes Across the Elementary School Curriculum.* White Plains, NY: Longman.

John, V. P. 1972. "Styles of Learning—Styles of Teaching: Reflections on the Education of Navajo Children." In *Functions of Language in the Classroom,* ed. C. B. Cazden, V. P. John & D. Hymes, New York: Teachers College Press.

Kuhn, T. 1963. *The Structure of Scientific Revolution.* Chicago, IL: University of Chicago Press.

Labov, W. 1972. *Language in the Inner City: Studies in the Black English Vernacular.* Philadelphia, PA: University of Pennsylvania Press.

Malmstad, B.J., M. B. Ginsburg & J. C. Croft. 1983. "The Social Construction of Reading Lessons: Resistance and Social Reproduction." *Journal of Education* 165: 359–73.

Mandler, J. & M. DeForest. 1979. "Is There More Than One Way to Recall a Story?" *Child Development* 50: 886–89.

Mandler, J. & N. Johnson. 1977. "Remembrance of Things Parsed: Story Structure and Recall." *Cognitive Psychology* 9: 111–54.

Martin, A. 1988. "Teachers and Teaching." *Harvard Educational Review* 58: 488–501.

Mather, N. 1992. "Whole Language Reading Instruction for Students with Learning Disabilities: Caught in the Cross Fire." *Learning Disabilities Practice* 7: 87–95.

Mayher, J., N. Lester & G. Pradl. 1983. *Learning to Write/Writing to Learn.* Portsmouth, NH: Boynton/Cook.

McGee, L. 1982. "Awareness of Text Structure: Effects on Children's Recall of Expository Text." *Reading Research Quarterly* 17: 581–90.

Mills, H., T. O'Keefe & D. Stephens. 1992. *Looking Closely: The Role of Phonics in a Whole Language Classroom.* Urbana, IL: National Council of Teachers of English.

Moffett, J. & B. J. Wagner. 1992. *Student Centered Language Arts, K–12.* Portsmouth, NH: Boynton/Cook.

Morrow, L. M. 1982. "Relationships Between Literature Programs, Library Corner Designs and Children's Use of Literature." *Journal of Educational Research* 75: 339–44.

National Association for the Education of Young Children. 1991. "Guidelines for Appropriate Curriculum Content and Assessment in Programs

Serving Children Ages 3 Through 8: A Position Statement of the National Association for the Education of Young Children and the National Association of Early Childhood Specialists in State Departments of Education (adopted November 1990)." *Young Children* (March): 21–38.

Newman, J., ed. 1985. *Whole Language: Theory in Use.* Portsmouth, NH: Heinemann.

Pappas, C., B. Kiefer & L. Levstik. 1990. *An Integrated Language Perspective in the Elementary School.* White Plains, NY: Longman.

Piaget, J. 1971. *Psychology and Epistemology,* trans. by A. Rosin. New York: Grossman.

Probst, R. 1992. "Five Kinds of Literary Knowing." In *Literature Instruction,* ed. J. Langer. Urbana, IL: National Council of Teachers of English.

Rand, M. 1984. "Story Schema: Theory, Research and Practice." *The Reading Teacher* 37: 377–82.

Reid, L. & J. Golub. 1991. "An Interactive Approach to Composition Instruction." In *Composition and Resistance,* ed. C. M. Hurlbert & M. Blitz, Portsmouth, NH: Boynton/Cook.

Rief, L. 1992. *Seeking Diversity.* Portsmouth, NH: Heinemann.

Rose, M. 1989. *Lives on the Boundary.* New York: Free Press.

Rosenblatt, L. M. 1978. *The Reader, the Text, and the Poem: The Transactional Theory of the Literary Work.* Carbondale, IL: Southern Illinois University Press.

Shaughnessy, M. 1977. *Errors and Expectations.* New York: Oxford University Press.

Short K. & C. Burke. 1991. *Creating Curriculum: Teachers and Students as a Community of Learners.* Portsmouth, NH: Heinemann.

Skinner, B. F. 1953. *Science and Human Behavior.* New York: Macmillan.

———. 1957. *Verbal Behavior.* New York: Appleton-Century-Crofts.

Smith, F. 1983. *Essays into Literacy: Selected Papers and Some Afterthoughts.* Portsmouth, NH: Heinemann.

———. 1988a. *Insult to Intelligence: The Bureaucratic Invasion of Our Classrooms.* Portsmouth, NH: Heinemann.

———. 1988b. *Joining the Literacy Club: Further Essays into Education.* Portsmouth, NH: Heinemann.

———. 1988c. *Understanding Reading.* 4th ed. Hillsdale, NJ: Lawrence Erlbaum.

Smith, F., & K. Goodman. 1973. "On the Psycholinguistic Method of Teaching Reading." In *Psychological Factors in the Teaching of Reading,* ed. E. E. Ekwall, Columbus, OH: Charles Merrill.

Stires, S. 1991. *With Promise: Redefining Reading and Writing for "Special" Students*. Portsmouth, NH: Heinemann.

Strauss, A. & H. Werner. 1942. "Disorders of Conceptual Thinking in the Brain Injured Child." *Journal of Nervous and Mental Diseases* 96: 153–72.

Strickland, D., & L. Morrow. 1989. *Emerging Literacy: Young Children Learn to Read and Write*. Newark, DE: International Reading Association.

Strickland, K. 1991a. "Changes in Perspectives: Student Teachers' Development of a Reading Instruction Philosophy." Eric Document Reproduction Service ED 331 037.

———. 1991b. "Review: *Learning Denied* by Denny Taylor." *English Leadership Quarterly* 13(2): 14–15.

Strickland, K. & J. Strickland. 1993. *Un-covering the Curriculum: Whole Language in Secondary and Postsecondary Classrooms*. Portsmouth, NH: Boynton/Cook.

Taylor, D. 1991. *Learning Denied*. Portsmouth, NH: Heinemann.

"Theme cycles." 1994 (January). *Primary Voices K–6* 2 (1).

Tucker, J. A. 1980. "Ethnic Proportions in Classes for the Learning Disabled: Issues in Nonbiased Assessment." *Journal of Special Education* 14: 93–105.

U.S. Office of Education. 1973. *Number of Pupils with Handicaps in Local Public Schools, Spring, 1970*. Washington, D.C.: Government Printing Office.

Vacca, R. & T. Rasinski. 1992. *Case Studies in Whole Language*. Fort Worth, TX: Harcourt Brace Jovanovich.

Vygotsky, L. 1978. *Mind and Society*, ed. M. Cole, V. J. Steiner, S. Scribner & E. Souberman. Cambridge, MA: Harvard University Press.

Wayman, J. 1980. *The Other Side of Reading*. Carthage, IL: GoodApple.

Weaver, C. 1988. *Reading Process and Practice: From Socio-psycholinguistics to Whole Language*. Portsmouth, NH: Heinemann.

———. 1990. *Understanding Whole Language: From Principles to Practice*. Portsmouth, NH: Heinemann.

———. 1994. *Reading Process and Practice: From Socio-psycholinguistics to Whole Language*. 2nd ed. Portsmouth, NH: Heinemann.

Wells, G. 1986. *The Meaning Makers: Children Learning Language and Using Language to Learn*. Portsmouth, NH: Heinemann.

Whaley, J. 1981. "Story Grammars and Reading Instruction." *The Reading Teacher* 34: 762–71.

Willis, P. 1977. *Learning to Labor*. Lexington, MA: D.C. Heath.

Wood, G. H. 1988. "Democracy and the Curriculum." In *The Curriculum: Problems, Politics, and Possibilities*, ed. L. E. Beyer & M. W. Apple, Albany, NY: State University of New York Press.

Young, R. 1978. "Paradigms and Problems: Needed Research in Rhetorical Invention." In *Research on Composing*, ed. C. R. Cooper & L. Odell, Urbana, IL: National Council of Teachers of English.

Zemelman, S. & H. Daniels. 1988. *A Community of Writers*. Portsmouth, NH: Heinemann.

INDEX

Hairston, Maxine, 13
"handicapped," xi, xii, 21
Harp, Bill, 28
Harste, Woodward, and Burke, 15
Heath, Shirley Brice, 59
heterogeneous grouping, 76
Hilgard, Ernest, 10
Hinton, S. E., 2, 20, 58, 63, 71, 72
Hollingsworth and Reutzel, 21
homogeneous grouping, 17, 19, 76
Hood, Wendy, 28
How to Eat Fried Worms, 88, 94–96

hyperactivity, 138
hyperkinesis, 138

IEPs (Individualized Education Plans), 2
"inclusion," 128
interacting with text, 31
invented spelling, 91, 113, 131

journals. *See* dialogue journal and
    response logs

Kuhn, Thomas, 9, 10, 13, 136

"Labeled Child, The," 123
labeling, the effects of, 133–34
labels, xi, xiii, 3, 21, 123–24, 133–34
language experience approach,47–48, 87,
    131
language learning, social aspect, 42, 130,
    131
Laurie, Anne Martin's student, 140
"learning disabled," xii, 16, 21, 40, 123,
    127, 134, 135, 139, 140
"learning support," 127
"learning workshop," 115
letter writing, 68
literacy, 18
    attitudes toward, 2
    purposes of, 35
    traditional approaches to, 23
"literacy club," 14, 33, 46, 82, 96
literate environment, 36, 104
literature response groups, 38
literature logs. *See* response logs
literature, as a vehicle to broadening
    schemata, xiii
literature, connecting worlds, 14, 99–100,
    104

literature-based approach, xiii, 20, 27,
    104, 112, 122
logs. *See* teacher's log and response logs

mainstreaming, 62, 67, 81, 128
Malmstad, Ginsburg, and Croft, 139
management, 19
Maniac Magee, 73
Martin, Anne, 140–41
Mather, Nancy, 16
Mayher, Lester, and Pradl, 111
McKissock, Rhonda, 129, 136
meaning-making, 3, 12, 13, 17, 20, 30, 35,
    46, 85, 111
medical-clinical model of reading, 17,
    135, 137–38
"minimally brain-injured," 133, 135
multiple readings of books, 95

National Association for the Education of
    Young Children, xii
National Council of Teachers of English
    (NCTE), 20, 26, 28
needs, supporting individual, 26, 88
neurological disorder, 135, 138

oral language, 87
oral sharing time, 40
organizing, as prewriting activity, 112–13
outlining, a prewriting strategy, 78–79
Outsiders, The, 2, 4, 7, 14–15, 20, 58,
    71–72, 77
"over-achiever," 137

paradigms, 2, 9, 11–13, 136
part-to-whole, 11, 15, 17
Paterson, Katherine, 27, 69, 85
peer response, 34, 66, 92
perception of self, 63, 81, 98
"percolating" prewriting activities, 111
philosophy, developing a, 23
phonics, 11, 16, 20, 25, 41, 43
politics of education, 133, 135, 136
populations with specialized needs, 127
prediction in reading, 12
    prewriting, 77, 111. *See also*
    brainstorming, categorizing, freewriting,
    organizing, outlining,
    "percolating," and webbing
progressive education, 12
publishing writing, 34

DATE DUE

DEC 1 7 2001			

graphic arts

First Edition

Lithographed in U.S.A.

DR. WILBUR R. MILLER
University of Missouri — Columbia
Columbia, Missouri

RICHARD J. BROEKHUIZEN
Nova High School
Ft. Lauderdale, Florida

DR. MARION E. MADDOX
University of Arkansas
Fayetteville, Arkansas

LAVON B. SMITH
Fayetteville, Arkansas

basic industrial arts

Copyright© 1978

ALKNIGHT

**Publishing Company
Bloomington, Illinois**

**Library of Congress
Card Catalog Number: 78-53390**

SBN: 87345-787-0 Paperback
SBN: 87345-795-1 Hardbound

TABLE OF CONTENTS

Chapter **1**

INTRODUCTION

Graphic arts is a broad term that includes printing, papermaking, binding, and photography. It includes all types of writing, drawing, and printing. Printed images may be in such forms as magazines, newspapers, books, and printed T-shirts. They may be in photographs, soda cans, wallpaper, or stationery. Printed materials have a great influence on our lives, Fig. 1-1. We look at calendars to check dates. We use road maps to locate routes for our travels. We buy goods and services as a result of printed advertisements. We use printed postage stamps for mailing letters and packages. We pay bills with printed money and checks. These and many other examples are all forms of graphic communication.

Graphic messages are prepared in these four stages:

1. **Design** — planning the message so that it communicates.
2. **Composition** — preparing the exact form of the words, symbols, or pictures. These must express the message as planned in the design stage.
3. **Preproduction and Production** — preparing the message to fit the method of printing that was selected. Also, printing the message as planned so that it can be mailed or shipped to consumers.
4. **Binding, Finishing, and Packaging** — forming the printed message into the size or shape that was selected in the design stage. It can then be shipped and later used by consumers.

To carry out these four stages of producing a graphic message, more graphic communications are needed. Written details and descriptions must be studied and used to produce the message. Also, order forms, labels, catalogs, displays, and other types of advertising materials must be designed and printed. As you can see, the need for graphic communication is

Fig. 1-1. People react differently to the same message.

Fig. 1-2.   Choose the kind of work you like to do.

huge. There is a constant need for many different kinds of skills in graphic arts. Many people find careers in this type of work. Will you?

CAREERS

"While you're in school," Mr. Jackson said to his class, "you should choose subjects that will help you develop some knowledge and skills to prepare for the world of work. This is important to planning your career. Do any of you have an idea of what you'd like to do? You'll be working for more than 40 years after high school."

The class moaned.

"John? What subjects do you want to take while in high school?"

John replied, "I don't know. Business courses, I guess."

"Why business courses, John?"

"Oh, my father owns an insurance agency. He thinks this would be a good place for me to work after I graduate."

"You don't sound very happy about it," said Mr. Jackson. "Is that what you really want to do?"

John's face lit up. "What I really like is photography. I'm good at it, too. But you can't make much of a living at that."

Mr. Jackson turned to the class. "What do you think? Do you have any advice for John?"

Tom raised his hand. "I think John is crazy not to want to go in with his dad. What a setup! I wish my father had a business waiting for me."

"I don't agree," said Mary. "It's more important to like what you do. Work should be what you like, not what you have to do. I don't think John should go into business with his father if he doesn't want to."

Bob raised his hand. "I think you can do what you enjoy and still make a good living." he said. "Have you looked to see what photography offers, John?"

"Well, not really," John replied.

"This relates to one of the three steps in good career planning," said Mr. Jackson.

Fig. 1-3.   It took years of careful planning to construct this rocket. It takes careful planning to construct a career, too.

Fig. 1-4.   These people are all different in their talents, interests, and needs. Working together, they become a vital and important team.

"What are these steps?" asked John.

"The three steps are **knowledge of self, knowledge of career opportunities,** and **trying out your choice,**" said Mr. Jackson.

"How do they work?"

"Well, first you must know yourself. You must know what kind of a person you are, what you like, what you don't like. John, you like photography, for instance. The next step is to gain knowledge about careers that you think fit you. What jobs are available in photography? When you find something that interests you, try it out. Test it by getting a summer job or part-time job. Perhaps you can get into a school work program. Try the job on for size, and see if it fits you."

"I'm going to do that," John thought as he gathered his books for his next class. "Maybe I really can have a career in photography and make a good living, too."

John is now on his way to planning his future career. He is going to start at the beginning — with himself. He will find that there is more to himself than he thought. John, like all of us, is a sum total of four types of traits. They are physical, mental, social, and emotional.

These traits have different importance in different people. One person likes to work with things. Another likes to work with ideas. Some people are not happy being alone. Others can only work alone. Certain types of people do their best when under pressure. Other people must be free from pressure to do well. People are different. The important thing is for them to know and understand themselves.

After John learns about himself, he can decide on the kind of job that will suit him best. It will fit into his physical, mental, social, and emotional makeup. Knowing what his needs are will also help him decide on the kind of working conditions that are best for him.

When John has an idea of **who he is** and **what he wants** from a job, he is ready to explore career opportunities. He is going to make the career fit him.

John already knows the kind of work that appeals to him. Now he is ready for the third step. He should try out the job by doing it. Or he can work in the environment of the job. This might be a photography store, lab, or printing company. He can take a summer job or part-time job or enroll in a school work program. This could mean the beginning of a long and an interesting career.

Fig. 1-5.   Exploring career opportunities is one of the steps in good career planning.

Fig. 1-6. The production of nearly all products begins with a design.

Fig. 1-7. Often, people first notice a product because of its design. Product designs must make a good impression.

People Who Design

Just about everything you see around you was designed. Designing is an important graphic art. It is used in the production of nearly all products, Fig. 1-6. Designers must have the skill to express ideas. They must be able to arrange lines, words, sentences, pictures, and colors so that an idea is understood.

Designers in the graphic arts design many different kinds of things. They design what you see and read on boxes, bottles, and cans of food. They design advertisements used in newspapers and magazines. They create signs for display in stores. They design wallpaper, greeting cards, and record album covers. They design wrapping paper, calendars, floor tile, and coloring books. Some designers work for publishing and printing firms where they design book covers and illustrations.

People in the Office

In graphic arts, as in other fields, the office is an idea and fact center. Some people in the office write. **Advertising writers** write about the value and purpose of a product or service. **Technical writers** use their scientific knowledge and writing skill to help people understand technical subjects. **Copy editors** deal with other people's writing. They check to see that their ideas are expressed clearly. They also check for grammar and writing style.

Clerical people are fact people. The facts that they handle must be accurate if the graphic business is to do well. **Secretaries** take facts through dictation, mail, or phone. Either they or **typists** organize the facts on paper. **File clerks** and **computer programmers** store the facts.

Another person in the office is the **estimator.** The estimator decides how much it will cost to produce a product in terms of material, machines, and human labor. This worker must know how much it costs to operate machines and pay salaries and benefits. He or she must also know the cost of materials to estimate prices for customers.

The overall success of a business depends on the skills of its managers. They must have

Fig. 1-8.   Good clerical workers are needed in the office.

Fig. 1-10. Customers depend on the service the salesperson gives.

Fig. 1-9.   The manager organizes people to do the work.

knowledge of the whole graphic arts field. They must know how to organize people and plan the work to be done.

People in Sales

Salespeople serve both the company and people who buy its graphic products. They must be dependable. They must be able to work with people. Salespeople may sell the services of designers or writers. Those who work for a printing company may sell machine time. Other salespeople may sell advertising space in newspapers or magazines. Still others may sell such items as paper or ink for producing graphic products. Or they may sell clip art, photographs, or books.

People in Production

Production managers guide the work through the production process. They make things happen on time.

Plant managers organize workers and machines. They must know something about every type of work that is done.

Plant engineers watch equipment and methods of doing things to see that operations go smoothly. If they do not, these workers must find out why.

Layout people organize art, illustrations, and copy. They get everything ready for other processes in printing to begin. This includes stripping, platemaking, presswork, and binding which you will learn more about later.

Camera operators photograph the work to be printed. **Strippers** arrange the negative films and strip them to size. The **platemaker** then exposes the sheets onto offset plates.

In photoengraving, the **etcher, finisher,** and **proofer** all play a part in turning the original idea into a real product.

People and machines make the finished product happen. The **typesetter** turns copy into type. The **press operator** turns type into product. The **binder** packages the product. Trucks, trains, and planes take the product to the consumers.

The product is made. But other people are needed so that the process can start all over again for other graphic products. Buyers purchase new materials for workers and machines. Storekeepers organize and maintain the graphic arts materials until they are purchased.

Some people work to find new and better ways to make products and offer services in graphic arts. This work is called **research and development.** Some of these people seek to improve methods of printing. Some of them are chemists. They do research to improve products, such as inks, color, or paper. Others work to improve film. Or they develop new tools for the graphic artist. There are researchers in sales, too. They find out how well a product will sell and what people want to buy.

How You Can Enter

Several weeks had passed since Mr. Jackson first told his class about the three steps to career planning. He wondered if his advice had helped John.

"I think so," said John. "I really thought about myself — what kinds of interest and abilities I have. Photography was still my big interest. So I looked at careers in that field. I found an area that really appealed to me. It has variety and good working conditions. And I'd be working with people. But I want to learn more about it. How do I find a job when I'm ready to test it?"

Fig. 1-11. The production manager and the press operator are action people who make the finished product happen.

Fig. 1-12. The talents of many people were involved in developing and producing this paper.

Fig. 1-13. Completion of school — and the beginning of a career.

"You can learn more about your field right here in school." Mr. Jackson said. "You can take classes in the subject. Later, you can go to a junior college or university. Or you can go right to work and learn on the job.

"How do I find a job?"

"There are a lot of ways. You can find a job through an employment agency or a state employment office. Or you can watch newspaper ads. You can go to the business itself and apply for work. The counselor at school also can help you. Another way is to talk to someone who works in the field you're interested in."

"That's what I'm going to do," said John. "I'm glad it's possible to do what you enjoy and still have a career. It just takes a little planning."

DEVELOPMENT OF PRINTING

Movable type was invented in 1439 by Johann Gutenberg. Before that time, printing was done from a solid piece of wood. A message was hand cut or **engraved** on the wood piece. With movable type, letters and figures that were cut in **separate pieces** of wood could be used time after time. When a printing job was done, the type could be taken apart and stored for the next job.

Printing presses used during the 1400's were made of wood. They were very crude. The press had two large blocks of wood fixed so that the type or engraved blocks could be placed between them. Ink was applied to the printing surface with a piece of padded leather. Paper was then placed on the engraving between the two blocks. It was pressed against the inked type by means of a lever or screw. Production was slow. These early presses were important in beginnings of the printing press.

Friedrick Konig, a German, invented a cylinder press early in the 1600's. Revolving cylinders pulled the paper from rolls. In this way, printing was done on continuous lengths. Our newspapers and many magazines are printed on rolls of paper.

THE PRINTING INDUSTRY

Printed materials play a big part in our daily lives. Yet we often take for granted the newspapers, magazines, books, paper money, business forms, and labels we use. Printed materials give everyone a chance to gain knowledge. Printing is a huge business. It ranks among the 10 largest industries in the United States.

More than one million people work in the printing industry. Many jobs are open each year to people who are prepared for them. One of these jobs could be yours. You can gain the know-how and skills through school printing classes and special training programs.

DESIGNING AND PRINTING METHODS

Chapter **2**

WHY DESIGN?

A printed message that has good design is effective in these ways:

1. It attracts the attention of the reader.
2. It is easily read and understood.
3. It makes the reader remember it.

People react well to objects or printed messages that have good designs. There are few set rules for designing. But there are certain basic ones that you should understand.

One of the most important things to think about in designing is **function.** A printed message must function, or serve its purpose, as intended. It must contain useful, correct information. As an example, companies often need business cards for their salespeople. The business card gives the name of the company, address, and phone number. It gives the salesperson's name and job title. It may also state what services the company offers. The business card's size must also make it useful or functional, Fig. 2-1.

Businesses make use of many different kinds of printed products. Before these products can be designed, designers must know for whom the messages are intended. They must decide on the sizes and shapes so that the products can be used in the best ways.

Think about a business such as the Holiday Inn. It uses many printed products. Some are used by the motel's workers. Others are used by the motel's guests. Look at how graphic art is used by the Holiday Inn in Fig 2-2. Note how each is designed to serve a special purpose.

Designers should know the many ways of designing. They should know how to prepare copy and art for printing. They should have some knowledge of the different printing processes and types of packaging. Money is wasted if knowledge and skill are lacking. It can happen in these ways:

1. The design is not appealing.
2. The design is high quality, but the production method is low quality.
3. The design is low quality, but the production method is high quality.

Designers who know about the different printing processes are better able to plan and design good, functional graphic products.

Fig. 2-1. This salesperson's business card is too big to be functional.

A. The design that identifies this business serves as a beacon.

D. Door knob signs are a useful item.

B. Printed guest registration card and key ring meet needs of guests and management.

E. These printed products are for the customer's use.

C. Printed guides are a convenience to guests.

F. Attractive printed material identifies the business and decorates a table.

Fig. 2-2. Many businesses, such as the Holiday Inn, need different kinds of printed products.

Fig. 2-3.   The message must be designed for the age
            of the people who are to read it.
            A. Elementary school children.
            B. High school students.

ANALYZING THE MESSAGE

A graphic message must be planned and prepared carefully. Many things are considered. First, the **people who will see and read the message** are thought about. Their age, interests, and sex are considered. How much money they have to spend and how well they read are also considered. Thinking about these things is called **analyzing the message.** For example, a message for young school children must be easily read and understood. The same message to high school students may have different words and art, Fig. 2-3.

How easily a message is read often depends on the **typeface,** or style of type, used. Messages for young children and elderly people are most often in a large typeface. In messages having lots of type, such as this book, the typeface should be simple, free of decorative lines, and easy to read.

The size, shape, and **material** for printing the message must also be considered. Size and shape may depend on how the graphic product will be used. Or it may depend on how it will be distributed. The function of a product is important when choosing material. A printed paper product would not be a functional item for carrying a bowling ball, Fig. 2-4. Letterhead stationery printed on heavy paper, such as poster board, would not be functional. It would be hard to fold and costly to mail.

The **ink color and paper color** chosen depend on the purpose of the message and who is to read it. Colors can be thought of as either cool or warm. Colors that give a feeling of coolness are violet, blue, and green. Red, yellow, and orange are considered warm colors. They catch the eye more than cool colors do. They are often used to point up something in a message. Using warm and cool colors together must be planned to work together. Printed things held close, such as books and pamphlets, should have great contrast in the colors for ink and paper. The most contrast is achieved by using black ink on white paper. Notice how colors are used on products in boxes, cans, and bottles. They are designed to interest you in what is inside.

Fig. 2-4.   A graphic product cannot function well if
            the wrong material is chosen.

The **content** of a message must also be analyzed. The message should be brief, complete, and to the point, Fig. 2-5. What the message says will influence the design of a product. Its purpose will influence size and shape.

Other things to be analyzed before designing can begin are **cost, quantity,** and **quality.** There are different ways of printing a message. There are different ways of binding, finishing, and packaging. All cost different amounts of money. Each produces a different effect. All this can be better understood after you learn more about the graphic arts industry.

DESIGN PRINCIPLES

Designers are always guided by certain principles when they create the design for a product. These are balance, contrast, rhythm, proportion, and unity. Using them helps the designer gain an overall pleasing effect.

Balance

There are two types of balance: formal and informal. Each does something different to a design. If a line were drawn through the exact center of a design, both sides of the graphic message would be alike. This is **formal balance,** Fig. 2-6A. It gives a sense of dignity, order, and

Fig. 2-5.   These messages say the same thing, but the first one has unnecessary wording.

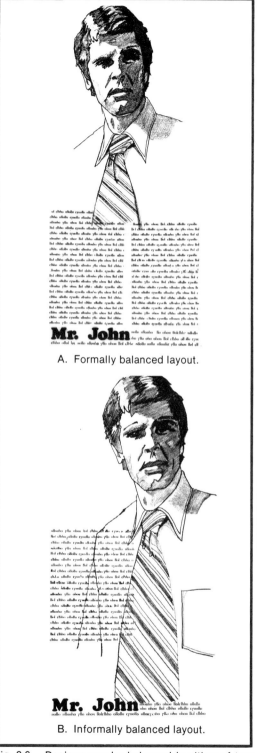

A. Formally balanced layout.

B. Informally balanced layout.

Fig. 2-6.   Designs can be balanced in either of two ways.

strength. In **informal balance,** the parts of the design are not centered, Fig. 2-6B. Balance is achieved in some other way than placing the parts in equal halves. The designer is free to place the parts as desired, as long as they balance each other.

Contrast

Contrast makes a design lively and gives variety. It calls special attention to certain parts of the message. Contrast can be achieved with the type chosen. The type might be underscored. *Italic typefaces,* **bold typefaces,** and LARGER TYPEFACES can be used to call attention to parts or words in a message.

Color also brings contrast. It points up key words or phrases. A **screen tint** is often printed as a background color. It contrasts with the color that is printed over it, Fig. 2-7. Using color and screen tints can help balance an informal layout in a design. Also, a small dark area will balance a larger light area, Fig. 2-8.

Another way of getting contrast in a graphic message is with **reverse lettering,** Fig. 2-9. This creates white letters in a black or color background.

Combining any of these methods of achieving contrast will increase the effect. For example, reverse lettering can be set in italic type to get greater contrast. Or bold-face type

can be set in a second color. Changing the size and shape of any part of a layout also brings about contrast to catch the eye. See Figs. 2-10, 2-11, and 2-12.

Fig. 2-8.   A large light area balances a small dark area.

Fig. 2-9.   Reverse lettering provides contrast.

Fig. 2-10. Parts are positioned to suggest eye movement.

Screen tints may also be used to provide contrast and variety. Screen tints are available in values from 5% through 90% in each of the seven rulings from 65 lines through 150 lines. The number of lines and different percentages of screens allow for better flexibility and permit control over the impact of the screened area as well as the color. A large area for example, when printed in a solid second color, may become overpowering and distract from the remainder of the message. If a color is desired in the larger area, a lesser percent screen tint may be used to reduce the overwhelming power of the color.

Fig. 2-7.   Screen tints provide contrast and variety.

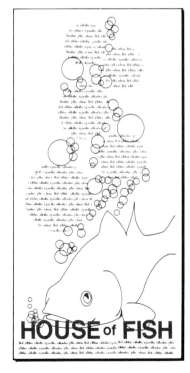

Fig. 2-11. Numbers suggest eye movement.

Rhythm

Rhythm in a design causes the eyes to move smoothly from part to part. The position of the parts may cause your eyes to move upward or downward. This is called **vertical positioning.** Or the parts may be placed so that your eyes move to the left or right or at an angle. This is called **horizontal positioning.** See Fig. 2-10. Numbers can also be used to guide your eyes from one part to the next, Fig. 2-11. Contrast also helps achieve rhythm. Contrast may be in the sizes of the parts and where they are placed. Their sizes and locations can cause your eyes to move in a desired direction, Fig. 2-12.

Proportion

Proportion has to do with how the sizes of different parts relate to each other and to the whole design. This is based on certain mathematical dimensions in layout.

A sheet size that has good proportion is known as a **regular oblong.** It is about two parts wide by three parts long, Fig. 2-13. How the

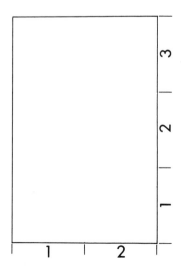

Fig. 2-12. The size and position of parts suggest eye movement.

Fig. 2-13. Regular oblong sheet size.

designer places parts of a design on the sheet makes the difference between a good design and a bad one. If you can **see** how the parts relate to each other, the layout is dull and dead, Fig. 2-14A. This design seems cut in half. But when you are not aware of a design's mathematical dimensions, the design is more interesting, Fig. 2-14B.

To achieve interest, the designer uses the **line of golden proportion.** This line is found by dividing the height of a sheet into eight equal parts. The third line from the top is the line of golden proportion, Fig. 2-15. A word or group of words should be placed so that one half of the area extends above this line. The other half extends below it. Sometimes, this line is located near the bottom of a sheet for interest, as in Fig. 2-14B. The dots are located close to the line of golden proportion.

Unity

When all of the parts blend together in a pleasing way, the design has unity. This can be achieved by designing the parts and areas in similar shapes. It is also achieved by controlling the number of typefaces used in the design. If several different type styles and sizes are used, a design seems confusing. It does not look organized. There is unity if not more than two different type styles are used, Fig. 2-16. Beginning design work is often done better if the type used is limited to one type family. Different styles in one type family are shown in Fig. 2-17.

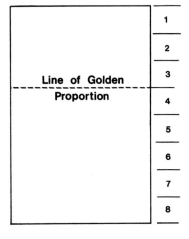

Fig. 2-15. Single words or small groups of words are placed at the golden line of proportion.

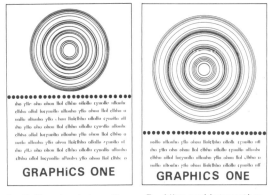

A. Dull and uninteresting.   B. Alive and interesting.

Fig. 2-14. Proportion is controlled by the way the parts are placed on the layout.

Fig. 2-16. Unity is achieved by using not more than two different type styles.

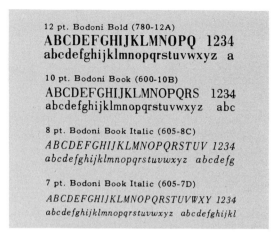

12 pt. Bodoni Bold (780-12A)
ABCDEFGHIJKLMNOPQ 1234
abcdefghijklmnopqrstuvwxyz a

10 pt. Bodoni Book (600-10B)
ABCDEFGHIJKLMNOPQRS 1234
abcdefghijklmnopqrstuvwxyz abc

8 pt. Bodoni Book Italic (605-8C)
ABCDEFGHIJKLMNOPQRSTUV 1234
abcdefghijklmnopqrstuvwxyz abcdefg

7 pt. Bodoni Book Italic (605-7D)
ABCDEFGHIJKLMNOPQRSTUVWXY 1234
abcdefghijklmnopqrstuvwxyz abcdefghijkl

Fig. 2-17. Sample of type styles and sizes from one type family.

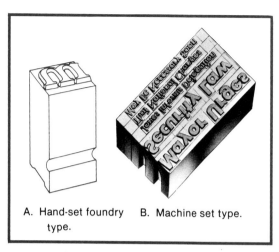

A. Hand-set foundry type.   B. Machine set type.

Fig. 2-18. Hot Composition

COMPOSING THE MESSAGE

After a graphic product is designed, the next step is to **compose** the message. This is the process of making an image that can be reproduced or printed. The image can be a letter, number, symbol, sketch, or photograph. It can be anything else that has a message. The image can be the color and lines an artist uses to design a message. It can be a picture taken by a photographer using a camera and film. It can be type produced by a typist or typesetter (one who sets type) on a machine.

There are two methods by which type can be composed for a graphic message:
1. By hot composition.
2. By cold composition.

In **hot composition,** type can be set by hand or by machine. By hand, each letter is lifted from a tray of type to compose the message. By **machine,** typesetters press the keyboard of a machine that casts the letters and numbers in hot metal. See Fig. 2-18.

In **cold composition,** the images are produced in other ways than with hot metal type forms. This includes linoleum block carving, clip art, and preprinted type. Also included are strike-on (typewriter), photocomposition, and continuous tone photography. These methods are discussed in Chapter 4.

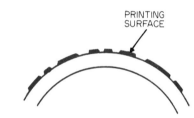

PRINTING SURFACE

Fig. 2-19. In relief printing, the image to be printed is above the plate surface.

PRINTING PROCESSES

Five basic processes are used in printing. These are relief, intaglio, planographic and stencil printing, and office duplicating.

Relief Printing

In relief printing, the printing surface is raised on the printing plate, Fig. 2-19. The plate may be a flat surface or a cylinder. Ink is applied to the printing surface. Paper is then pressed against the printing surface. This makes an impression of the image on the paper. Relief printing is called **letterpress** printing. It is often used for printing newspapers, magazines, and books. Business forms, labels, catalogs, and advertising are also printed by this process.

Intaglio Printing

Intaglio printing is the opposite of relief printing. The printing surface is formed by depressions engraved or etched in the printing plate, Fig. 2-20. The entire plate is covered with ink and then wiped clean. This leaves the depressed areas filled with ink. Paper is pressed against the plate. This lifts the ink from the depressions onto the paper. Intaglio printing works well for long runs and in jobs where the images have fine detail. Paper money, labels, and advertising are often printed by this process.

Planographic Printing

In planographic printing, the printing surface and background are on the same level, Fig. 2-21. A common type of planographic printing is **lithography.** This printing process is based upon the fact that grease and water do not mix. The printing areas of the plate are covered with a greasy substance. The entire plate is then covered with water. The water will not stick to the parts covered with grease. When the ink is rolled over the plate, only the parts covered with grease will take the ink. The rest, covered with moisture, is free of ink. Paper is then pressed against the surface. The inked printing areas are impressed upon it.

A common machine that prints by the planographic process is the **spirit duplicator.** It is also known as a ditto machine and is used in many offices and schools.

Businesses that print by the planographic process often use the **offset lithography** method, Fig. 2-22. The image is first transferred from the plate to a rubber blanket. The paper is then pressed against the rubber blanket. Since ink is transferred to the rubber blanket and then to the paper, the printing plate is made to be read normally. The impression from this plate, when transferred to the rubber blanket, is in reverse. The rubber blanket then transfers the image to the paper. The image again reads correctly. This process is called **photo-offset lithography.** This is because the plates are made by a photographic process, and printing is done by the offset methods. This process is often used for magazines, books and advertisements.

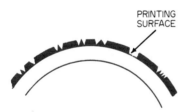

Fig. 2-20.   In intaglio printing, the image to be printed is below the surface.

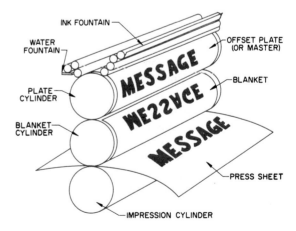

Fig. 2-22.   In offset printing, the image is transferred from plate to blanket to paper.

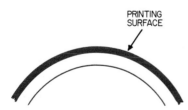

Fig. 2-21.   In planographic printing, the image and the plate surface are on the same level.

Stencil Printing

Mimeograph, office duplicating, and screen process (silk screen) are examples of stencil printing. One of the simplest methods of stenciling is used in making labels for containers. The image is cut in the stencil. Paint or ink is then forced **through** the stencil. This transfers the image to the container.

Some advertisements and some art work are printed by silk screening. A stencil is cut by hand or prepared by a photographic process. It is then fastened to a fine mesh screen stretched tightly over a frame. This blocks out all parts of

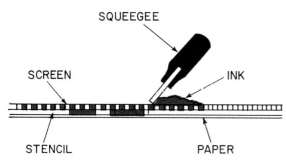

Fig. 2-23. In screen stencil printing, ink is pressed through a screen and stencil to make the print.

the screen except those to be printed. Paint is then moved over the screen and stencil with a rubber blade. This forces the paint through the open part of the screen onto the surface being printed, Fig. 2-23.

Office Duplicating

Offices, schools, and duplicating plants reproduce information by using an office copier. It is quick and easy, and it costs little. One such machine makes copies of original documents by **xerography,** which means dry writing. A toner, instead of ink, is used to create the message. Electrostatic forces are created between the original and the copy paper. This causes the toner to be attracted to the copy paper in the image areas.

Refer to the schematic of the office copier in Fig. 2-24. The original message is placed face down on the platen (1). The reflected light from the message is measured by the photocell which signals the lens (2) to open or close, depending on the light. The oscillating mirror (3) scans the message. It reflects the image through the lens to the mirror (4). The mirror reflects the image to the selenium drum (5). The

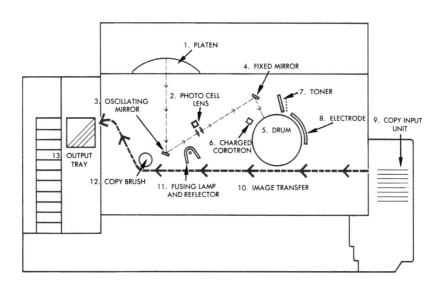

Fig. 2.24. This is how the Xerox 3600 III makes copies of information for offices and schools.

drum receives a positive charge from the corotron (6). The positive charge on the drum has the same pattern as the reflected image. Toner (7), negatively charged, is poured between the drum and electrode (8). The toner is attracted to the positively charged image. Paper from the copy paper input (9) is positively charged. The image is transferred to the paper as it passes under the drum (10). The paper moves to the fusing lamp (11) where the toner is heated and fused to the paper. Excess toner is brushed away by the copy brush (12). Copies are stacked on the output tray (13).

CHOOSING THE PRINTING PROCESS

Printing is done to suit customers' needs for products. This is called **custom work.** Printing also allows the graphic message to be mass produced. Custom work is everything that is done to prepare for printing. Mass production is the printing, folding, and binding work done to complete the job. The printing process chosen will depend largely on how many copies are to be printed. The table in Fig. 2-25 shows which process is best for the number of copies needed. The kind of work to be done is also important. A few thousand copies of a graphic message with many pictures may cost less if

PRINTING PROCESSES

Number of Copies	Process Recommended
1-5	Typing (custom work) with carbon paper
5-150	Type once, then reproduce on office copier such as the Thermofax, Xerox, etc.
10-1000	Spirit duplicator
50-5000	Mimeograph
100-5,000/15,000	Letterpress
500-25,000/250,000	Offset Lithography
50,000-250,000/up	Rotogravure

Fig. 2-25. These are the printing processes suggested according to the number of copies desired.

printed by offset lithography. A message that is all type is often printed by letterpress in many thousands of copies.

PAPER CUTTING

Paper and paper products are the most widely used materials for producing printed messages. There are many types of paper. They run from **fine** to **coarse.** Design and printing methods often dictate the type of paper chosen. They also determine how paper will be cut.

Paper can be ordered in basic sheet sizes. This might be 17″ × 22″ (432 × 559 mm), 20″ × 26″ (508 × 660 mm), and 25″ × 38″ (635 × 965 mm). The printer can then cut the paper to needed sizes.

Paper sizes are indicated in inches (″) or millimeters (mm). The **basic size** is the standard size of any given type of paper. But the basic size is not the only size in which paper is available. For example, bond paper has a basic size of 17″ × 22″ (432 × 559 mm). It is also available in regular sizes of 17″ × 28″ (432 × 711 mm), 19″ × 24″ (483 × 610 mm), 22″ × 34″ (559 × 864 mm), and 24″ × 38″ (610 × 965 mm).

Paper is available in different weights. The weight chosen is decided by the type of product to be printed. Thickness or heaviness of paper is shown by **weight** per ream (500 sheets) of a standard size of paper. One ream of 20 pound (9 kilogram) bond paper in the basic size of 17″ × 22″ has a basic weight of 20 pounds. The 20 pound bond is much like the paper chosen for school textbooks.

The grain direction of the paper may be shown by underlining one of the dimensions on the label. This might be shown as 17″ × <u>22</u>″. The grain direction may also be printed on the label as **grain short** or **grain long.** Grain refers to the fiber direction or structure of the paper. Grain direction must be considered if the paper is to be folded. Paper folded **with the grain** makes a smooth and longer lasting fold. Folding against the grain will crack the paper,

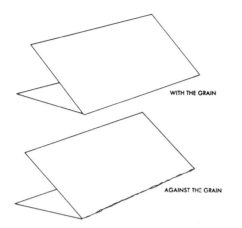

WITH THE GRAIN

AGAINST THE GRAIN

Fig. 2-26. Paper has a clean fold with the grain and a ragged fold against the grain.

Fig. 2-26. The grain normally runs the long dimension of the printed product.

FIGURING PAPER CUTS

Consider this problem: Suppose 550 copies of a letterhead are to be printed on 8½" × 11" (216 × 279 mm) bond paper. How many basic size sheets are required? The basic size of bond paper is 17" × 22" (432 × 559 mm).

First, you must find how many sheets of the desired size can be cut from one basic size sheet. To do this, write the basic sheet size over the desired sheet size and divide. To get an accurate figure that shows the least amount of waste, you must divide both straight up and diagonally. See Fig. 2-27.

As you can see, either two or four desired size sheets can be obtained from one basic size sheet. This will depend on the cutting technique. The first method of cutting shown in Fig. 2-28 has the least amount of waste. It therefore costs less.

Four desired size sheets can be cut from one basic size sheet, and 550 sheets are needed. You must divide 550 by 4 to find the number of basic size sheets required. See Fig. 2-29. When paper cuts are figured, you must add a full sheet if a fraction appears in the final

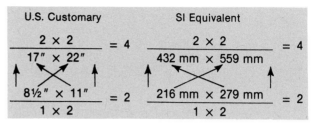

Fig. 2-27. Divide straight up and diagonally.

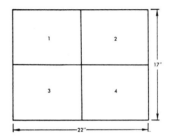

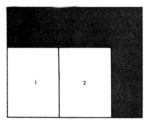

U.S. Customary	SI Equivalent
17 in.	432 mm
22 in.	559 mm

Fig. 2-28. Cut the paper with the least amount of waste.

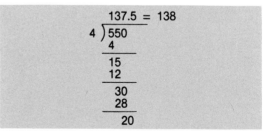

Fig. 2-29. Divide the number obtained from one sheet into the total number desired.

answer. In this case, 138 basic size sheets (17" × 22" or 432 × 559 mm) would be needed to cut 550 sheets that are 8½" × 11" (216 × 279 mm).

PAPER CUTTERS

The paper cutter can accurately cut large sheets of paper into the size sheets needed. Paper cutters range from the small cutter having a hand lever (Fig. 2-30) to the power-driven cutter (Fig. 2-31).

The depth of cut is set by turning the hand wheel on the front of the paper cutter. This sets the distance between the blade and the back fence. This distance may be shown by a measuring tape. If the cutter does not have a measuring tape, a soft wooden measuring stick may be used to find the depth of cut. Place the measuring stick on the bed of the cutter and up against the back fence. Measure the distance from the back fence to the front edge of the paper clamp. The thumbscrew on the hand wheel should be tightened to maintain an accurate setting.

Safety Note

Only one person should operate the paper cutter. Take great care to keep your hands out of the way of the cutter.

The paper to be cut is placed on the **cutter bed.** It is jogged to the back fence and the left side, Fig. 2-32. Lower the paper clamp by turning the paper **clamp wheel** on top of the cutter. The **clamp** will hold the paper securely in place while it is being cut. Lower the **blade** in one motion to obtain a smooth, even cut. Most paper cutters are equipped with a built-in safety device. This device requires the operator to use both hands. After the cut has been made, raise the paper clamp. Remove the paper. Before leaving the paper cutter, lower the clamp to the bed. Remove all scraps. Be sure the power is **off** if you are using an electrically powered cutter.

Safety Note

Do not leave any machine running while it is unattended.

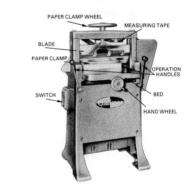

Fig. 2-31.   Hydraulic paper cutter.

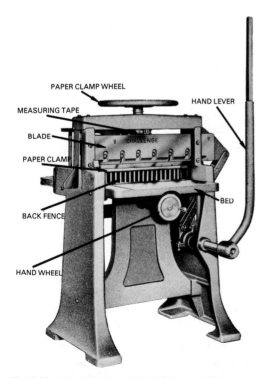

Fig. 2-30.   Hand-lever paper cutter.

Fig. 2-32.   Jog the paper to the left side and back fence.

Chapter **3**

Relief printing, or letterpress, as you have learned, is printing from a raised surface. The printing surface extends above the body that holds it. It is cast in reverse, Fig. 3-1. Hand-set foundry type, machine set type, and carved linoleum block are common printing surfaces.

TYPOGRAPHY

Hand-set foundry type is cast with single characters on separate bodies. The standard height of type in the United States is close to 1 inch or 25 millimeters.

Type is sold in **fonts.** Fonts are complete assortments of any one size and style of type, Fig. 3-2. Each font includes capital letters and lowercase letters. It also includes figures and punctuation marks. There are more of some characters than others in a font. This is because they are used more often in printing. More letter **e**'s, for example, are supplied in a type font than **y**'s. The **e**'s are used more often. Special characters are also included in some type fonts. This would include ligatures (ffi), fractions (¼), diphthongs (ae).

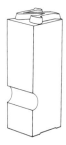

Fig. 3-1.   The relief printing surface is raised above the supporting body.

HOT COMPOSITION AND RELIEF PRINTING

THE PRINTER'S POINT SYSTEM

The line gauge is the printer's rule, Fig. 3-3. The gauge most commonly used is 1 foot or 305

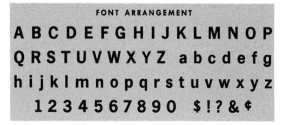

Fig. 3-2.   A font of type.

Fig. 3-3.   Line gauge.

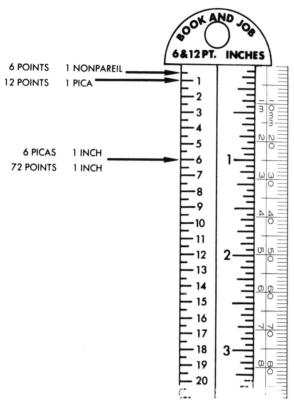

6 POINTS   1 NONPAREIL
12 POINTS   1 PICA

6 PICAS   1 INCH
72 POINTS   1 INCH

Fig. 3-4.   The printer's point system. Compare it to the metric scale.

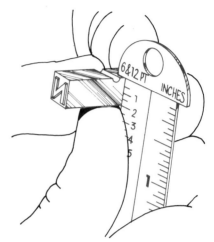

Fig. 3-5.   Measuring type from the nick side to the back.

ABCDEF
1948-C / 48 pt.

ABCdefg
1942-CL / 42 pt.

ABCDEFGhijklmn
1924-CL / 24 pt.

ABCDEFGHIJklmnopqrstu
1916-CL / 16 pt.

ABCDEFGHIJKLMN opqrstuvwxy
1912-CL / 12 pt.

ABCDEFGHIJKLMNOpqrstuvwxyz1234567
1908-CL / 8 pt.

Fig. 3-6.   A series of type.

millimeters long. It has inch or millimeter graduations along one edge and pica divisions along the other. The pica is the standard unit of measure of the printer's point system. It is equal to 1/16 in. (1.6 mm). The pica can be subdivided into twelve equal parts called **points.** The printer's measure is shown in Fig. 3-4.

Type is measured in points from the nick side to the back, Fig. 3-5. Type sizes larger than 72 point are measured in lines. Each line is equal to 1 pica or 12 points. A six-line type, for example, is equal to 6 picas or 72 points.

Typefaces that measure 12 points or smaller are called **text** or **body type.** Text types are used to compose general reading material. This includes newspapers, magazines, and book pages. The typeface you are now reading

is a text typeface. Typefaces larger than 12 points are known as **display types.** The typeface used for chapter headings in this book is a display typeface.

The most commonly used type sizes are 6, 8, 10, 12, 14, 18, 24, 30, 36, 42, 48, 60, and 72 point. The complete size range of one type design is called a **series,** Fig. 3-6. A family of type consists of two or more series. Each has the same general characteristics. The type styles in one family bear the same name. They vary slightly in printed design. The **Century** family includes these styles:

1. Century.
2. *Century Italic.*
3. **Century Bold.**
4. Century Expanded.
5. *Century Expanded Italic.*
6. Century Schoolbook.
7. *Century Schoolbook Italic.*
8. **Century Schoolbook Bold.**
9. Century Schoolbook Expanded.

PARTS OF A HAND-SET FOUNDRY TYPE CHARACTER

The names of the parts of a type character are shown in Fig. 3-7. The **face** is the part of the type character that is printed on the paper. The thick stroke of the typeface is called the **stem.** The thin strokes are called **hairlines. Serifs** may also appear on the typeface. The serif is a short cross line at the end of each unconnected line of the typeface.

The **body** makes up the largest portion of the type. It supports the typeface. The **belly** or front of the type body has a groove across its surface. It is called a **nick.** The nick serves as a guide when type is set. It shows that all the characters are from the same font. It also shows us they are positioned right side up.

At the base of the type body are the **feet.** The feet are flat surfaces on which the type stands. The recessed area between the feet is known as the **groove.** The flat area at the top of the type body is called the **shoulder.** The shoulder supports the relief typeface. The beveled part reaching from the shoulder to the face is called the **neck** or **beard. The counter** is the depressed part that is enclosed by the lines of the typeface. The **fillet** is the rounded corner that connects the letter strokes of a typeface and the serifs. Fillets do not appear on all typefaces. Any part of a typeface that extends over the edge of the type body is called a **kern,** Fig. 3-8. A kern may be found on such characters as the italic letters "f" and "i".

CLASSIFICATIONS OF TYPEFACES

There are seven different kinds of typefaces. They are Old Style, Modern, Sans Serif, Square Serif, Text, Cursive, and Occasional. Each kind has unique design features. Knowing the different kinds of type helps people choose the right type for their needs. Typesetting companies have books that show the different kinds of typefaces, display faces, and sizes of type.

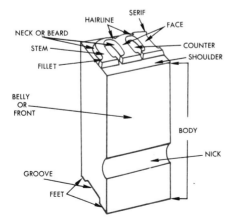

Fig. 3-7.   Parts of a hand-set foundry type character.

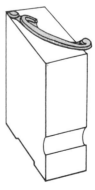

Fig. 3-8.   A kerned piece of hand-set foundry type.

OLD STYLE TYPE

Old Style typefaces are generally used when legibility and readability are important factors of design, which is the reason they are often used for text composition. Old Style typefaces have only slight variations in the thick and thin strokes of the letter. Rounded serifs and fillets are also common characteristics of this classification.

MODERN TYPE

Modern typefaces have considerable contrast between the thick and thin strokes of the letter and are identified by fine serifs with no fillets. The modern types are used in advertising, book composition, and commercial printing.

SANS SERIF TYPES

"Sans" is a French word which means without. Sans serif type, therefore, is type that does not have serifs. These typefaces have little or no variation in the thickness of the letter strokes. They are often used for display advertising, headlines, and captions in books and magazines.

OCCASIONAL TYPE

Occasional types are also called decorative or novelty types. These are the attention-getters used in advertising. Each typeface in this classification has individual and distinct characteristics for expressing a particular mood.

SQUARE SERIF TYPES

Square serif types can easily be identified by the square serif. The serifs have the same weight or thickness as the letter strokes. The letter strokes of square serif types have little or no variation in thickness. Square serif types are durable and are used mainly for display composition, headlines, and short pieces of text material.

TEXT TYPES

Text typefaces are sometimes referred to as Old English. The letters resemble those used by the scribes and are patterned after the earliest types used by Gutenberg. Text types are difficult to read because of the complex design of the letter strokes. These types are used primarily for announcements of special occasions and for Christmas greeting cards. Text types should not be composed in forms of all uppercase (capital) letters.

CURSIVE TYPE

Cursive types resemble handwriting and are often called script types. Many cursive types have uniform line weight while others have both thick and thin letter strokes. Cursive types are used for special effects in advertising and for announcements and invitations. Because they are sometimes difficult to read, cursive type forms should not be composed in all capital letters.

HOT COMPOSITION

Hot composition, as you have learned, uses molten metal. It is cast into relief printing type characters or symbols. The two methods of hot composition are (1) hand-set foundry type, Fig. 3-9, and (2) machine-set type, Fig 3-10.

Type characters are prepared by heating a metal alloy of lead, antimony, and tin to a molten state. It is then cast in prepared typeface molds. Each typeface mold has a symbol cavity. It is in reverse of the printed symbol. After the alloy has been cast in the mold, it is allowed to cool. It hardens in the shape and

Fig. 3-9. The image can be generated by using hand-set foundry type.

design of the mold. The cast symbol, when removed from the mold, has a raised surface that carries the ink. This surface is supported by the body of the type, Fig. 3-11.

HAND-SET FOUNDRY TYPE

Hand-set foundry type characters or symbols are made on individual type bodies. They are produced by hot metal production plants called **foundries.** A complete font of type is stored in a **California Job Case.** The case is made with separate places for each character. Each character is taken from the case by hand and placed in a **composing stick,** Fig. 3-9. This operation is known as composition. The type, after use, must be placed back into the California Job Case by hand. It is then ready to be reused to produce new printing images.

THE CALIFORNIA JOB CASE

The California Job Case is divided into three major sections, Fig. 3-12. Each type

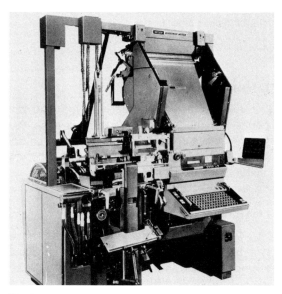

Fig. 3-10. Typesetting machine.

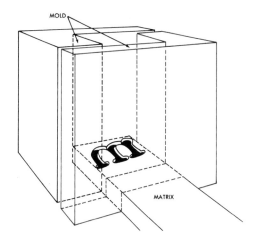

Fig. 3-11. Type is cast by pouring molten metal into a mold.

ffi	fl	5-EM	4-EM	'	k		1	2	3	4	5	6	7	8		$						
j		b	c	d		e		i	s	f	g		ff	9		A	B	C	D	E	F	G
?													fi	0								
!		l	m	n	h		o	y	p	w		,	EM QUADS	EM QUADS		H	I	K	L	M	N	O
z																						
x		v	u	t	3-EM SPACES		a	r			;	:	2-EM AND 3-EM QUADS			P	Q	R	S	T	V	W
q											.	-				X	Y	Z	J	U	&	ffl

Fig. 3-12. The lay of the California Job Case.

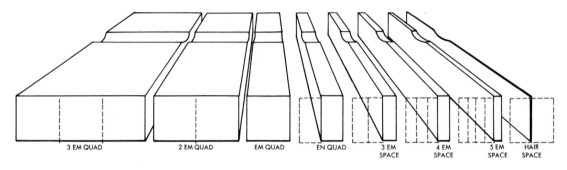

Fig. 3-13. Spaces and quads as related to each other in size.

character is stored in a special place within the case. It is important that letters are always stored in their proper places.

The right hand one-third of the case holds the CAPITAL letters. These letters are arranged in the order of the alphabet, except J and U which follow the Z.

The lowercase letters are placed in the left two-thirds of the case. They are arranged according to how often they are used. The letters most used are located near the middle of the case. Places for numbers, punctuation marks, spaces, quads, and ligatures are mixed in with those for lowercase letters.

Spaces and Quads

Words must be separated in a line of type set by hand. To do this, the typesetter places metal spaces between the words. Spaces are pieces of type metal that are shorter than type. They have no printing face. These pieces of metal are called spaces and quads, Fig. 3-13.

Demon Characters

As you look at a piece of type, you will notice that the typeface is cast in reverse. For this reason, some characters appear to be different letters than they really are. These are called the demon characters, Fig. 3-14.

Ligatures

Two or more connected typefaces on one type body is called a ligature, Fig. 3-15. Typical examples found in most California Job Cases are fi, ff, fl, ffi, and ffl.

TYPE COMPOSITION

The **type bank,** Fig. 3-16, serves as a storage unit for California Job Cases. Most type banks also provide a slanted work surface. The typesetter can place the case on this surface while setting type. See Figs. 3-17 and 3-18.

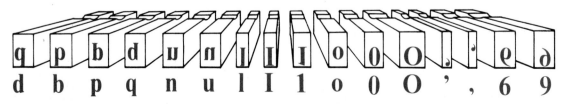

Fig. 3-14. The demon characters.

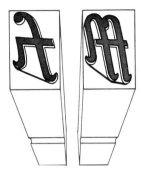

Fig. 3-15. Ligatures have two or more connected typefaces on one type body.

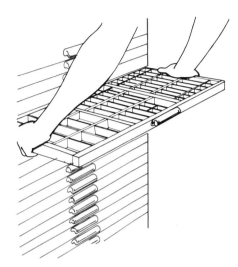

Fig. 3-17. Removing the California Job Case from the type bank.

Fig. 3-16. Type bank with lead and slug rack.

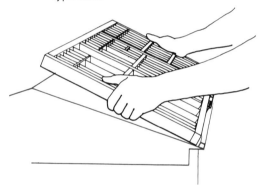

Fig. 3-18. Placing the case on the slanted type bank surface.

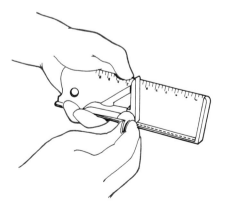

Here is how to begin setting type. First, adjust the composing stick to the desired pica measure, Fig. 3-19. Select a slug that is the same length as the line to be set. Insert it in the composing stick. **Leads** and **slugs** are metal strips of spacing material. They are placed between lines of type. Slugs are generally six

Fig. 3-19. Adjusting the composing stick to the desired measure.

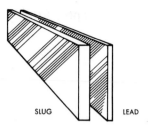

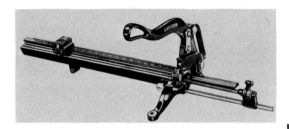

SLUG   LEAD

Fig. 3-20. Slugs are six points in thickness. Leads are two points in thickness.

Fig. 3-21. Lead and rule cutter.

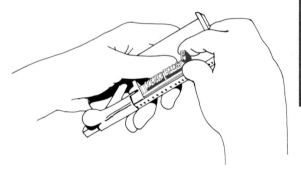

Fig. 3-22. Composition of hand-set foundry type.

points in thickness. Leads are two points in thickness, Fig. 3-20. Leads and slugs may be cut to the desired length on the lead and rule cutter, Fig. 3-21.

Hold the composing stick in the left hand. Hold it at a slight angle so the type will not fall out. Use the right hand to pick up the type from the case. Place the type in the composing stick. Left-handed persons may use the left hand to pick up the type. The right hand holds the composing stick.

As you pick up each piece of type, note the position of the nick and the typeface. The type

must be placed in the composing stick from left to right. The nick is up and the typeface pointing out. The thumb catches and holds each piece of type as it is placed in the composing stick, Fig. 3-22.

Justifying the Line

If the line of type characters does not fill the measure, it must be justified in the stick. Justifying is the spacing out of lines of type so that each line is of equal length. Each line must be equally tight in the composing stick. To place all the spaces at the end of the lines would make an uneven right-hand margin, Fig. 3-23. Figure 3-24 shows how lines look when correctly spaced.

If the line of type characters does not fill the measure it must be justified in the stick. Justification is the process of spacing-out lines of type so that each line is of equal length and equally tight in the composing stick. Justification at the end of the lines results in an uneven right-hand margin.

Fig. 3-23. Justifying by placing all the spaces at the ends of the lines gives an uneven right-hand margin.

Justification of type forms that are to have a flush left and right margin is accomplished by regulating the spacing between the words. This is called spacing-in or spacing-out. The last word in the line must extend to the end of the line measure. Some words may have to be divided between syllables. A hyphen is placed after the syllable of the word at the end of the line and the remaining syllables of the word are then set in the next line.

Fig. 3-24. Justifying by spacing between the words makes even lines.

When there is not enough spacing between words, the words run together. They are hardtoread.Thislineoftypedoesnothaveenough spacing between words. But too much space between words produces a large white space called a **lake.** If too much spacing between words appears for several lines, white streaks called **rivers** show up. See Fig. 3-25.

Besides spacing-in or spacing-out, a line of type must sometimes be letter-spaced. This also helps the words fill the measure and be justified. **Letter-spacing** is the placing of spaces between the letters of words. Unless there is a special reason for it, do not letter-space. It may cause the line to look stretched out. Letter-spacing is also useful when letters or words are to be used in a certain shape or to create a desired effect. Never l e t t e r-s p a c e lowercase words.

Center the line of type in the composing stick. Do this by placing an equal amount of spacing material on each side of the type. When centering type, keep the small spaces on the inside of the line, Fig. 3-26.

Justify each line of type before starting the next line of type. Before starting the next line, place a lead in the composing stick. It should be equal in length to the measure being set, Fig. 3-27. If you want to place more than two points between lines, you can insert more than one lead.

Printer's rule are type-high strips of metal which print on the paper. Rule can be set in type form. They print as lines in a line of type and as borders around a form, Fig. 3-28. The mitering

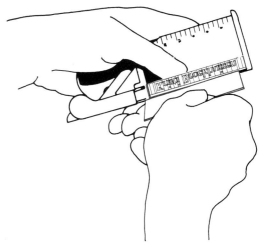

Fig. 3-27. Place a lead on top of the completed line before starting the next line.

Too much space between words, on the other hand, produces a large white space called a **lake.** If too much spacing between words continues for several lines, white streaks called **rivers** may appear.

Fig. 3-25. Lakes and rivers are caused by too much spacing between words.

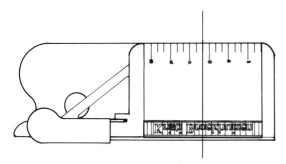

Fig. 3-26. A line of type is centered in the composing stick.

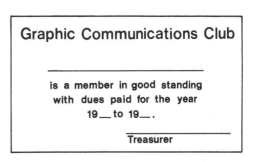

Graphic Communications Club

_____

is a member in good standing with dues paid for the year 19__ to 19__ .

_____

Treasurer

Fig. 3-28. Rule can be used to print lines and borders.

Fig. 3-29. A mitering machine.

Fig. 3-30. A galley is used to store type forms.

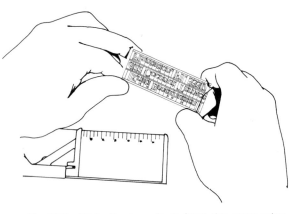

Fig. 3-31. Slide the type form from the composing stick onto the galley.

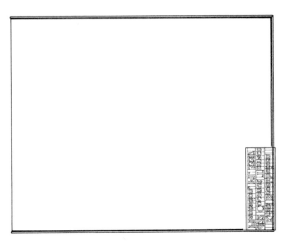

Fig. 3-32. Position the form in the corner of the galley.

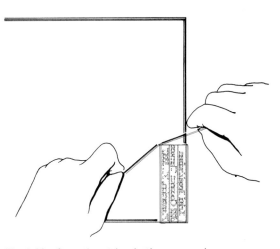

Fig. 3-33. Start the string in the exposed corner.

machine, Fig. 3-29, is used to cut or miter the rule at different angles. Rule for borders around a type form should be mitered at 45° angles on both ends.

For ease of handling, do not fill the composing stick more than three-fourths full of type. Place a slug in the composing stick when you finish.

TYING A TYPE FORM

A galley, Fig. 3-30, is used to store or carry type forms. Place the galley on the slanted work surface of the type bank. The open end should be to one side.

Place the composing stick in the galley. Pinch the lines of type between the thumbs and index fingers. Carefully slide the form from the composing stick onto the galley. See Fig. 3-31. Place the form in the galley, Fig. 3-32.

Cut a piece of string long enough to go around the type form four or five times. Start the string in the exposed corner, Fig. 3-33. Wind it clockwise around the form. The first winding should overlap the beginning end, Fig. 3-34. This binds the string in position. Keep winding the string around the type form. Tuck the end of the string under the windings in the open corner. Use a **makeup rule** to do this, Fig. 3-35.

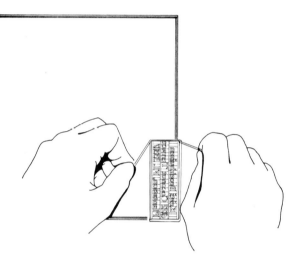

Fig. 3-34. Overlap the string end with the first winding.

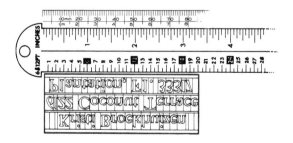

Fig. 3-35. Use the makeup rule to tuck the end of the string under the windings.

PROOFING A TYPE FORM

The proof press, Fig. 3-36, is used to pull proofs of composed type forms. **Proofs** are impressions of the type. They are read to check for errors in typesetting. The **brayer,** Fig. 3-37, is an ink roller on the proof press. It inks the printing surface of relief forms for proofing.

To "pull" a proof, place the galley on the bed of the proof press. It should be at a slight angle. The open end of the galley should be toward the cylinder. In this slanted position, the type form will be supported by two galley sides.

Fig. 3-36. Relief forms are proofed in a proof press.

Fig. 3-37. The brayer is used to ink relief forms for proofing.

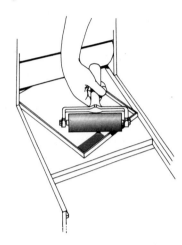

Fig. 3-38. Ink the type form to be proofed.

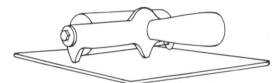

Fig. 3-39. Place the brayer on its feet to keep the roller from becoming flat or sticking to the ink plate.

This prevents the type from being pushed off its feet as the cylinder is passed over the form.

To ink the proof press, place a small amount of ink on the ink plate. Spread the ink evenly over the ink plate with the brayer. Then ink the type form. Do this by rolling the brayer lightly over the type, Fig. 3-38. Replace the brayer on the ink plate. Rest it on its feet, as shown in Fig. 3-39.

After inking the form, carefully place one sheet of proof paper on the form. Roll the cylinder over the form once. This transfers ink to the paper. Carefully lift the paper from the form. Inspect the proof to be sure it is clear and readable. Now clean the type. Moisten a cloth pad with solvent. Use it to wipe the type. Remove the galley from the proof press. Replace the galley on the slanted surface of the type bank.

∧	MAKE INDICATED CORRECTION IN MARGIN
Stet	RETAIN CROSSED OUT LETTER OR WORD
⫫⫫⫫	UNEVENLY SPACED
no ¶	NO PARAGRAPH
¶	MAKE PARAGRAPH
tr	TRANSPOSE LETTERS OR WORDS INDICATED
Dr	DELETE
⊄	LINE THROUGH CAP MEANS LOWER CASE
ϱ	UPSIDE DOWN, REVERSE
⊂	CLOSE UP, NO SPACE
#	INSERT SPACE HERE
⌐	MOVE TO THE LEFT
⌐	MOVE TO THE RIGHT
sp	SPELL OUT
w.f.	WRONG FONT
Qu.?	QUESTION, IS THIS RIGHT?
l.c.	PUT IN LOWER CASE
s.c.	PUT IN SMALL CAPITALS
caps.	PUT IN CAPITALS
ital	CHANGE TO ITALIC
≡	BENEATH LETTER OR WORD MEANS CAPS
—	BENEATH LETTER OR WORD MEANS ITALICS
⋏	INSERT COMMA
⊙	INSERT PERIOD
bf	BOLD FACE TYPE

Fig. 3-40. Sample proof marks and their meanings.

Safety Note

Place cloths that contain solvent and ink in metal safety cans.

Carefully read the proof. Check it against the original copy. Errors are marked on the proof copy by using symbols called **proof marks,** Fig. 3-40. Figure 3-41 shows how corrections are marked on the proof.

Most corrections can be made with the type form in the galley. Suppose a letter is to be

Carefully read the proof, checking it against original copy, errors are marked on the Proof Copy by using symbols called proof marks.

The proof marks are usually placed in the margin either on left right or left side of the error. A line may not be drawn from the proof mark to the specific location of the error.

Fig. 3-41. Proof marks are used to correct errors.

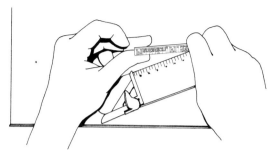

Fig. 3-43. Place the line of type to be corrected into the composing stick with slugs on each side to hold the line.

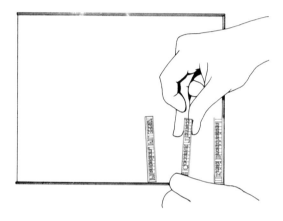

Fig. 3-42. Separate the line of type containing the error.

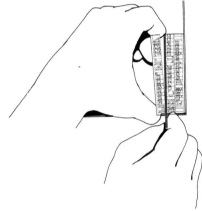

Fig. 3-44. Remove the slugs that were added when the line to be corrected was taken out of the type form.

replaced by a letter of equal width. Carefully remove the letter and insert the correct letter. Suppose a letter or space is to be replaced by a letter or space that is not the same width. Then the line of type is returned to the composing stick. See Figs. 3-42 and 3-43.

After making corrections, return the line to the galley. Place it in its proper position in the type form. Remove the extra slugs that were used, Fig. 3-44. Tie the form with string and pull another proof. Check the second proof for errors.

To store the type form for future use, place the galley in the galley rack. The open end should be out. This shows that there is a type form on the galley. When the galley is empty, it

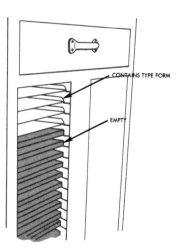

Fig. 3-45. Storage of galleys in the galley rack of the imposing table.

should be placed in the galley rack upside down. The open end should be inward. See Fig. 3-45.

LOCKUP TOOLS AND EQUIPMENT

A relief printing image must be locked up so it can be placed in position in the press. Lockup means clamping the lines of type or other relief form in a **chase.** Seven basic tools and pieces of equipment are used in the lockup.

1. The size of the **chase,** Fig. 3-46, varies with the press size being used.
2. **Quoins,** Fig. 3-47, are locking devices. They expand and help tighten a relief form in the chase.

3. The **quoin key** is used to expand the quoin.
4. The wooden **planing block,** Fig. 3-48, is placed on top of the relief form and gently tapped. This levels the locked up relief surface. It makes all characters the same height.
5. The **imposing table,** Fig. 3-49, is a smooth, flat top table used as a lockup surface.

Fig. 3-48. Planing block.

Fig. 3-49. Imposing table with storage space for furniture.

Fig. 3-46. A chase is used to lock up type forms.

Fig. 3-47. High speed quoin and quoin key.

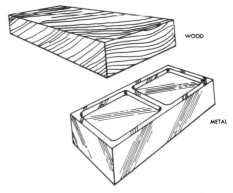

Fig. 3-50. Furniture is made of either wood or metal.

6. **Furniture,** Fig. 3-50, is made of wood or metal. Wooden furniture is used to lock up press relief forms. The metal furniture is used to lock up rubber stamp forms where heat is a factor. Furniture is measured in length and width by picas. The length is stamped on the ends of the furniture. It is shown in five-pica multiples from 10 to 60. The width of furniture is 2 picas, 3 picas, 4 picas, 5 picas, 6 picas, 8 picas, and 10 picas.

7. **Reglets,** Fig. 3-51, are measured in 6 and 12 point thicknesses. Reglets are used in lockup to fill spaces that are too small for wooden furniture.

METHODS OF LOCKUP

There are two common methods of lockup. One is the chaser method. The other is the furniture within furniture method. See Fig. 3-52. The furniture within furniture method is useful only when the line length of the relief form is in multiples of five picas. If the line length is not in five-pica multiples, the chaser method is used. See Figs. 3-53 and 3-54.

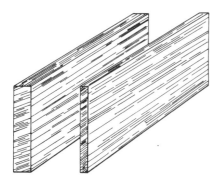

Fig. 3-51. Reglets are 6 and 12 points in thickness.

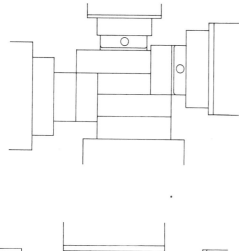

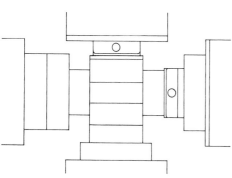

Fig. 3-52. Two methods of lockup for relief printing.

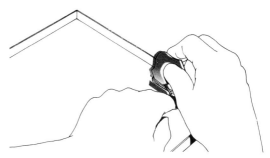

Fig. 3-53. Measure the length of the form to determine the method of lockup to be used.

Fig. 3-54. Position the type form in the center of the chase.

THE PLATEN PRESS

In relief printing, the platen press is used to produce the printed message. There are three types of platen presses:

1. Hand-lever press, Fig. 3-55.
2. Power-driven press, Fig. 3-56.
3. Automatic press, Fig. 3-57.

Parts of the Press

The main operating parts of the platen press are shown in Fig. 3-58. The purpose of each part is described.

Fig. 3-57. Automatic platen press used for jobs that run for a long time.

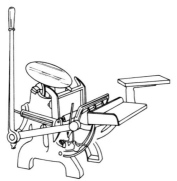

Fig. 3-55. Hand-lever platen press used for small runs and small jobs.

Fig. 3-56. Power-driven platen press used for small jobs that run for a limited time.

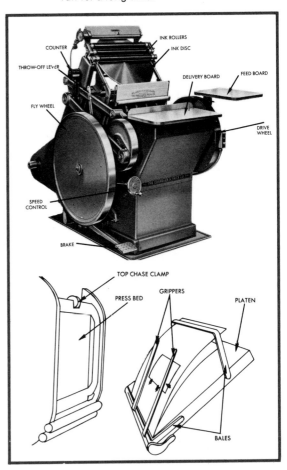

Fig. 3-58. Parts of the power-driven platen press (part B shows details of pressboard).

1. The **feedboard** holds the paper stock that is to be printed.
2. The **delivery board** is a surface for piling the printed paper that is removed from the press.
3. The **grippers** hold the paper to the platen after the impression is made. This prevents the paper from sticking to the face of the relief form.
4. The **platen** is a smooth, flat surface. It holds the paper to receive the impression from the relief form.
5. The **throw-off lever** regulates the impression of the platen press. When the throw-off lever is pushed away from the operator, the relief form and the paper do not make contact. Therefore, no impression is made. When the throw-off lever is pulled toward the operator, contact is made between the form and the paper.
6. The **fly wheel** keeps the press running smoothly and evenly.
7. The **drive wheel** transfers the power from the motor to drive the press.
8. The **brake** slows or stops the press. Pressure on the brake is applied with the left foot.
9. The **ink disc** supplies the rollers with fresh ink before each impression.
10. The **press bed** is a smooth, flat surface. It holds the locked up chase in position.
11. The **ink rollers** transfer the ink from the ink disc to the relief printing form before each impression.
12. The **counter** counts the number of printed impressions.
13. The **bales** hold the drawsheet and the packing sheets to the surface of the platen.
14. The **speed control** regulates the operating speed of the press.
15. The **top chase clamp** holds the chase to the bed of the press.

The platen press must be oiled to run smoothly. Oiling also reduces bearing wear. Turn the press over by hand until the rollers rest on the ink disc. Begin oiling at the feed board.

Work around the press, oiling each bearing. Check with your instructor to find out whether the press needs oiling.

Safety Note

Under no circumstances should the press be oiled or adjusted while it is running.

PREPARING THE PLATEN PRESS

Dressing the press means to position the drawsheet and the packing on the surface of the platen. The **drawsheet** is made of a tough, oily, manila-colored paper. It is called **tympan paper.** The packing generally consists of (1) one piece of pressboard and (2) a specified number of book paper sheets. These sheets are called **hanger sheets,** Fig. 3-59. The amount of packing varies with the adjustment of the platen. Check with your instructor for the proper amount of packing to be used.

Cut the drawsheet to a size that is 4 in. to 5 in. (102 to 127 mm) wider than the sheet to be printed. It should be long enough to extend under both bales. Cut the hanger sheets to a size large enough to cover the platen. It should not extend under the bales. Raise the top and bottom bales. Place the drawsheet under the lower bale. Lock it in position. Now place the

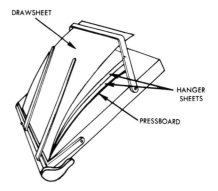

Fig. 3-59. Dressing the platen.

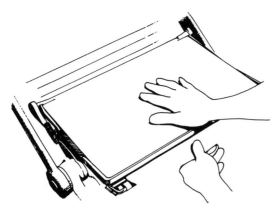

Fig. 3-60. Stretch the drawsheet and lock it under the top bale with the heel of the hand.

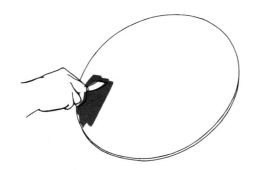

Fig. 3-61. Place the ink on the left side of the ink disc.

pressboard and hanger sheets under the drawsheet. Stretch the drawsheet tightly over the platen by placing both hands on the drawsheet. Press down and pull up toward the top bale. Lock the top bale in the same motion using the heel of the hand, Fig. 3-60. Tear off any excess paper that extends beyond the bales.

The press should be inked before the locked up chase is placed in the press. The press should be in the **off** position. The rollers should be at their lowest point of travel. Place a small amount of ink on the left side of the ink disc, Fig. 3-61. Use an ink spatula to scrape the ink from the surface. Do not dig holes in the ink. This will cause the ink to dry out.

Safety Note

Roll up shirt sleeves and tuck in shirt tail before turning press on. Remove jewelry, such as rings and watches.

Start the press on a slow speed. Allow the rollers to distribute the ink evenly over the surface of the ink disc. Stop the press with the rollers at their lowest point of travel. With the rollers in this position, the bed is fully exposed.

Place the locked up chase in the bed of the press. The quoins should be to the top right. Rest the bottom of the chase against the lugs. Lift the top chase clamp. Push the chase back against the press bed. Lower the top chase clamp until it firmly engages the top of the chase, Fig. 3-62.

Check the **gripper** position. If the grippers are in front of the relief form, they will crush the type. Move the grippers by loosening the bolt. Slide them along the gripper bar, Fig. 3-63. Mover the grippers away from the form and tighten the bolt. Stand in front of the press and double-check the gripper position in relation to the form.

Turn the press on. Let it run slowly with the throw-off lever in the **off** position. Let the press

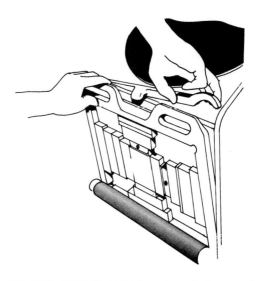

Fig. 3-62. Place the locked up chase in the press bed.

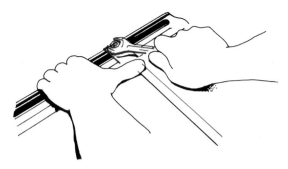

Fig. 3-63. Loosening the bolt on the gripper.

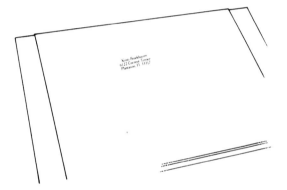

Fig. 3-64. The kiss impression should show the type outline.

turn over several times. Then pull the throw-off lever to the **on** position. Allow the relief form to come in contact with the drawsheet only once.

After one impression on the drawsheet is made, push the throw-off lever to the **off** position. Stop the press with the rollers at the lowest point of travel. In this position the platen is fully opened. The print on the drawsheet can now be inspected. This is called the **kiss impression.** The impression on the drawsheet should be clear enough to show the outline of the relief form, Fig. 3-64. If no impression appears on the drawsheet, there is not enough packing. Add one more sheet of book paper. Pull the kiss impression again. Add only one sheet of book paper at a time. If the impression is dark and heavy, there is too much packing. This may damage the type. Remove some of the book paper hanger sheets.

The guides for paper are called **gauge pins,** Fig. 3-65. They are placed in the drawsheet to hold the paper in the correct position during the impression. Three gauge pins are usually used. Two are located at the bottom of the platen. One is on the left hand side.

If the image is to be centered on the paper, follow this procedure. Place the edge of the sheet to be printed on the edge of the impression on the drawsheet. On the sheet of paper, mark the length of the longest line of type. See Fig. 3-66.

Divide the remaining amount in half to determine the side margins. Fold the edge of

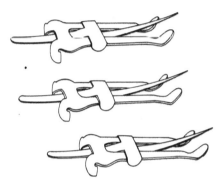

Fig. 3-65. Gauge pins hold the paper during the impression.

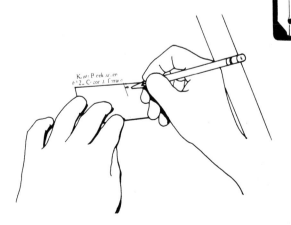

Fig. 3-66. On the paper, mark the length of the longest line.

the paper over to the mark on the paper and crease, Fig. 3-67. Now place the fold crease on the right side or end of the longest line of the impression on the drawsheet. The edge of the sheet should run parallel with the impression. Use the paper as a straightedge to scribe a pencil line along the edge of the paper, Fig. 3-68. Repeat this process to determine the placement of the two bottom gauge pins. Use the widest part of the impression on the drawsheet when marking the paper.

Suppose the impression is not to be centered on the sheet. The margins can then be found by measuring and then marking the drawsheet. On the drawsheet, mark the actual position of the gauge pins. To do this, place a piece of paper on the scribed lines. The two bottom pins should be located about one-fourth the length of the sheet in from each side. Place an "X" at these points. The position of the gauge pin on the left side should be marked with an "X" about one-fourth the distance up from the bottom of the sheet, Fig. 3-69.

Start the point of the gauge pin through the drawsheet about ¼ in. (6 mm) away from the scribed line. This should be at the point marked with the "X". Push the gauge pin down about ½ in. (12 mm). The gauge pin must be kept from

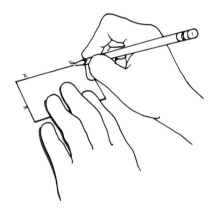

Fig. 3-69. Mark the position of the gauge pins.

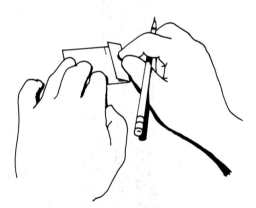

Fig. 3-67. Fold the paper to the mark and make a crease.

Fig. 3-68. Scribe a line along the edge of the paper.

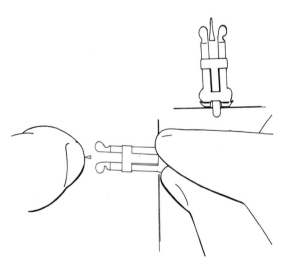

Fig. 3-70. Bring the point of the gauge pins back through the surface of the drawsheet.

moving during printing. Bring the point back through the surface of the drawsheet. Push the drawsheet down with your thumb in front of the gauge pin. Now bring the point back through the surface, Fig. 3-70. Keep pushing the pin down until the small feet on the bottom of the gauge pin are on the scribed line. Check the position of the tongue of the gauge pin. Make sure it will not touch the type during impression. Repeat this process to position each of the three gauge pins.

You must prevent offset of ink on the back of the printed sheets. To do this, remove the wet ink on the drawsheet. Use a cloth with solvent to remove the ink. Then dust with talcum powder.

PLATEN PRESS MAKEREADY AND PRODUCTION

Before production can start, the last adjustments must be made. This is called **makeready.** The amount of packing is adjusted so there are no high or low areas in the impression.

Makeready

Place a sheet of paper to be printed against the gauge pins on the platen. Put the throw-off lever in the **off** position. Start the press on a slow speed. After it turns several times, pull the throw-off lever to the **on** position. Allow the relief form to contact the paper once.

After you have made one impression, return the throw-off lever to the **off** position. Stop the press. The rollers should always be at the lowest point of travel when the press is stopped. Remove the paper from the gauge pins. Inspect for three things.

1. Impression location.
2. Amount of impression.
3. Ink coverage.

Measure with a line gauge to check the location of the impression on the paper. The impression should be located on the printing stock as it was planned. Adjust the gauge pins to correct the location of the impression.

Remember that **you** move and readjust the paper. The form remains in place.

The impression on the paper should print clearly. Too little packing behind the drawsheet will cause a light, spotty impression. See Fig. 3-71. Thicken the packing under the drawsheet to improve the evenness of the impression. One sheet of tissue paper often provides the needed extra packing. Never add more than one sheet of book paper.

Too much packing will cause a raised impression on the back of the paper. This may damage the relief form. Run your finger over the back of the paper. If you can feel the impression, reduce the thickness of the packing sheets.

Suppose the ink is too heavy on the press. The impression will smudge very easily during the finger test, Fig. 3-72. Rub your finger over

Fig. 3-71. A light, spotty print usually shows the need for more packing.

Fig. 3-72. An easily smudged print shows that there is too much ink.

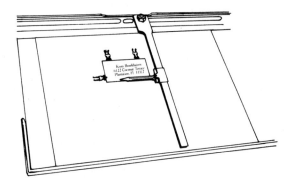

Fig. 3-73. Position a gripper and gripper finger to prevent the paper from sticking to the type.

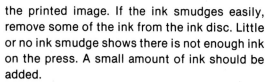

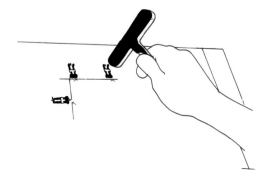

Fig. 3-74. Set the pins by gently tapping them with a quoin key.

the printed image. If the ink smudges easily, remove some of the ink from the ink disc. Little or no ink smudge shows there is not enough ink on the press. A small amount of ink should be added.

Print another sheet to check your location, packing, and ink adjustments. Check the impression for the same three points just described. Repeat this procedure until there is a good impression on the paper.

During printing, the paper often sticks to the surface of the relief form after the impression. This causes the paper to be pulled from the gauge pins as the platen opens. To prevent this, place a gripper over the margin of the sheet being printed. Use a gripper finger if there is not enough margin for the gripper, Fig. 3-73. Position the gripper so that the relief form or the gauge pins are not crushed during the impression.

Double check the location of the printed impression on the paper. If it is right, set the gauge pins firmly in the drawsheet. This keeps them from slipping during production. Do this by gently tapping the gauge pins with a quoin key. Imbed the two small points on each pin into the drawsheet, Fig. 3-74.

Production

Set the impression counter at zero. Place the paper to be printed on the feed board.

Fig. 3-75. With the right hand, pick up the sheet to be printed.

Remove all other tools and materials from the press.

Start the press at a slow speed. The throw-off lever should be in the **off** position. With the right hand, pick up one piece of paper from the feed board. The thumb should be under the paper and the fingers on top, Fig. 3-75. As the platen opens, place the paper first against the bottom pins. Then slide it over to the left side pin, Fig. 3-76. Withdraw your hand as the platen begins to close.

Pull the throw-off lever to the **on** position. The printed sheet is removed with the fingers of the left hand as the platen opens after the impression has been made. See Fig. 3-77. The

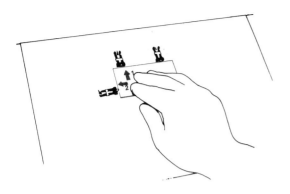

Fig. 3-76. Place the sheet against the bottom pins, and then slide it over to the side pin.

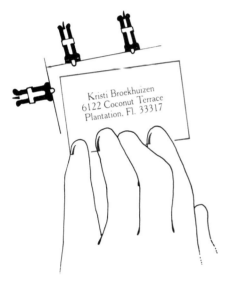

Fig. 3-77. Remove the printed sheet from the pins with the left hand.

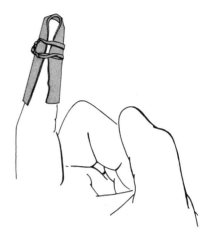

Fig. 3-78. A sandpaper finger will prevent ink smudging when you remove the printed sheet.

> **Safety Note**
> Only one person should operate the press at one time. If you must leave the press, push the throw-off lever to the **off** position. Stop the press. **Always** stop the press before making any adjustments.

Speed is not important to the beginning press operator. Take your time. Think about feeding and delivering the paper in a smooth and even way. Speed and skill will come with experience.

CLEANING THE PLATEN PRESS

When a production run is done, the press must be cleaned.

> **Safety Note**
> Do all cleaning with the press power to the **off** position.

Begin cleaning by removing the chase from the bed of the press. Place the chase on the imposing table. Remove the ink from the surface of the relief form.

sheet then is placed on the delivery board. If at any time a sheet is not properly positioned in the gauge pins, push the throw-off lever to the **off** position. This will prevent printing on the drawsheet.

If the fingers touch the printed area after the impression, they may smudge the ink. To prevent this, use a sandpaper finger, Fig. 3-78.

When operating the press, stand erect. Stand squarely on both feet at the delivery board.

Remove the gauge pins. Lift the bales and remove the drawsheet and packing. Be sure to lock the bales back in position on the platen.

Moisten a clean cloth with solvent. Fold it neatly into a pad. Use it to clean the ink from the ink disc, Fig. 3-79. Turn the fly wheel with your hand. Stop when the rollers are up in a position just below the ink disc where they can be cleaned. Clean the ink from the first roller, Fig. 3-80. Keep turning the fly wheel by hand

Fig. 3-79. Clean the ink disc with a cloth dampened with solvent.

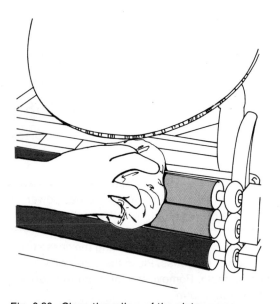

Fig. 3-80. Clean the rollers of the platen press.

and clean the rest of the rollers. Make sure that the ends of the rollers are also cleaned. You may need to repeat this process several times before all the ink is removed from the press. Clean the ink spatula. Cover the ink that was used.

Safety Note

Cloths that contain solvent and ink should be placed in metal safety cans.

Leave the press with the throw-off lever in the **off** position. The rollers should be at their lowest point of travel. Do not leave the rollers on the ink disc. This causes them to become flat at the point of contact over a period of time.

TYPE DISTRIBUTION

Distribution is the process of returning the type to their places in the California Job Case. Place the chase on the imposing table. Loosen the quoins. Return all quoins, reglets, furniture, and the chase to their proper storage places. Slide the form into the corner of a galley, Fig. 3-81. The nicks should be toward the open end. Place the galley on the slanted surface of the type bank.

Remove the proper typecase from the type bank. Place it on the slanted surface next to the

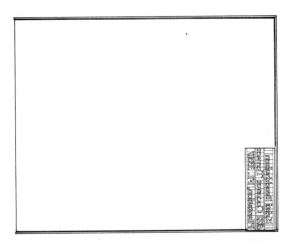

Fig. 3-81. Place the form in the corner of the galley.

galley. Compare the size, face, and nick position of the type in the form with the type in the case before you distribute the type.

Select the first one or two lines of the type form. Carefully move it away from the remaining portion of the form, Fig. 3-82. A lead or slug must be on the top and bottom of the selected line. Pinch the line together by putting pressure on all four sides. You can then lift the line without the pieces of type dropping out.

Transfer the type to the left hand if you are right-handed (or to the right hand if you are left-handed). The type should be held between the thumb and second finger. The index finger should be under the line for support, Fig. 3-83.

Distribute type by starting from the right-hand side. (A left-handed person starts from the left side.) Pick up a word or syllable at a time between the index finger and thumb. Separate the individual pieces of type. Do this by rocking the pieces back and forth, Fig. 3-84. Read each letter, space, or quad. Then drop it in the proper

compartment of the California Job Case. Work to have a clean case. A clean case is one in which all the characters are in their proper places. After all the type has been distributed, store the leads and slugs. Place the typecase in the type bank.

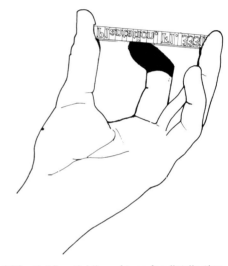

Fig. 3-83. Holding the line of type for distribution.

Fig. 3-82. Separate the line to be distributed from the form.

Fig. 3-84. Rock the type between the fingers.

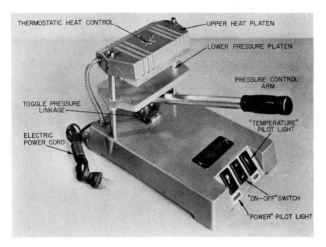

THERMOSTATIC HEAT CONTROL
UPPER HEAT PLATEN
LOWER PRESSURE PLATEN
PRESSURE CONTROL ARM
TOGGLE PRESSURE LINKAGE
"TEMPERATURE" PILOT LIGHT
ELECTRIC POWER CORD
"ON-OFF" SWITCH
"POWER" PILOT LIGHT

Fig. 3-85. Rubber stamp press.

RUBBER STAMPS

A rubber stamp is a relief printing image. It is cast or molded in rubber. Its raised surface is pressed against an ink pad. Then it is pressed on the surface to receive the image. Rubber stamps are used by individuals and in offices for different kinds of labels and markings on packages and business forms.

Equipment

Rubber printing stamps are made on vulcanizing presses. The press shown in Fig. 3-85 has all the features needed for good production. Type used for making rubber stamps is the same as that used for relief printing. It is available in any size or style needed. The quads, spaces, leads, and furniture are also the same. The type can be set by machine or by hand. The composed type is used to make a matrix or mold. The matrix will have a recessed impression of the type. The matrix is then used to prepare the rubber stamp relief surface.

The chase is made to fit the vulcanizing press. A combination type chase fits most needs. One side is used to vulcanize the matrix. The chase is then turned upside down. This furnishes a surface for vulcanizing the rubber over the matrix.

A special thin **plastic molding board** is used to make the matrix. The plastic is a thermosetting type. This means that after it is once heated, formed and cured, it will keep its shape.

The **rubber** used for making stamps is not vulcanized. It is available in sheets of the required thickness. The rubber sheet has a thin, cloth, protective cover on the front side. The front side forms the printing surface when the stamp is made. A **mold-release powder** is sprinkled over the rubber to prevent it from sticking to the matrix.

Setting and Locking Type in the Chase

The image for most rubber stamps is small. This allows type to be set in the chase with the lines running crosswise, Fig. 3-86. This often leaves much open space around the type form. If the form is centered in the chase, even pressure can be exerted on it by the press.

1. Tip the chase at an angle as shown in Fig. 3-86. This keeps the type from falling over as it is set.
2. Place enough metal furniture in the end of the chase to take up slightly less than half the expected open space.
3. Lay a 2-point lead against the furniture.
4. Set the first line of type. Begin at the left side of the chase and work toward the right,

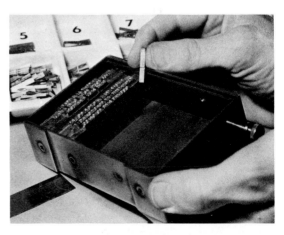

Fig. 3-86. Placing type in the chase.

Fig. 3-86. Place the type in the chase with the nick visible.

5. Center the line of type in the chase by placing an equal number of quads and spaces on each side. The line should have a snug fit.
6. Place a 2-point lead against the line of type. This makes the spacing between the first and second lines. In some jobs, more space between lines is needed.
7. Set and center the second line of type.
8. Set the remaining lines of type in the same way as the first two.
9. Place a 2-point lead against the last line.
10. Fill in the remaining open space with furniture.
11. Tighten the lockup screws slightly.
12. Plane the type form by placing a flat wood block on top and tapping it lightly with a mallet.
13. Tighten the lockup screws at intervals during the planing until the form is held securely in place.

Making the Matrix

The matrix is made from a thermosetting plastic. It is used to take an impression of the type form. The sheet of rubber is then forced into the impression and vulcanized. This makes a rubber stamp of the same shape as the type.

1. Cut the plastic sheet to size.
2. Place the chase and type in the vulcanizing press and let them preheat for a few minutes, Fig. 3-87.
3. Remove the chase from the press. Center the plastic sheet over the type with the shiny side down, Fig. 3-88.
4. Place the chase back in the vulcanizing press. Raise the lower platen until the plastic is resting snugly against the upper heat platen. Hold for about a minute.
5. Push down on the pressure-control arm. Gradually increase the pressure, as the plastic softens.
6. When the lower platen reaches the maximum height, leave it for 9 minutes to permit the plastic to cure. After curing, the plastic will always keep its shape.
7. Remove the chase from the press.
8. Carefully pry the matrix from the type, as shown in Fig. 3-89.

Fig. 3-88. Applying plastic sheet over type.

Fig. 3-87. Preheating type.

Fig. 3-89. Matrix and type.

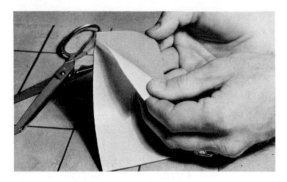

Fig. 3-90. Removing protective covering.

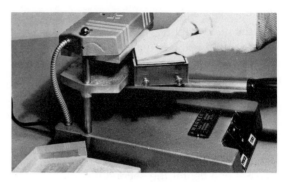

Fig. 3-92. Placing paper over the rubber.

Vulcanizing the Rubber Form

1. Turn the chase upside down.
2. Arrange the matrix in the chase.
3. Cut a sheet of unvulcanized rubber slightly larger than the matrix.
4. Remove the protective covering from the front side of the rubber, Fig. 3-90.
5. Sprinkle mold-release powder over the front side of the rubber.
6. Arrange the rubber over the matrix with the powdered side down, Fig. 3-91.
7. Lay a sheet of paper on top of the rubber to keep it from sticking to the upper heat platen, Fig. 3-92.
8. Place the chase in the press.
9. Raise the lower platen to the maximum height. Force the rubber against the upper heat platen.

10. Leave the chase and rubber in the press for 10 minutes.
11. Remove the chase from the press.
12. Peel the paper from the top of the rubber.
13. Pull the rubber form from the matrix, as shown in Fig. 3-93.

Safety Note

Be very careful in removing the matrix from the form. The chase, type, and form are **very hot.** They could cause severe burns.

Securing the Rubber Stamp to a Wood Mount

1. Select a stamp mount that is slightly wider than the rubber stamp.
2. Saw the wood mount to length.

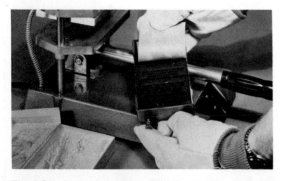

Fig. 3-91. Arranging rubber over the matrix.

Fig. 3-93. Removing rubber from the matrix.

Fig. 3-94. Applying rubber cement to the mount.

A. Positive print.   B. Negative print.

Fig. 3-95. Linoleum Block Prints

A. Line print.   B. Textured print.

Fig. 3-96. Linoleum Block Prints

3. Sand, stain, and apply a finish to the ends of the mount.
4. Apply a coating of rubber cement to the bottom of the mount and the back side of the rubber stamp, Fig. 3-94.
5. Let the cement dry for 3 to 4 minutes.
6. Press the rubber stamp to the wood mount with firm pressure of the fingers.
7. Trim the rubber to the edges of the wood mount.
8. Press the rubber stamp against an ink pad. Then make an impression on paper.
9. Check the impression to make sure there are no unwanted smudges around the printing.

LINOLEUM BLOCK PRINTING

Block printing is one of the oldest and simplest forms of printing. Linoleum is now used to do block printing. It is easy to carve and costs little. It is often mounted on a wooden block. The best linoleum for printing has no finish coat on the surface. The natural color is usually gray or brown.

Either positive or negative prints may be carved into linoleum blocks. **Positive printing blocks** are made by cutting the background areas away from the image, Fig. 3-95A. **Negative printing blocks** are made by cutting the image to a lower lever. This leaves the background standing. At printing, the background serves as the printing surface. The figure remains the color of the material being printed. See Fig. 3-95B.

Fig. 3-97. Transferring the design to tracing paper.

Line cuts may also be made. A small cutter is used to remove the linoleum along the lines of the design. The entire surface of the block does the printing. Only the lines do not print, Fig. 3-96A. Often, the background area is textured. See Fig. 3-96B.

Cutting a Linoleum Block

1. Transfer the design to tracing paper, Fig. 3-97.

2. Cut a sheet of carbon paper to the same size as the block.

3. Place the carbon paper over the block with the carbon side down, Fig. 3-98.

4. Turn the traced pattern upside down and place it over the carbon paper. Turning the pattern upside down will transfer the pattern to the surface of the block **in reverse.** When the print is made from the block, the design will again be reversed to the original pattern.

5. Adjust the tracing to leave the proper margins all around, Fig. 3-99. Then secure it to the block with masking tape.

6. Transfer the design to the block by tracing over the lines with a pencil or ball point pen, Fig. 3-100.

7. Remove the tracing paper and carbon paper.

8. Place the block on a bench hook, as shown in Fig. 3-101.

Fig. 3-100. Transferring design to the block.

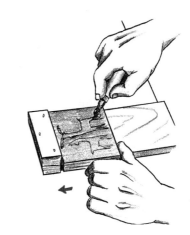

Fig. 3-101. Using a bench hook.

Fig. 3-98. Placing carbon over the block.

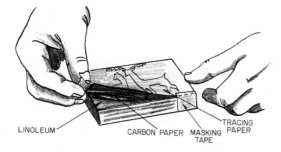

LINOLEUM   CARBON PAPER   MASKING PAPER
TAPE   TRACING

Fig. 3-99. Adjusting margins.

9. Cut all around the outside edge of the design with a small V veiner. Hold the block securely to the bench hook with the left hand. Keep your hand in such a position that you will not be hurt should the tool slip.

10. Remove the background areas with a large gouge tool, Fig. 3-102. Remove any parts of the design that are to remain white. The area of the background need not be smooth. But it must be cut enough below the level of the printed area so there will be no smudges of ink when the print is made.

11. Cut in the textures within the design using the proper tool. Various textures can represent shading and other design details.

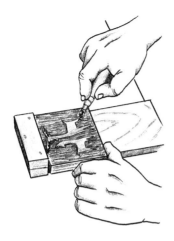

Fig. 3-102. Cutting the background.

Fig. 3-104. Spreading ink.

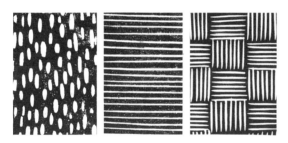

Fig. 3-103. Textures.

Fig. 3-105. Inking the block.

Figure 3-103 shows several of the more common methods of texturing.

12. Check the carved block to make sure there are no unwanted high places.

Printing with a Linoleum Block

1. Place a small amount of ink on a flat smooth surface such as a sheet of glass.
2. Spread the ink evenly by rolling it with a brayer, Fig. 3-104.
3. Roll the brayer over the printing surface of the linoleum block, Fig. 3-105.
4. Lay a sheet of printing paper on the bed of the press.
5. Place the inked block carefully on the paper. Lower the upper pressure plate. Apply pressure to the block by pushing down on the handle, Fig. 3-106.

Fig. 3-106. Making an impression.

6. Raise the upper pressure plate and remove the block from the paper.

7. Apply more ink to the printing block and repeat Steps 4-6 for each print.

8. Spread the inked prints out until they dry thoroughly.

9. Clean the ink from the printing block, brayer, inking surface, and other tools.

Blocks can also be printed in many other ways. A proof press or a platen press is excellent for printing. A screw press or even a large vise can be used. A very simple method is to stand on the back of the block, which is face down on the sheet and a pad of newspapers lying on the floor.

Rub-off prints create interesting effects. First, the inked block is covered with paper and then a sheet of soft plastic or an old drum head held tautly in a frame. The printing area is then rubbed with a spoon or other smooth object to make the print.

MAKING MULTICOLOR PRINTS

Linoleum blocks can also make attractive prints with two or more colors. The general procedures are the same as those followed for making single-color prints. A separate block must be made for printing each color. The paper must be run through the press for each color.

Registering devices must be used to align the paper and block exactly the same on each run.

The following procedures are for making a two-color print. The same procedures may be followed for making prints with any number of colors.

1. Select two blocks of the same size.

2. Draw a rectangle on the paper which is exactly the same size as the linoleum blocks.

3. Transfer the design to the paper. Arrange it properly within the rectangle, Fig. 3-107.

4. Color the design with crayons or colored pencil. This design is used as the master copy.

5. Transfer the design of the first color to tracing paper. Draw in the lines of the rectangle.

6. Transfer the design of the first color to one of the blocks, Fig. 3-108. Check to make sure the lines of the rectangle and the sides of the block coincide. Allow for the colors to overlap slightly where they touch. This will prevent open spaces.

7. Remove the tracing from the block.

8. Cut around the outside of the design with a small veining tool.

9. Cut away the background from around the design with a large gouge tool.

10. Add textures to the design as desired.

Fig. 3-107. Transferring the design to paper.

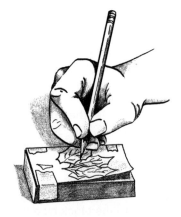

Fig. 3-108. Design of the first color.

11. Prepare a tracing of the second color and transfer it to the second block. Use the same procedures as used on the first block. One block for each color to be printed, Fig. 3-109.
12. Cut two register guides from cardboard that is thicker than the material to be printed.
13. Attach these two register guides to another piece of cardboard that is slightly smaller than the printing press bed, Fig. 3-110. Check these guides to make sure they are at a 90° angle to each other.
14. Cut two more register guides from wood that is somewhat thinner than the linoleum blocks, Fig. 3-111.
15. Place a sheet of printing paper against the two cardboard register guides.
16. Arrange the master copy of the design over the sheet of printing paper. Leave the desired margins all around.
17. Secure the wood register guides on top of the first guides with rubber cement. Align the inside edges of the wood guides with the lines forming the rectangle on the master copy, Fig. 3-112. These guides hold the blocks exactly the same on each print. The bottom guides hold the paper exactly the same on each impression.
18. Place the cardboard base and guides on the bed of the printing press.
19. Select the linoleum block which is to print the lighter of the two colors.
20. Place a sheet of printing paper under the top wooden guides and against the bottom cardboard guides.

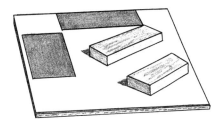

Fig. 3-111. Wood register guides.

Fig. 3-109. One block is made for each color.

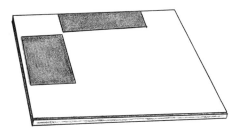

Fig. 3-110. Cardboard register guides.

Fig. 3-112. Aligning the wood guides.

Fig. 3-113. Positioning the block against the guides.

Fig. 3-114. Checking the register of two colors.

21. Ink the block and place it carefully against the top register guides making sure it does not touch the paper in the process, Fig. 3-113. Lower the block down on top of the paper while holding it against the top register guides.

22. Lower the top pressure plate of the press. Make an impression by applying heavy pressure to the handle.

23. Print the first color on all the sheets. Spread the prints out. Let them dry before printing the second color.

24. After the first color has dried, print the second color in the same way as the first. Check the first print of the second color to make sure the two colors are registering properly, Fig. 3-114. If they fail to coincide, adjust by moving the top register guides.

25. Clean all the equipment and return it to its proper storage place.

COLD COMPOSITION AND PLANOGRAPHIC PRINTING

Chapter **4**

Cold composition methods are those which do **not** use molten metal to cast the image. These methods may be used for planographic printing. In this process, the image on the printing plate surface is on the same level as the background or non-image area.

One type of planographic printing is **lithography.** It is also known as photo-lithography, photo-offset lithography, and offset lithography. It is often called **offset.** This term describes the transfer of the image from the plate to a rubber blanket and then to the paper, Fig. 4-1. The paper never makes contact with the plate.

Basic to offset printing is the fact that grease and water do not readily mix. The ink carriers or plates are flat. Image area and background area are at the same level. Image areas have a grease surface. The non-image does not. When water is applied to the plate surface, it is repelled by the grease image. But a thin layer of moisture forms on the background or non-image area. When ink is applied, it sticks to the grease image area. It is repelled by the moisture over the non-image areas. The water must be applied to the plate surface first. If there were no moisture present to repel the ink, the whole surface will accept the ink.

Offset plates may be made of metal, plastic, or paper. Some of these plates can be prepared by writing, drawing, or typing the image directly on the flat surface. Pens, pencils, and typewriter ribbons are designed for that purpose. Most often the image is prepared by a photographic process. Clip art and preprinted

type may be used in the photographic process to produce an image for printing. These are cold composition methods of making an image. Only cold composition methods of making an image for planographic printing are discussed here. But remember that type images prepared by hot composition methods may also be used for planographic printing.

CLIP ART AND PREPRINTED TYPE

Clip art and preprinted type are designed and printed on sheets for use in designing a message. A design or type can be chosen, cut out, and placed on the layout. Clip art and preprinted type are prepared in many kinds of designs. They are attractive, easy to use, and meet different needs, Fig. 4-2.

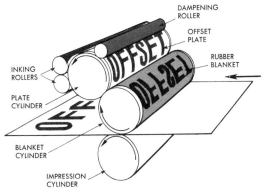

Fig. 4-1. Offset printing.

Fig. 4-2.   Clip art encyclopedia.

Fig. 4-3.   Samples of transfer type lettering styles.

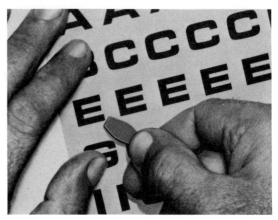

Fig. 4-4.   Rub the surface of the letter with a burnishing tool.

styles and sizes, borders, illustrations, symbols, and designs, Fig. 4-3.

To use transfer type, draw guidelines to show character placement on the surface to receive the image. Then place the sheet of transfer type over the guidelines. Put the desired character in position. Use a burnishing tool to rub over the surface of the sheet, Fig. 4-4. The smooth end of a ball point pen or pencil top can also be used. Burnishing transfers the characters to layout.

Tab Type

Display lines of type may be composed by using Fototype.® Fototype is supplied on tabs of paper pads. There are many type styles and sizes as well as borders, symbols, reverse lettering, and screen patterns.

As you remove each letter from the pad, snap it into position in the composing stick. The blue side should be up. Start at the left side of the stick. Push each new letter tab snugly to the left against the one before it, Fig. 4-5. To space between words, insert a blank tab.

After all the desired characters have been placed in the stick and proofread, apply tape. Cut a piece of tape about 1 in. (25 mm) longer than the type line. Lay it over the letters, Fig. 4-6.

Preprinted Type

Three different kinds of preprinted type are available. They are (1) transfer type on sheets, (2) individual letters on tabs, and (3) pressure sensitive type in sheets and rolls.

Transfer Type

Transfer type is made on a transparent plastic sheet. It has a wide variety of letter

Fig. 4-5. Place the letter tabs in the composing stick.

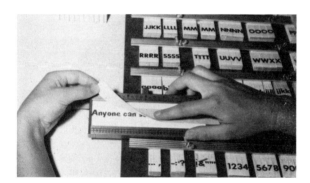

Fig. 4-6. Place tape over the letters in the composing stick.

Fig. 4-7. The desired letter is lifted from the backing sheet.

Fig. 4-8. Several IBM Selectric typewriter elements.

Pressure Sensitive Type

Pressure sensitive type is self-adhesive. Letters can be applied directly to the layout. The desired letter and guideline under it are cut out and lifted from the backing sheet, Fig. 4-7. It is placed in position. The letter's guideline is aligned with the drawn guideline. The letter is burnished down (but not the guideline). The guideline is cut away.

STRIKE-ON COMPOSITION

Strike-on composition (by typewriter) is used in office work to prepare letters, stencils, memos, and other matter. Several copies may be typed by using carbon paper between the sheets of paper. A message to be printed can be prepared on a typewriter quickly and at low cost. The kind of typefaces is often limited unless a machine like the IBM Selectric is used. This machine uses type fonts that can be interchanged, Fig. 4-8. Thus, typefaces can be intermixed on one message.

PROCESS PHOTOGRAPHY

Most often, images are placed on offset plates by **process photography.** This is a means of producing negative images which will result in positive images when printed. Figure 4-9 shows a positive image (A) made from a negative image (B). Process photography

A. Photograph.

B. Halftone negative.

Fig. 4-9.   Photographs are continous tone copy.

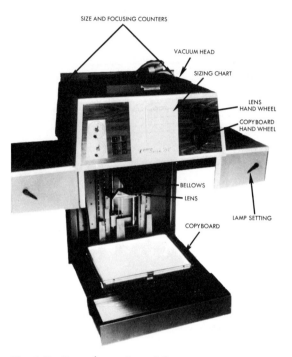

Fig. 4-10. Operating points of the process camera.

negatives are either line negatives or halftone negatives.

Line negatives are produced by shooting line copy. This is copy that is black and white with no gradations of tone. The line negative is black or opaque in the non-image areas. It is transparent in the image areas. Lines of type, hand lettering, clip art and preprinted type, and typewritten copy are all examples of line copy artwork.

Halftone negatives are produced by exposing sensitized film, through a halftone screen, to reflected light from continuous tone copy. Continuous tone copy, such as a photograph, has gradations of tone from white to black. The half-tone negative registers the gradations in tone by a series of **dots**.

Process cameras are either horizontal or vertical. The horizontal camera has the copyboard, lens, and vacuum head in a horizontal line. On the vertical camera, the copyboard, lens, and vacuum head are in a vertical line, Fig. 4-10.

CHEMICAL PREPARATION

Before any copy is photographed (shot), processing chemicals are prepared. These chemicals should be placed in order from left to right. Four individual trays are often used. They contain (1) developer, (2) stop bath, (3) fixer, and (4) running water.

Safety Note

When preparing the stop bath, always add the acid to the water. Prepared stop bath should be stored in a clearly labeled container.

CAMERA PREPARATION

If the copy is to be shot at 100% or 1:1, the size and focus counters must be set at 100% or 1:1. If the copy is to be enlarged or reduced, the shooting percentage must be determined. The copy size is compared to the desired size required on the layout. The shooting percentage is found with a **proportional scale.** This scale is adjusted so that the original copy dimension is directly under the desired reproduction dimension on the outside scale. The percentage of enlargement or reduction is shown by the arrow in the window of the scale, Fig. 4-11.

After the shooting percentage has been determined, refer to the **sizing chart.** Opposite the percentage are shown both the lens and copyboard size and focus counter setting numbers. Set the lens and copy counters by turning the matching control hand wheels.

Before positioning the copy, clean both the inside and outside surfaces of the copyboard glass. Use glass cleaner and a soft cloth pad to remove dust and fingerprints.

Position the copy in the center of the copyboard. Use the size markings as guide-lines. A **sensitivity guide,** also called a **gray scale,** should be positioned on the copyboard for each exposure. For the best results, place the sensitivity guide near the center of the copy, Fig. 4-12.

Set the lens f-stop by turning the diaphragm ring to the best setting for the exposure. The f-stop setting may vary with exposure time and type of film being used. It may also vary with the shooting percentage and the copy being shot. The f-stop refers to the size of the lens opening or aperture, Fig. 4-13. The higher the f-stop number, the smaller the opening.

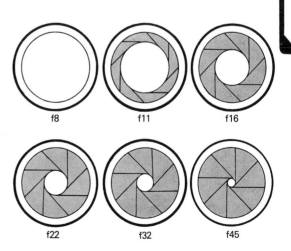

Fig. 4-12. Position the sensitivity guide near the center of the copy.

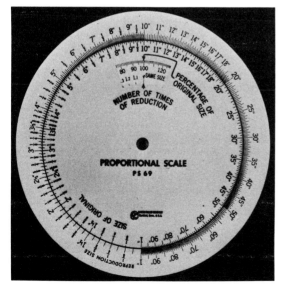

Fig. 4-11. Computing shooting percentage with the proportional scale.

Fig. 4-13. Different f-stop openings as related in size.

Adjusting Exposure Time and f-Stop

When the image is to be enlarged or reduced, the exposure time and/or f-stop must be changed. To figure the change, use an **exposure guide.** It shows the basic exposure time at a given f-stop for shooting a line negative at 100%. For example, suppose the basic exposure time of 20 seconds at f/22 is used for shooting a 100% line negative. If the copy is to be enlarged to 150%, the exposure factor is 1.42. This is found on the exposure guide. The exposure factor is then multiplied by the basic exposure for shooting at 100%. This gives the new exposure time.

Exposure factor	1.42
Basic exposure at 100%	$\times 20$
New exposure time	28.40 or 28 seconds

Exposures may also be varied by changing the lens f-stop. By opening the lens one f-stop without changing the timer, the film is exposed with twice the amount of light. By closing the lens one f-stop without changing the timer, the film is exposed with one-half the amount of light. A 30-second exposure at f/22 allows the same amount of light to expose the film as a 15-second exposure at f/16. Remember, the higher the f-stop number, the smaller the lens opening.

EXPOSING A LINE NEGATIVE

The next step is to expose the negative. By this time, all camera adjustments have been made. Chemicals have been prepared to process the film. The copy is positioned. Now select the desired exposure lighting. Turn the on-off switch to the timer position.

Under the proper safelight conditions, position the film in the center of the vacuum head. Emulsion side should be facing out. See Fig. 4-14. The emulsion side of the film is the lighter of the two sides. If the film is notched, the emulsion side is facing out when the notch is in the upper right-hand corner. Turn on the vacuum pump.

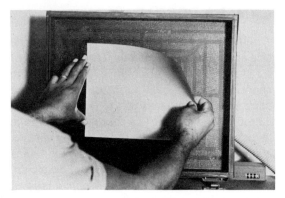
Fig. 4-14. Place the film in the center of the vacuum head.

Fig. 4-15. Place the halftone screen over the film on the vacuum head.

Close the vacuum head. Press the exposure button to make the exposure. At the end of the exposure time, open the vacuum head. Turn off the vacuum pump and remove the film. The film is now ready for processing. If no other negatives are to be made, cap the lens. The vacuum head should also be closed when the camera is not in use. This prevents dust from settling in the bellows.

Exposing a Halftone Negative

The method for shooting a **halftone negative** is about the same as that used for preparing a line negative. A halftone screen, however, must be placed in direct contact with the film. Place the halftone screen over the film on the vacuum head, Fig. 4-15. The emulsion side of the screen should be against the emulsion side of the film. This is emulsion to emulsion. The reflected light must pass through the density of the screen. The exposure time and/or f-stop opening, therefore, may have to be increased.

FILM PROCESSING

Safe lights used during processing are turned **on** in the darkroom. The exposed film is immersed in the developer with the emulsion side up. Be sure the entire sheet of film is under the surface of the developer. Gently rock the tray during development by raising and lowering one edge. This action will keep the chemicals moving. It keeps supplying new developer to the surface of the film.

A properly exposed Kodalith Ortho Type negative should develop a solid step 4 on the sensitivity guide. This would occur in 2¾ minutes using Kodalith developer at 20° C (68° F). Step 5 will appear as light gray before solid 4 has been reached.

When good development has been achieved, lift the negative from the developer. Allow it to drain a few seconds. Then immerse it in the **stop bath.** The stop bath stops the action of the developer. The negative should be agitated in the stop bath for 10 seconds. Then allow it to drain.

Then place the negative in the **fixing bath.** The fixing solution removes the unexposed silver particles from the film. It also removes the milky white appearance of the image area. Let the negative remain in the fixer for 2 to 4 minutes with agitation. The normal room lights may now be turned on.

Remove the negative from the fixer. Immerse it in a running water rinse for 10 minutes to remove all trace of chemicals. Negatives that are not well rinsed may discolor when dried.

To dry, remove the negative from the water rinse. Allow it to drain for a few seconds. Hang the negative in a dust-free area. Be sure the negative is not touching another negative when drying. Negatives may stick together. Handle the film by the edges. Since the negative emulsion is soft, it will show scratches and fingerprints.

STRIPPING

In stripping, process negatives are arranged and mounted on goldenrod paper. This produces a **flat.** The flat holds the negatives in position for "burning" or exposing the offset plate. Goldenrod paper is generally an 80 pound (36 kilogram) double-coated paper. It is ruled in ¼ in. (6.5 mm) graduations. The worker who makes up the flat is called a **stripper.**

Place the flat on the light table. Locate and mark on the masking sheet the outside dimensions of the paper size to be used for printing. Within this area, locate and mark the exact location of the image area to be printed, Fig. 4-16.

Position the image (transparent areas) of the negative in the designated image area on the masking sheet. To position correctly, use a T-square and triangle. Or align the image by using the graduation lines printed on the masking sheet.

When the masking sheet and negative have been properly placed, hold them in position. With the other hand, cut a small oval shape in the masking sheet. Cut it near the center of the

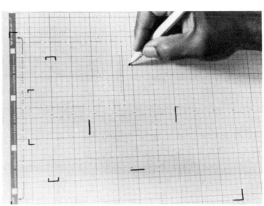

Fig. 4-16. Mark the location of the image area on the masking sheet.

image area. Apply pressure to cut through the masking sheet only. **Do not** cut through the negative.

Keeping a downward pressure, remove the oval-shaped cutout. Place a piece of red lithographer's tape over the opening, Fig. 4-17. The tape should contact both the masking sheet and the negative.

Turn the masking sheet over so that the negative is now on top. Tape the four corners of the negative to the back of the masking sheet. Use transparent tape. The flat must be turned over again. With a sharp razor blade or stencil knife, cut a **window** in the masking sheet. The window should be between 1/8 in. and 1/4 in. (3

and 5 mm) larger than the image area on all sides. Use very light pressure so that the negative is not cut. Remove the window from the masking sheet and inspect the negative, Fig. 4-18. Be sure all the desired image area is exposed by removal of the window.

OPAQUING THE FLAT

You will often find some unwanted transparent areas in the negative. These are called **pinholes.** They are usually caused by careless negative handling. Or they show that small dust particles were not cleaned off the camera lens or copyboard glass. If these pinholes are not blocked out, they will appear as a printing image on the plate.

Work on the **light table** so that you can locate pinholes easier. **Opaquing** should be done on the readable or non-emulsion side of the negative. Use a small brush and photographic opaquing solution to block out the pinholes, Fig. 4-19.

PHOTO-OFFSET PLATE PREPARATION

Presensitized Paper Photo-Offset Plate

Suppliers offer several kinds of presensitized paper plates. They also carry chemicals

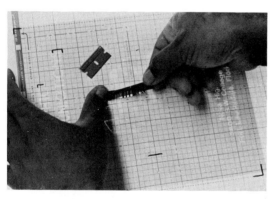

Fig. 4-17. Tape the masking sheet to the negative by placing a piece of tape over the oval cutout.

Fig. 4-18. Cut out and remove the windows.

Fig. 4-19. Opaque any pinholes.

and materials needed for a certain brand of plate.

Prepare or select the material you wish to reproduce. Lines, letters, symbols, etc. can be placed on tracing paper to be exposed on the presensitized paper plate. Art and type may be photographed and stripped. They can then be exposed on the plate.

Remember these facts about paper plates:

1. They are treated in the same manner as any other plate on the press.
2. They can be gummed and stored.
3. Packages of presensitized paper plates should be opened in subdued light.
4. Packages of presensitized paper plates should be sealed after removing a plate.
5. Presensitized paper plates should be used by the expiration date marked on the package.

The same general steps are used to prepare a presensitized paper plate as other plates.

PLATEMAKING

The **platemaker,** Fig. 4-20, is used to "burn" the plate. Open the vacuum frame. Clean both sides of the glass to remove any dust or fingerprints. Place the metal plate in the vacuum frame with the presensitized side up.

The flat is positioned face up on top of the plate. It is in a readable position. Align the gripper margin end of the masking sheet with one end of the plate. The edge of the masking sheet nearest the operator should also be aligned with the corresponding edge of the plate, Fig. 4-21. You will notice that the plate is slightly smaller than the flat.

Carefully close the vacuum frame. Check to see that the flat does not slip from position. Turn on the vacuum pump. Double check the position of the flat to the plate. Flip the vacuum frame over so that the flat is now between the plate and the light source. Set the timer and expose the plate for the desired length of time.

Fig. 4-20. NuArc platemaker.

Fig. 4-21. Position the flat on top of the plate in the vacuum frame.

Safety Note
Do not look directly at the exposure light. It may result in damage to the eyes.

The exposure time may vary with (1) the type of plate being used, (2) the type of light source, and (3) the distance between the light source and the plate. During the exposure time, the light passes through the transparent areas of the negative. It hardens the presensitized plate coating. Where the plate is not struck by the exposure light (in the opaque negative places), the plate coating remains soft.

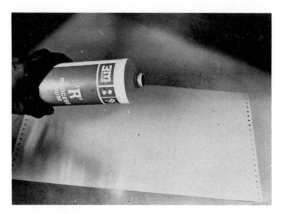

Fig. 4-22. Pour a small puddle of process gum into the surface of the plate.

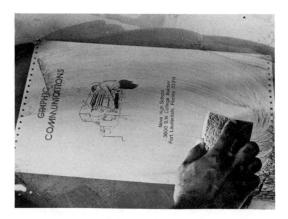

Fig. 4-23. Wipe the developer over the plate with a soft sponge.

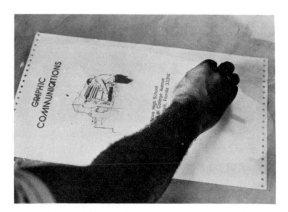

Fig. 4-24. Wipe the plate with a cotton pad while rinsing.

After exposure, the plate is **rubbed up** or developed to bring the image into view. Turn off the vacuum. Remove the plate, placing it on a flat work surface. Pour a small puddle of process gum in the center of the plate, Fig. 4-22. Use a clean, soft sponge to wipe the process gum over the entire plate surface. The process gum removes the unhardened plate coating.

While the process gum is still wet, pour a small puddle of developer on the plate. A second clean, soft sponge should be used to spread the developer over the entire plate surface, Fig. 4-23. For best results, use very light pressure and long, even wiping strokes. The image will begin to appear as the plate is rubbed with the developer. A solid step 6 on the sensitivity guide in the gripper margin usually shows that the plate has been properly exposed and developed. Repeat the rub-up procedure for the second side of the plate. Apply running water to both sides of the plate. This removes all traces of the developer. Wipe the plate surface lightly with a cotton pad during the rinsing, Fig. 4-24.

Allow the plate to dry. The plate is now ready to be placed on the offset duplicator. If it is to be stored, gum arabic is used to coat the surface of the plate. This prevents oxidation of the non-image areas. Gum arabic may be applied with a cotton pad to the entire plate surface, Fig. 4-25.

Fig. 4-25. Coat the plate with gum arabic.

OFFSET PRESSWORK

It is best that a qualified teacher show how the press is operated. The instructions in this section apply in general to most duplicators and presses. See Figs. 4-26 and 4-27.

Ask your instructor for a checklist that fits your equipment. The following instructions are a general guide to offset presswork.

Preparing the Press

> **Safety Notes**
>
> Never operate a press without having **complete knowledge** of how to operate it. Know how to operate it **safely.** Always get permission to operate the press.
>
> Never adjust a press until properly instructed and judged capable of doing it right by the instructor. Do not hesitate to ask questions. Ask for help or more instruction.

Press Instruction Manuals

The operator's instruction manuals for the particular presses in the shop should be on hand for students.

Personal Dress

Remove coats and sweaters. Roll shirt sleeves above the elbows. Remove or tuck in neckties. Remove jewelry, such as rings and bracelets. Do not wear gloves or loose aprons.

Visual Inspection

Remove the fabric press covering. Examine the press carefully. See that all parts are in place and that all settings and controls are in **off** position.

Turn by Hand

As an added check, be certain there is no interference. Turn the press by means of the handwheel for a revolution or two.

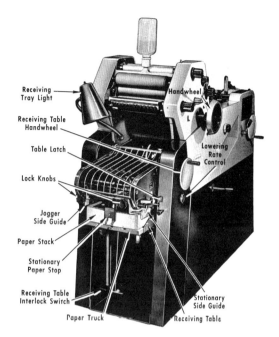

Fig. 4-26. Duplicator equipped with chain delivery and receding stacker.

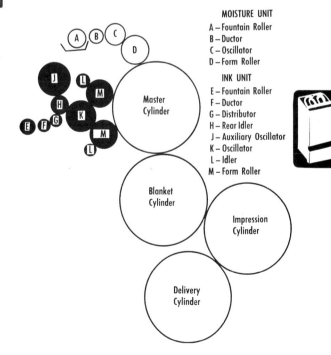

MOISTURE UNIT
A – Fountain Roller
B – Ductor
C – Oscillator
D – Form Roller

INK UNIT
E – Fountain Roller
F – Ductor
G – Distributor
H – Rear Idler
J – Auxiliary Oscillator
K – Oscillator
L – Idler
M – Form Roller

Fig. 4-27. Schematic of roller and cylinder arrangement.

Lubrication

Lubricate the press daily before operation. Do this **while the press is stopped! Never** try to lubricate a moving press.

Turn On the Press (Power Check)

If all is clear, turn on the power. Allow the press to revolve for a few times. Check that all parts are working correctly.

Check Specifications

Check the job specifications. Do you have the correct ink? Is the correct paper stock at hand, and cut to the correct size? Are the plates ready? What other "specs" are there? If, in doubt, ask your instructor.

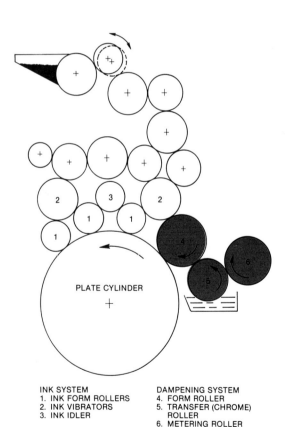

INK SYSTEM
1. INK FORM ROLLERS
2. INK VIBRATORS
3. INK IDLER

DAMPENING SYSTEM
4. FORM ROLLER
5. TRANSFER (CHROME) ROLLER
6. METERING ROLLER

Fig. 4-28. Ink and dampening system.

SETTING UP FOR OPERATION

If the press has been prepared as described above, set up for operation as follows.

Prepare the Ink Unit

Install the ink fountain and all rollers which may have been removed. See Fig. 4-28. If an ink fountain liner is used, install it now.

Decide how much ink is needed. It is better to start with too little ink on the rollers than too much. More can be added easily.

Prepare the Water (Dampening) Unit

Install the water fountain, fountain roller, and all other water system rollers that may have been removed. Fill the fountain bottle with the recommended solution. Invert the bottle to make sure no solution leaks out from between the cap and the bottle. Place the bottle in its recess in the fountain. Allow the solution to reach its level.

Install the Plate

When doing pressure checks, use either the gummed plate to be used on the job or a test plate. The plate should be of the same thickness as the plate for the job.

Perform the Pressure Checks

Perform the pressure checks in this sequence:
1. Dampener form roller to plate.
2. Ink form roller to plate.
3. Plate cylinder to blanket cylinder.
4. Impression adjustment (or squeeze).

Prepare the Feeder, Sheet Controls, and Delivery

Setting up for the "paper cycle" (feeder, sheet controls, and delivery) is not hard if done the right way. Always center the printing sheet (not necessarily the image) on the flat from left to right. Also, always see that the leading edge of the sheet is the same distance down from the leading edge of the flat.

Feeder Setup

Set up the feeder by placing stiff cardboard on the supports to hold the paper. Align the paper with the center of the scale. Set the guide 1/32 in. (0.8 mm) from the paper. Follow your instructor's demonstration to make final adjustments. Adjust the following: left and right pile guides, sucker feet, tail guide, sheet separator combs, air pump, vacuum, and pile-height governor.

Conveyor Board and Sheet Controls

The conveyor board and sheet controls include the pullout roll and wheels, the sheet caliper (double-sheet detector), the conveyor tapes, the riders (steel balls or metal bands). They also include front stops, side jogger, stationary side guide and forwarding rollers. See Figs. 4-29 and 4-30.

Delivery

Set the delivery tray, jogger, or stacker for maximum width. Feed a sheet through. Turn the press by hand until the jogger is in a closed position. Set the jogger, tray, or stacker to this sheet position.

Inspection of Test Sheet

These are some of the important points to inspect on the test sheets:

1. Is the ink coverage correct? Is it too heavy or too light?
2. Is the ink coverage consistent across the sheet?
3. Are the clear areas free of ink?
4. Is the entire image printing?
5. Is the image square on the sheet?
6. Is the image correctly placed horizontally?
7. Is the image correctly placed vertically?
8. Is the overall impression satisfactory—not too light or too heavy?
9. In the halftones, are highlight dots visible and shadow dots unplugged?

Adjustments

If the answer to any of the above questions is "no," then adjust to correct problems. The operator should be alert to detect printing troubles as they occur. This avoids wasting paper and time. Also, in making adjustments, do as many corrections at one time as possible.

Obtaining Ink and Water Balance

A good printed image should be dense and the non-printing areas clear. If the clear areas tend to "scum," cut back some ink. Increase the flow of water a bit, and then increase the ink gradually. Water level should be just enough to prevent scumming. If the image is too light, increase the ink supply by small degrees. If the increase causes scum, add more water.

Fig. 4-29. Multiple-sheet detector.

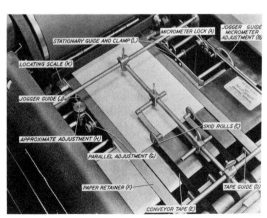

Fig. 4-30. Conveyor board (register table).

Fig. 4-31. Vertical positioning control.

Correcting Image Position on the Sheet

When the position of a plate or plate cylinder must be adjusted, the image must be washed from the blanket. This is because the next test impression on most presses will be in another place on the blanket.

1. **Lateral Adjustment.** The image is moved to the left or right on the printed sheet. Reset the side jogger and the stationary guide on the feed board, Fig. 4-30. If needed, make a minute adjustment of the jogger guide micrometer adjustment wheel. For large adjustments, reposition the feed pile.

2. **Cocked Image.** A cocked image, if not overly crooked, is straightened this way. Adjust the leading and trailing plate clamp lateral adjusting screws, if the press has them.

   For straight edge plates, release the plate from the trailing clamp. Then loosen and twist at the lead clamp. Tighten the plate again at the lead and trailing ends.

   For a badly cocked image, have the plate remade.

3. **Vertical Adjustment.** On some presses a vertical adjustment is made by moving the plate around the plate cylinder. Loosen the tension on the set of plate clamp screws at one end of the plate. Then tighten the plate

clamp screws at the opposite end of the plate.

On other presses, the plate cylinder or the impression cylinder may be moved without involving its driving gears. When moved, the plate image will print on the blanket either up or down from its earlier location. See Figs. 4-31 and 4-32.

Impression. Too little impression will result in too light an image. Highlight dots may also be missing. Too heavy an impression will result in a squashed out image. This causes individual highlight dots to spread and halftone shadow areas and fine reverses to fill in.

On some presses, the impression is adjusted by means of a micrometer lever or handscrew. This moves the impression cylinder closer to or away from the blanket cylinder.

Refer to a press manual for details for your specific press. Your instructor will show the proper way to use the presses in your shop.

Operating the Press

If something goes wrong during press operation, stop the press. Suppose you do not know what is wrong or cannot correct the prob-

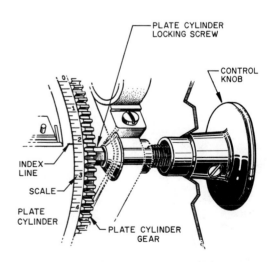

Fig. 4-32. Cut-away view of the vertical positioning control.

lem. Then ask your instructor for help. Much paper can be wasted if you experiment.

Suppose you must stop a press for more than a few seconds while running a metal plate. Then gum the plate right away. Sponge off with water before starting the run again.

Press Wash-Up

Assume that the offset plate has been "run-down," gummed, and removed from the press. Proceed to wash up the press.

1. Turn off all operating controls.
2. Remove the paper stock.
3. Clean the water fountain and all dampening rollers.
4. Clean the blanket.
5. Clean the ink fountain and ductor.
6. Clean the ink rollers.
7. Replace the rollers in the same holders they were removed from.
8. Check the above items again. Wipe all surfaces clean.
9. Turn the night latch for the ink and water form rollers to the vertical position.

```
——————————— Safety Note ———————————
   Place cloths with solvent and ink in
metal safety cans.
```

SILK SCREEN PRINTING

Chapter 5

Screen-process (silk screen) printing is a stencil method of printing. Fine mesh silk cloth, or screen, is stretched over a frame. Open screen areas are printing areas. This leaves the open screen in only those places to be printed. The screen is lowered over the material. Ink is forced through the screen openings with a squeegee. See Fig. 5-1. This transfers the design to the surface of the material. Screen-process printing is mostly used for posters, billboards, cards, labels, and textiles. It is also used on three-dimensional items such as milk bottles.

PAPER STENCIL METHOD

The paper stencil method costs the least and is easiest to prepare. The stencil is cut from paper, Fig. 5-2, and attached to the screen. Paper used for making stencils must be tough to prevent tearing and rough edges. If a water base ink will be used for printing, the paper stencil should be made of waterproof paper.

The paper stencil method is mostly used for short runs of less than 100 impressions. It is commonly used for simple designs. It is often of one color. This method is not good for

Fig. 5-1.　Screen-process printing.

Fig. 5-2.　Cutting a paper stencil.

designs that have loose centers such as the letters "o," "p," "b," and "d." In multi-color printing, a separate stencil is prepared for each color.

The paper stencil is quick and easy to attach and remove from the screen. Glue or gummed tape are used to fasten it. The paper stencil is prepared to a size that is equal to the size of the frame. The block-out operation is not needed.

HAND-CUT FILM METHOD

The hand-cut film method of screen printing reproduces designs of sharp, clear cut lines. There can be much precise detail as well as large solid places. Much care and skill are needed to cut film stencils accurately.

Hand-cut stencil film is flexible and durable. Up to 10,000 impressions can be made from a single stencil. The stencil film is easy to cut, Fig. 5-3. It is also easy to adhere it to and remove it from the screen fabric.

Designs of many colors may be printed with good registration. A separate stencil must be cut for each color.

EQUIPMENT

The equipment used for screen-process work costs little. Much of it is easy to make in a home workshop, if desired.

Printing Frame

Printing frames can be made in any size needed. The frame shown in Fig. 5-4 is made from 2 in. × 2 in. (50 × 50 mm) white pine stock. It is mitered at the corners. A groove is cut around the bottom side of the boards. It is used in stretching the silk tightly across the bottom of the frame. A cord or rope is cut just long enough to reach around the groove. The silk is stretched across the frame. It is held in place by tapping the cord and silk down in the groove. See Fig. 5-5. The cord is tapped down gradually all around to tighten the silk evenly. The deeper the cord is forced into the groove, the tighter the silk is stretched.

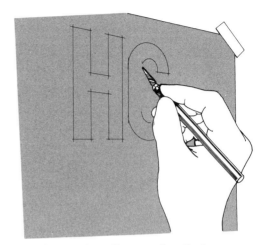

Fig. 5-3.   Hand-cut film stencil method.

Fig. 5-4.   Screen-process printing frame.

Fig. 5-5.   Stretching silk.

Fig. 5-6.   The frame is hinged to a base board.

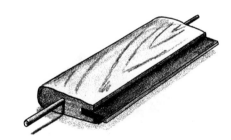

Fig. 5-7.   Squeegee.

The frame is attached to a base board with hinges, Fig. 5-6. The hinges should have removable pins. This allows the screen frame to be easily removed from the base for cleaning.

Several frames of various sizes can be made to fit the same base. A small board attached to the side of the frame with one screw will permit it to be lowered. This supports the frame and holds the screen above the base.

Silk

A wide range of silk meshes is available. They range from 6XX, which is coarse, to 18XX, which is very fine. The coarse meshed silk is used for designs that require very little detail. The fine meshed silk is used for intricate designs that require sharp details. The 10XX to

12XX mesh is good for most printing jobs. After it is stretched, new silk should be washed in warm water. This removes the starch and helps tighten the screen.

Squeegee

The squeegee is a rubber blade that fits in a groove on the bottom edge of a board, Fig. 5-7. The rubber should extend out from the wood about ¾ in. (20 mm).

CUTTING A LACQUER FILM STENCIL

The lacquer film has a thin layer of lacquer adhered to a special sheet of transparent plastic paper backing. The lacquer film can be cut without cutting through the backing. After the lacquer stencil is adhered to the silk screen, the plastic backing can be peeled off.

1. Prepare the design on a sheet of paper. Lay it on a smooth surface, Fig. 5-8.
2. Attach the lacquer film over the design with the lacquer side up, Fig. 5-9. The design can be seen through the lacquer film and plastic backing.
3. Cut around the areas of the design which are to be printed. Use a sharp knife similar to the stencil knife shown in Fig. 5-10. Use just enough pressure to cut through the film without cutting through the backing.

Fig. 5-8.   Prepared design.

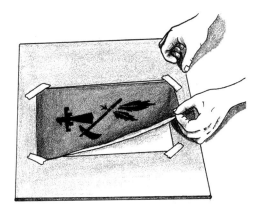

Fig. 5-9.   Attaching lacquer film over the design.

Fig. 5-10. Cutting through the lacquer film.

Fig. 5-11. Stripping lacquer film from the design.

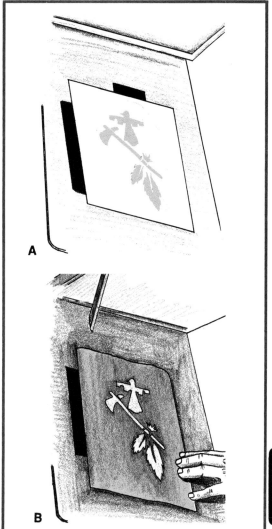

Fig. 5-12. View A shows the position of the register
           guides and view B how the stencil is
           aligned over the pattern.

4. Lift the lacquer film at one edge with the
   knife. Peel it carefully from the backing
   paper in the design areas, Fig. 5-11. Continue in this way until the film has been
   removed from all parts of the design to be
   printed.

Adhering the Film to the Screen

1. Place the prepared design on the base
   board.
2. Cut two register guides from heavy paper.
3. Attach the register guides to the base
   board in line with the back and left edges of
   the design sheet. See A of Fig. 5-12. Rubber

cement may be used to hold the guides in place.

4. Lay the lacquer-film stencil over the pattern and align the two designs. See B of Fig. 5-12.
5. Lower the silk screen onto the stencil.
6. Get two clean cloths and dampen one with adhering liquid.

7. Cover a **small area** of the lacquer film with the damp cloth. Then wipe it dry right away with the second cloth, Fig. 5-13. If too much adhering liquid is applied, the stencil may be dissolved around the edges. The film will turn dark when adhered to the screen. Light spots on the film show that more adhering liquid should be applied.
8. Dampen another section of the film. Wipe it dry with the clean dry cloth. Continue covering small parts until the entire stencil has been adhered to the silk.
9. Let the lacquer stencil dry for about 20 minutes. Then peel the plastic backing from the bottom side of the film, Fig. 5-14.
10. Cut four lengths of gummed paper to fit the inside of the frame. Fold them lengthwise down the center. Dampen the gummed paper and stick it to the silk and frame. See Fig. 5-15.
11. Apply block-out solution over the gummed paper and the open places of the screen between the stencil and frame. The entire area may be covered with gummed tape in place of the block-out solution. This is needed if the printing is to be done with water soluble colors. Most block-out solutions are also water soluble. They would be dissolved if water soluble paint were used.

Fig. 5-13. Using an adhering liquid.

Fig. 5-14. Removing backing paper.

Fig. 5-15. Blocking out corners with gummed tape.

PRINTING WITH THE SILK SCREEN

1. Lay a clean sheet of printing paper on the base board against the register guides, Fig. 5-16.
2. Apply a generous amount of ink near the back side of the frame.
3. Place the squeegee blade behind the ink. Tip the top of the squeegee forward at about a 60° angle, Fig. 5-17.
4. Pull the squeegee forward with a smooth, even stroke. In this way, move the ink over the stencil area to the front side of the screen, Fig. 5-18. Press hard enough to keep the squeegee pressed firmly against the screen.
5. Lift the frame just enough to replace the printed sheet with a clean sheet, Fig. 5-19.
6. Lower the screen. Move the ink back across the stencil to the back side.
7. Continue in this way until all sheets have been printed. Do not stop printing for more than 3 or 4 minutes at a time without washing the screen. If you do not do this, the ink may dry enough to clog the screen.

Fig. 5-16. Laying paper against register guides.

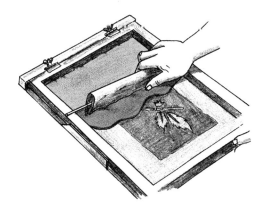

Fig. 5-18. Pulling squeegee over stencil design.

Fig. 5-17. Placing squeegee behind paint.

Fig. 5-19. Replacing printed sheet with clean sheet.

8. Remove the excess ink from the screen and return it to the container. Close the lid to keep the paint from forming a scum on top.

9. Remove the frame from the base board. Wash the screen thoroughly with solvent. Scrub the screen from both sides. A slight coloring of the screen can be expected. This will not be harmful if the mesh is free of ink. Hold the screen up to the light to see whether all the ink has been removed.

10. If the stencil is to be saved, store it where there will be no danger of damage.

11. Clean the squeegee.

> ─── **Safety Note** ───
> Place cloths with ink and solvent on them in metal safety cans.

REMOVING THE STENCIL FROM THE SCREEN

1. To remove the water soluble, block-out material, soak and wash the screen with warm water, Fig. 5-20. Remove the gummed tape. Scrub both sides of the screen with a wet cloth.

2. Place the screen over a pad of newspapers.

3. Apply lacquer thinner over the screen, Fig. 5-21. Keep the stencil wet for 4 or 5 minutes.

Fig. 5-21. Applying the lacquer thinner.

Fig. 5-22. Lacquer film adhered to newspaper.

4. Lift the screen from the newspapers. Most of the stencil will adhere to the newspapers, Fig. 5-22. Get fresh newspapers and repeat step 3.

5. Scrub the remaining stencil material from the screen with a cloth filled with lacquer thinner.

6. Hold the screen up to the light to make sure no lacquer remains.

> ─── **Safety Note** ───
> Place soiled cloths and newspapers in metal safety cans.

Fig. 5-20. Removing block-out solution.

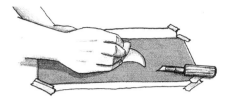

Fig. 5-23. Cutting design of first color.

MAKING MULTICOLORED PRINTS

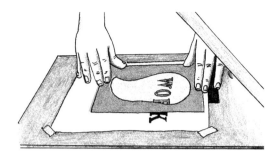

Fig. 5-24. Arranging stencil over the master copy.

Prints made with more than one color require a separate stencil for each color used. If there are enough frames to fit the same base, all the stencils may be cut and adhered to separate screens before any of the printing is done. If only one screen is available, each stencil must be printed and then removed from the screen. In either case, the general procedures are the same. Each color must be printed separately and then allowed to dry before the next color is printed.

Fig. 5-25. First color printed.

1. Prepare a master copy of the design. Color it with crayons or colored pencils.
2. Secure the stencil material over the master copy. Cut out over all areas of the first color to be printed, Fig. 5-23. Print the lightest colors first. If opaque colors are used, overlap the parts slightly where two colors join. (Opaque colors are those you cannot see through.)
3. Place the master copy against the register guides on the base board.
4. Arrange the lacquer stencil over the master copy. The cutout areas must align exactly with the design, Fig. 5-24.
5. Lower the screen and adhere the stencil.
6. After the stencil dries, remove the plastic backing.
7. Remove the master copy and print the first color on all the sheets, Fig. 5-25. Make sure that each sheet is lined up correctly against the register guides before printing.
8. Spread the prints out or place them in a rack to dry.

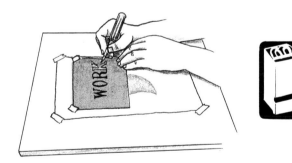

Fig. 5-26. Cutting second color design.

9. Clean the ink from the screens and tools.
10. If the same frame is to be used for the second color, remove the lacquer stencil from the screen.
11. Secure a new piece of stencil film over the master copy.
12. Cut out all the areas of the second color, Fig. 5-26.

Fig. 5-27. Checking register of two colors.

Fig. 5-28. Attaching design to base board.

13. Place the master copy against the register guides on the base board.
14. Line up the stencil on top of the master copy so that the designs coincide.
15. Adhere the stencil to the screen.
16. Block out the screen between the stencil and frame.
17. Place one of the sheets already printed with the first color against the register guides.
18. Print the second color on the sheet.
19. Check to make sure the second color registers properly with the first color, Fig. 5-27.
20. Make any necessary adjustments of the register guides. Then print all the sheets with the second color.
21. Do all this for each color used.
22. Clean all the equipment. Store it properly.

MAKING STENCILS BY OTHER METHODS

Other methods of making stencils can be used. The design dictates which method can or should be used.

Paper and Glue Method

Stencils with simple designs may be applied to the silk screen by the glue method.

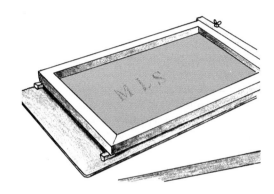

Fig. 5-29. Placing blocks under front edge.

These designs should have no fine detail.
1. Transfer the design to a sheet of paper.
2. Attach the design to the base board with masking tape, Fig. 5-28.
3. Lower the screen over the design.
4. Place a small object under each side of the frame to hold the screen slightly above the design, Fig. 5-29.
5. Paint around the design with silk-screen glue, Fig. 5-30. Leave all areas open which are to be printed.
6. Block out the screen between the glue stencil and the frame.
7. Let the glue dry.
8. Place register guides on the base board against the back and left side of the prepared design.

Fig. 5-30. Painting with silk-screen glue.

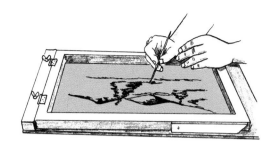

Fig. 5-31. Applying tusche.

9. Replace the design sheet with clean printing paper.
10. Check the stencil to make sure no pinholes appeared during the drying. Touch up the stencil with more glue as required.
11. Make the first print. Make any needed adjustments and then start printing.
12. Remove glue stencils from the screen by soaking and washing them in warm water.

Glue and Tusche Method

Tusche stencils can be used for fine art printing.

1. Paint the design to be printed directly on the screen with an oil-base tusche, Fig. 5-31.
2. After the tusche dries, apply a coating of glue over the entire screen. Include the tusche design, Fig. 5-32.
3. Allow the glue to dry. Then wash the tusche from the screen with paint thinner. The glue on top of the tusche will also be removed while that on the rest of the screen will remain. The open screen is left in the design areas which were painted with tusche, Fig. 5-33.
4. Make the prints. Use the same procedure as with lacquer film stencils.
5. Clean all equipment. Then remove the glue stencil with warm water.

Photographic Film Stencil Method

Designs having fine detail can be transferred to the silk screen by the photographic

Fig. 5-32. Coating with glue.

Fig. 5-33. Washing off tusche.

direct film method. In one procedure, the silk screen is coated with an emulsion. It is sensitive to light and causes the design to be exposed directly onto the screen. The photographic indirect method, however, is more common. It uses a light sensitive film which is transferred to the screen after being processed. The film has a plastic backing covered with a light sensitive emulsion. When the film is properly exposed to light, the emulsion becomes hard. It will not dissolve out during the developing and washing processes. The parts of the emulsion protected from the light will be removed when processed. After the design is adhered to the silk and allowed to dry, the plastic backing is peeled off. This leaves the open screen in the areas to be printed.

1. Prepare the design on a sheet of paper, Fig. 5-34.
2. Lay a sheet of acetate tracing paper over the pattern. Secure it with masking tape.
3. Transfer the design to the tracing paper with acetate ink, Fig. 5-35.
4. Lay the photographic stencil film on a smooth flat surface. The emulsion side (shiny side) should be up.
5. Arrange the traced pattern face up over the film.
6. Lay a piece of glass over the pattern and film to press them firmly together, Fig. 5-36.

7. Expose the film to the light of a No. 2 photo-flood bulb for about 12 minutes. Place the bulb about 2 ft. (52 cm) from the film, Fig. 5-37. The film may also be exposed to direct sunlight for 1½ or 2

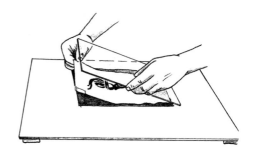

Fig. 5-36. Laying glass over the film.

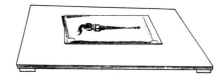

Fig. 5-37. Exposing film to light.

Fig. 5-34. Making the design.

Fig. 5-35. Inking the design.

Fig. 5-38. Developing film.

Fig. 5-39. Washing film with warm water.

Fig. 5-40. Placing film on the base board.

minutes. However, the photo-flood bulb is more accurate.

8. Mix the film developer as directed by the manufacturer. The amount mixed will be determined by the size of the developing tray. The developer should be at least ½ in. (12 mm) deep.

9. Place the film in the developer and leave it for 1 minute, Fig. 5-38. Agitate the solution constantly while the film is developing.

10. Remove the film and place it on the piece of glass. The emulsion side should be up.

11. Wash the emulsion side of the film with very warm water until the design shows clearly, Fig. 5-39.

12. Place a padding of paper on the base board of the silk screen press.

13. Lay the film on the padding with the emulsion side toward the screen, Fig. 5-40.

14. Lower the screen on the film.

15. Lay a sheet of paper over the screen and film.

16. Rub the paper with heavy pressure of the fingers to cause the soft emulsion to imbed in the mesh of the silk, Fig. 5-41.

17. Raise the screen and let the film dry for about 30 minutes.

18. Peel the backing from the film, Fig. 5-42.

Fig. 5-41. Embedding stencil in silk-screen mesh.

Fig. 5-42. Removing backing paper.

FINISHING AND BINDING   Chapter **6**

Very few printed jobs are ready to use when they come off the press. They need to be finished or bound. There are many finishing processes. Cutting, drilling holes, rounding, gathering, counting, numbering, and wrapping are some of the most common.

The fastening of pages together to form a single unit is called **binding.** Almost all commercial binding is now done by machines. Hand bookbinding remains a popular leisure-time activity. It is also used for the custom hand binding of magazines, business records, manuscripts, and the like.

There are four types of commercial binding. These are padding, stitching, mechanical, and case binding.

Padding

Padding is a simple method of binding. It is used to secure the sheets of memo pads, labels, writing tablets, and so on.

The sheets are first jogged to align the edges. They are then compressed tightly. A liquid rubber substance called **padding compound** is brushed along the back edges of the pads. This fastens them together. Several pads may be stacked together and separated by cardboard before they are compressed. After the padding compound dries, the pads are cut apart. One of the cardboards is left attached to the bottom of each pad.

Paperbacks, such as novels, catalogs, and phone directories, are often bound by a method called **perfect binding.** This is very similar to padding. The signatures are stacked together

and trimmed. Then they are cemented with a special glue developed for the purpose. The word **signature** refers to a large sheet of printed paper which is folded to the size of the book. The most common signatures have 16 or 32 pages. Figure 6-1 shows a method by which a 32 page signature may be folded. Before the signatures in a perfect binding are glued together, the back edges are trimmed. They are

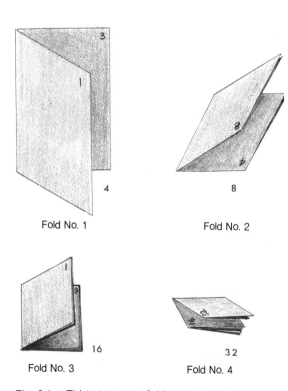

Fold No. 1   Fold No. 2

Fold No. 3   Fold No. 4

Fig. 6-1.   Thirty-two page fold.

then notched or perforated slightly to allow the glue to penetrate to the inside sheets of each signature. A gauze type cloth is sometimes glued along the back edge to furnish added strength. Covers are glued to the back before the pages are trimmed.

STITCHING

Most magazines, small catalogs, and pamphlets are fastened with wire staples. Machines cut wire into proper lengths. They force the ends through the pages and bend them down on the reverse side. In **saddle stitching,** Fig. 6-2, the book is opened in the middle. The wire is forced through the pages from the back side.

The wires are bent over on the inside at the middle of the book. Small books are usually fastened in this manner. Larger books are fastened by a method called **side stitching,** Fig. 6-3. The wire is forced through the entire book. It enters from the side near the back edge and is bent over on the reverse side. The covers may be attached in the same operation. The staples are then covered with tape. The backs are sometimes made from one piece of stock. They are then folded to fit the back edge and glued.

MECHANICAL BINDING

Mechanical bindings are used to secure the sheets of books, catalogs, and notebooks. There are several types. The best known of these are the loose-leaf notebooks. Other mechanical binders are made from spiral wire and plastics. The pages must be punched with holes or slots for these bindings, Fig. 6-4.

CASE BINDING

In case binding, signatures of a book are fastened together by one of three methods. These are sewing, stapling, or perfect binding. A **case,** or cover, is then attached to the book with glue. Books in most schools and libraries are bound by this method. Here are the typical steps in case binding.

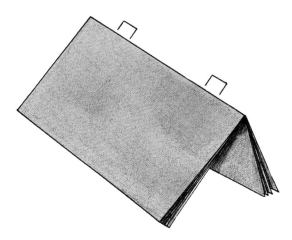

Fig. 6-2.   Saddle stitching.

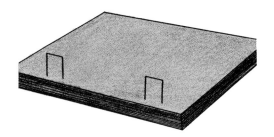

Fig. 6-3.   Side stitching.

Fig. 6-4.   Mechanical binding.

Fig. 6-5.   Folding machine.

Fig. 6-6.   An automatic sewing machine.

Folding of Signatures

The large printed sheets are folded by machines into signatures, Fig. 6-5. The layout of the printed pages on the large sheet must be planned. The page numbers must be in order when the signature is folded.

Gathering Signatures

After signatures are folded, they are gathered by machines. They are gathered one on top of the other. This puts the book in order by page numbers.

Attaching End Sheets

A folded sheet of heavier paper is secured with glue to the top and bottom signatures near the back edge. The outside fold of each end sheet is later glued to the inside cover of the book.

Sewing

Machines sew individual signatures together. They also attach the signatures to each other, Fig. 6-6.

Fig. 6-7.   A machine automatically trims the pages.

Gluing

The backs of the sewn signatures are then reinforced. Glue is applied along the sewn edge. The glue seeps between the signatures and into the sewing slightly to help bind the sheets together.

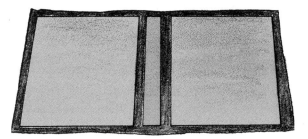

Fig. 6-9.   Arrangement of binding materials.

Fig. 6-8.   The back of the book is rounded by machine.

Trimming

After the first gluing, machines trim the books on three sides, Fig. 6-7. From 1/8 to 1/4 in. (3 to 6 mm) is allowed on the sheet sizes for this operation. The trimming cuts all edges so they are even. Also, it cuts away the folds made when the larger sheets were folded into signatures.

Rounding

The back of the book is rounded by machines. This eliminates some of the thickness caused by sewing, Fig. 6-8. Without this operation, the back of the book would be much thicker than the front edge.

Attaching the Super

A strip of heavy, coarsely woven cloth called a **super,** is cemented to the back of the book. It secures the coverings and furnishes a hinge for easy opening and closing of the covers. The super is long enough to extend almost to the top and bottom of the sewn edge. It is wide enough to extend out from each side of the book a little more than 1 in. (25 mm). These extensions serve as the hinges after the cover is attached.

Headbands made from cloth are often attached to each end of the back of the book. They furnish a trim to the ends of the sewn edge of the completed book. A lining paper of the same width as the thickness of the sewn edge is glued over the super. It prevents the cover from sticking to the sewn edge.

Making the Case

The case or cover for a book is made in a separate operation. It is made from binder's board or cardboard covered with binder's cloth. The cloth is sized with starch or plastic to make it stiff. This gives greater wear and helps the cover resist soil. The binding board, binding cloth, and back liner are cut to size. They are arranged as in Fig. 6-9. The cloth is cemented to the binding board. The edges are then folded over and glued to the inside of the covers. There are two methods of folding the corners in to make them neat and compact. The folding of

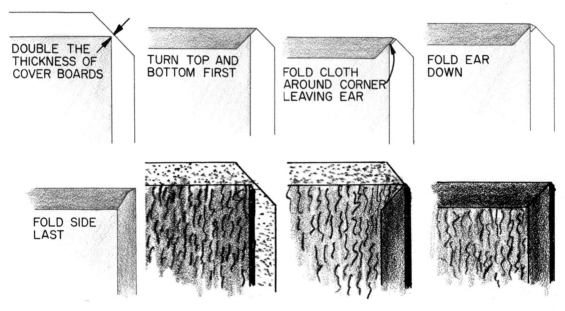

DOUBLE THE THICKNESS OF COVER BOARDS

TURN TOP AND BOTTOM FIRST

FOLD CLOTH AROUND CORNER LEAVING EAR

FOLD EAR DOWN

FOLD SIDE LAST

Fig. 6-10. Nicked corners.

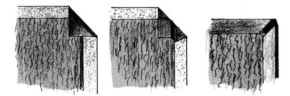

Fig. 6-11. Library corners.

the nicked corner is shown in Fig. 6-10. The library corner is shown in Fig. 6-11. The back liner is cemented to the binder's cloth to make the cover more rigid. The case is now ready to be compressed by special machines while it dries. The printing of the case is done before it is attached to the book. Sometimes the cloth is printed before the case is made.

Attaching the Case

After the case is completed, it is attached to the book. It is glued to the extending por-

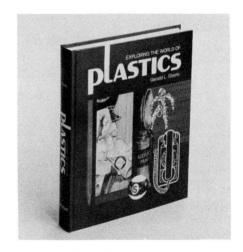

Fig. 6-12. Completed binding.

tions of the super and the end sheets. Open the cover of a clothbound book and notice how the end sheets are attached to it. Also, notice where the super extends out from the sewn edge of the book under the end sheet. Building-in machines are now used to compress the cover and book while the glue dries. The completed book is shown in Fig. 6-12.

Chapter 7

ACTIVITIES AND STUDY QUESTIONS

PROJECT 1 – LETTERHEAD

Design and set up in type a letterhead for stationery for your school or some school organization. An example is shown in Fig. 7-1.

Steps of Procedure

1. Make a rough layout.
2. Correct the rough copy and make a finished layout.
3. Set the type in a composing stick.
4. Transfer the type to the galley.
5. Tie up the form.
6. Lock the form in the chase.

PROJECT 2 – GREETING CARD

You may use your own design for this card or the one shown in Fig. 7-2. The design selected should lend itself to linoleum block printing.

Materials

1 linoleum block, 3 × 5 in. (76 × 127 mm)
linoleum block printing ink
paper

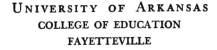

UNIVERSITY OF ARKANSAS
COLLEGE OF EDUCATION
FAYETTEVILLE

Fig. 7-1.   Layout and proof of a letterhead.

Fig. 7-2.   Block-printed card.

Steps of Procedure

1. Transfer the design to tracing paper.
2. Transfer the design to the linoleum block.
3. Cut the design into the surface of the linoleum.
4. Make a proof print.
5. Make any necessary corrections. Then proceed to print the cards.

PROJECT 3 — PEP RIBBON OR PEP BANNER

The mascot and slogan shown on the ribbon, Fig. 7-3, are suggestions. These should be changed to apply to your own school.

Materials

1½ in. (38 mm) ribbon (quantity needed)
silk screen ink, oil base
stencil material
stencil adhering liquid
solvent
rags
block-out solution

Steps of Procedure

1. Design the ribbon.
2. Transfer the design to tracing paper.
3. Cut the design in the lacquer stencil material.
4. Adhere the stencil to the silk screen.
5. Block out all the areas of the screen except the printing areas.
6. Make a jig to hold the ribbon in place as it is unrolled from the spool.
7. Strip the backing from the stencil.
8. Examine the stencil and make any corrections or repairs with block-out solution.
9. Print the ribbons and let them dry before stacking.
10. Clean all the equipment with solvent or other appropriate solvent.

PROJECT 4 — NAME AND ADDRESS STAMP

Design a rubber stamp to be attractive and useful for a variety of purposes, Fig. 7-4. It might be for return addresses on envelopes, school papers, and identification of personal items.

Materials

1 plastic molding board
1 sheet unvulcanized rubber
  mold release powder

Fig. 7-3.   Typical pep ribbons.

COLLEGE OF EDUCATION
UNIVERSITY OF ARKANSAS
FAYETTEVILLE, ARKANSAS

Fig. 7-4.   Print of a rubber stamp.

Steps of Procedure

1. Design the stamp on paper.
2. Set the type and lock it in the chase.
3. Make the plastic matrix.
4. Vulcanize the rubber over the matrix.
5. Secure the rubber stamp to a wood mount.

OTHER ACTIVITIES

1. Obtain a newspaper, a magazine, a paper-bound novel, and a school textbook. Describe the differences and list the advantages and disadvantages of the kind of paper, style of type, and the illustrations used in each.
2. Divide the surface of a 4″ × 5″ linoleum block into four equal parts. Cut a different textured surface in each part. Make a print of the block and explain how each textured surface could be used in a linoleum block print.
3. Collect several kinds of paper and fabric which have different textures. Make a silk-screen print on each using the same stencil and same kind of paint. Compare the qualities of the various surfaces.
4. Obtain three photographic negatives — one light, one medium, and one dense. Make a test strip for each negative, using the same paper and same time intervals. Develop the strips. Then compare the best exposure times of each.
5. Make a collection of books, magazines, pamphlets, or other publications representing the four basic methods of binding. Explain how each was bound.

STUDY QUESTIONS

Introduction

1. Define graphic arts.
2. Briefly describe the four stages in which graphic messages are prepared.
3. Briefly describe five careers in graphic arts.
4. How can you learn about a career field and whether it suits your needs?

5. When was movable type first used?
6. Why was movable type an important invention in the printing industry?

Designing and Printing Processes

7. In what ways is a good design effective?
8. How is function important to good design?
9. In what ways do designers analyze a graphic message they will design?
10. What are the five design principles?
11. Describe three ways to get contrast in a design.
12. Explain the "line of golden proportion."
13. How is unity achieved by the choice of typefaces?
14. Define hot composition and cold composition.
15. What are the five basic printing processes? Briefly describe each.
16. By what two measurements is paper chosen for a printing job?

Hot Composition and Relief Printing

17. Describe a piece of type used in relief printing.
18. What is the name of the measuring device used by printers?
19. How many points are there in 1 in. (25 mm)? How many picas?
20. How are quads and spaces used in setting type?
21. How is type stored?
22. Explain briefly how a composing stick is used.
23. What is a galley? How is type transferred to a galley?
24. How is a proof made? What is the purpose of a proof?
25. Explain how a form is locked up.
26. Explain what function each of the following parts of a platen press serves: ink disc, press bed, chase, ink-rollers, platen, throw-off lever, grippers, feed board.
27. What are the main steps in preparing a press for printing?

28. Explain the feeding of a platen press.
29. What are gauge pins? What function do they serve?

Rubber Stamp Making

30. How are rubber stamps used?
31. Explain the meanings of the following words and terms: plastic molding board, matrix, mold release powder, type chase, vulcanizing.
32. Explain briefly how rubber stamps are made.

Linoleum Block Printing

33. What is the difference between blocks for printing positive and negative prints?
34. Explain a third type of cut which may be used in block printing.
35. What are the steps in carving a linoleum block?
36. How is ink spread over a block to be used for printing?
37. Explain the precautions which must be taken when making linoleum block prints with more than one color.
38. How many separate blocks must be used for making multi-color prints?

Cold Composition and Planograph Printing

39. Explain how the image is transferred to paper in offset printing.
40. What are clip art and preprinted type?
41. How is the image transferred to the design using transfer type? Tab type? Pressure sensitive type?
42. What is strike-on composition?
43. How are images most often placed on offset plates?

44. Explain the difference between line negatives and halftone negatives.
45. Explain the use of the proportional scale.
46. What is the basic difference between exposing a line negative and a halftone negative?
47. Explain the steps in film processing.
48. Describe the stripping process.
49. Describe the platemaking process.
50. What are the steps for setting up operation of the press?
51. List the basic equipment needed for doing simple silk-screen work. What is the purpose of each piece?
52. How is lacquer film adhered to a silk screen?
53. Explain how a silk screen is cleaned.
54. What are the basic differences in making one-color silk-screen prints and multi-color prints?
55. Explain the procedure for making stencils by the glue method. By the glue and tusche method.

Binding and Finishing

56. What four basic types of bookbinding are used commercially?
57. What method of binding is generally used for binding paperback novels, telephone directories, and large catalogs?
58. List some of the uses of mechanical bindings.
59. How are most school books and library books bound?
60. Define the following terms: folding, gathering, collating, sewing, gluing, end sheets, trimming, rounding, super, headbands.
61. How is the case (cover) attached to a clothbound book?

INDEX